CATALAN NATIONALISM

Catalan Nationalism

Past and Present

Albert Balcells
Autonomous University of Barcelona

Edited and introduced by
Geoffrey J. Walker
Fitzwilliam College, Cambridge

Translated by Jacqueline Hall
with the collaboration of Geoffrey J. Walker

St. Martin's Press
New York

CATALAN NATIONALISM
Copyright © 1996 by Albert Balcells
Introduction copyright © Geoffrey J. Walker 1996

St. Martin's Press, Scholarly and Reference Division,
175 Fifth Avenue, New York, N.Y. 10010

First published in the United States of America in 1996

First published in 1991 in Castilian as *El nacionalismo catalán*
and in 1992 in Catalan as *Història del nacionalisme català*

Printed in Great Britain

ISBN 0-312-12611-5

Library of Congress Cataloging-in-Publication Data
Balcells, Albert.
[Nacionalismo catalán.   English]
Catalan nationalism: past and present / Albert Balcells; edited
and introduced by Geoffrey J. Walker; translated by Jacqueline
Hall.
p. cm.
Includes bibliographical references and index.
ISBN 0-312-12611-5
1. Nationalism—Spain—Catalonia—History.   2. Catalonia (Spain)-
-History.   I. Walker, Geoffrey J.   II. Hall, Jacqueline.
III. Title.
DP302.C67B3513   1996
320.5'4'0946—dc20   94-47389
                                                        CIP

Contents

Contents

List of Tables

Acknowledgements

The English translation of this book was promoted and sponsored by the Fundació Jaume Bofill, Barcelona, and thanks are due in particular to its Director, Sr Jordi Porta, for his interest and personal assistance at every stage in its production.

Introduction to the English Edition

Broadly speaking, there are two kinds of nationalism. The first is the raucous, assertive, overbearing nationalism we associate with major nations, cultures or languages which at different times and for various reasons go through phases of aggressive intolerance of people perceived of as aliens in their midst, of foreigners in general and often of neighbouring nations or cultures. When in this mood, as in the case of Germany in the 1930s, they become 'bloody-minded' towards all but their own, usually with very serious consequences for those who oppose them or even merely get in their way. The other kind of nationalism may be equally intolerant, potentially as assertive or even aggressive as the first; but it rarely has the chance to be raucous or overbearing, for it is the resentful, bitter, defensive nationalism not of a people deluded into believing its great language or culture or honour is under threat, but the nationalism of a people that knows its nationhood has been usurped by another, whose identity has been denied to it, whose language has been spurned and prohibited, whose cultural heritage has been derided or even denied altogether. Nevertheless, nationalism that arises for these reasons, given time and the right conditions, is also capable of overcoming the natural demoralization that such repression brings to a people, and if channelled towards positive goals it can be energetic, constructive, vitalizing, even optimistic. Catalan nationalism is of this second kind.

For nearly three hundred years now it has been usual in Europe to think of Spain as a unitary nation state, a country and a nationality whose existence as such is beyond reasonable doubt, and this has indeed been the case politically. We think of the people of Spain as Spaniards, and we react, however slightly, to those who call themselves first Basques or Catalans or Galicians before Spaniards as at best a shade prickly or at worst as potential troublemakers. But they are probably neither. They merely reflect the underlying eternal truth about the peoples of Spain, observed by the Roman geographer Strabo, that 'they are bad mixers who are difficult to unite'. During the Middle Ages the peoples of 'the Spains' as the country was often called (in English texts too sometimes) were gradually brought into two power blocks under the separate and independent crowns of Aragon, in the east, and Castile, in the centre of the Iberian Peninsula. But contrary to what countless history books quite mistakenly inform their readers, the marriage of Ferdinand of Aragon and Isabella of Castile, the 'Catholic Kings', in 1469 did *not* finally unify the country. It merely meant that the monarch of one country was consort in the other, and vice versa. That is not unification! Their royal heirs and successors, for more than two centuries, continued to be monarchs of both kingdoms separately and together, and the constitutional proof of this is that until the eigtheenth century the Principality of Catalonia was ruled over by a viceroy – not a royal governor or a crown minister – from its capital Barcelona, while the King himself was ruling the kingdom of Castile. But Castile ever regarded this situation as unsatisfactory, and throughout the seventeenth century it had the same kind of ambitions to unify Spain as Louis XIV was so successfully achieving in France. The chance came in 1700 when Louis' grandson, Philip of Anjou, inherited the Spanish thrones, and was challenged by some of the European powers to a war of succession that ended in 1714 with the military conquest of Barcelona by the armies of Castile. Reprisals and subjugation of the Catalans for their alliance with Philip's enemies (made in order to protect their threatened traditional constitutional status) were extremely harsh, and it was not until the mid-nineteenth century that the Catalan consciousness again dared to express itself.

Repression of the Catalan identity, then, has been a constant feature of the Spanish political scene since the seventeenth century. It was particularly fierce in the eighteenth century, in the early nineteenth century under Ferdinand VII, and under the dictators of the twentieth century, Primo de Rivera and Franco. While the *españolistas* (those who wished to force conformity on the whole of Spain) were intolerant of diversity and therefore resolutely anti-Catalan, the dreams of men such as Primo de Rivera and Franco went further and included the objective of turning the Catalans into right-thinking 'Spaniards': indeed Spanish policy in this regard came very close to the notion of the overbearing kind of nationalism outlined above. Everything Catalan was banned – books, press, theatre, radio, songs, folklore, flags, emblems, history – but supremely the language. At the height of the Franco repression one could even be legally thrown off a tram in Barcelona by a Spanish-speaking tramguard for speaking Catalan. This was not 'ethnic' cleansing, but it *was* a programme of 'cultural' cleansing. But cultural genocide is an impossible dream. The Catalan intellectual and nationalist thinker J. M. Batista i Roca once remarked, 'The Spaniards talk and write a lot about the so-called "Catalan problem"; but there is no such thing! We are alright! It is the Spaniards who have a problem because they want to turn us into something we are not. It should therefore more correctly be referred to as "the Castilian problem"'!

To a large extent the flagship of Catalan nationalism is the language and culture. Catalan is *not* a 'dialect of Spanish' as many would have us believe. It is not even the sister language of Spanish. Spanish (i.e. Castilian) and Portuguese make a pair, but certainly not Spanish and Catalan. Catalan is a relative of Occitan and Provençal, of Auvergnois and Limousin, and even Romansh, the language of the Swiss Grisons. It has its own dialects like Valencian and Majorcan and Rossellonès. It is one of the great Romance languages, and it has a vast body of splendid literature, both medieval and modern, to prove it. Over 5 million people speak Catalan as their native language, not as a 'party trick' or in order to annoy others who cannot speak it. Castilian does not come to them naturally. Most of those who are not born into bilingual families have actually to learn to speak Spanish. They rightly become indignant if foreigners belittle their language; or, as in Franco's times, when Castilian-speakers might easily have told them to 'stop barking like dogs and talk like Christians'. Sometimes it is said, rather condescendingly, that you have to tread carefully with the Catalans because they are a very proud people, proud of their traditions and of their language. Such observations seem to imply that they keep their language and their culture alive essentially as a means of distinguishing themselves from 'other Spaniards' or that they consider themselves to be special in some way. What nonsense! Of course they are proud of their language and their traditions, just as the English, the French, the Italians, and, dare one say it, the Spanish are proud of their language and traditions; but just imagine how the Dutch or the Danes, for example, would react if they had Germans and other nationalities constantly telling them to stop fooling around in their annoying local dialect and to be reasonable and speak and think in proper German because everyone knows that in their heart of hearts they really do live culturally and linguistically in German! This is the equivalent of what generations of Catalans have had to suffer day-in, day-out for over three hundred years now – from government, state officials, lawyers, censors, policemen, even tramguards and private Castilian-speaking citizens! Is it any wonder that Catalan nationalism was born, and that it continues to rise to greater cultural and political aspirations?

Not all Catalans are nationalists however. Not all Catalan nationalists are separatists. Not all Catalan separatists seek total independence from Spain. None of them advocate violence. The majority of Catalans accept that history cannot be denied or rolled back. They now wish to be allowed to run their own affairs within and *not* outside a Spain that forms part of the European Union; they wish to have Spanish and Catalan as the two official languages of their country without there being contrived ludicrous controversies about the use and teaching of Catalan; they wish to flourish economically and culturally as a people in their own right and to explore in their own way their special Catalan talents for design and technology; they wish to recover and retain their own rightful individual place in the European cultural tradition quite as much as any of the free peoples that form it. Their signal success in promoting and staging the Olympic Games of 1992 in Barcelona as a Catalan event within a Spanish and European context is eloquent testimony to this.

This book was originally written in Castilian by Professor Albert Balcells, one of Catalonia's leading historians, to place before Spanish-speakers historical material that under censorial régimes in Spain had been kept from them altogether, or at best distorted. Its intention was to inform objectively and analyse impartially, thus working towards a better understanding in Spain of the reasons for and the character of Catalan nationalism. The book was subsequently updated and translated into Catalan and it became a bestseller. The present edition has been slightly expanded and adapted for readers of English in the hope that they too may benefit from greater familiarity with facts that until recently have been known only – and that very imperfectly – in Catalonia itself.

Fitzwilliam College   Geoffrey J. Walker
Cambridge

Glossary of Catalan and Spanish Acronyms used in this Book

ACO	Catholic Workers' Action
ACR	Catalan Republican Action
ADPC	Popular Democratic Association of Catalans
AIT	International Working Men's Association
AP	Popular Alliance
APEC	Association for the Protection of the Teaching of Catalan
BOC	Labour and Agricultural Workers' Bloc
CADCI	Autonomist Centre of Shop Assistants and Industrial Employees
CC	Christ and Catalonia
CCMA	Central Committee of Anti-Fascist Militia
CCOO	Workers' Commissions (independent trade unions)
CDC	Democratic Convergence of Catalonia
CEDA	Spanish Confederation of Right-wing Forces
CEOE	Spanish Employers' Association
CFPC	Coordination Committee of Political Forces of Catalonia
CIC	Catholic Women's Information Centre
CiU	Convergence and Union (alliance of CDC and UDC)
CNC	Catalan National Council
CNDC	National Council of Catalan Democracy
CNR	Republican National Centre
CNS	National Union Confederation
CNT	National Confederation of Labour
CSC	Socialist Convergence of Catalonia
ERC	Republican Left of Catalonia
ETA	Freedom for the Basques
FAI	Iberian Anarchist Federation
FLP	Popular Liberation Front
FMA	Autonomous Monarchist Federation
FNC	National Front of Catalonia
FOC	Workers' Front of Catalonia

FSFC	Federal Socialist Force of Catalonia
IC	Initiative for Catalonia
IEC	Institute for Catalan Studies (the Catalan Academy)
IU	United Left
JOC	Young Catholic Workers' Association
LOAPA	Organic Law for Harmonization of the Self-government Process
MSC	Socialist Movement of Catalonia
PCC	Communist Party of Catalonia
PCE	Spanish Communist Party
PCP	Catalan Proletarian Party
PCR	Catalanist Republican Party
PNRE	Nationalist Republican Party of the Left
PNV	Basque Nationalist Party
POUM	Workers' Party of Marxist Unification
PP	Popular Party (successor of the right-wing Popular Alliance)
PRC	Catalan Republican Party
PSA	Socialist Party of Andalusia
PSAN	Socialist Party of National Liberation of the Catalan Countries
PSC	Party of the Socialists of Catalonia
PSOE	Spanish Socialist Workers' Party
PSUC	United Socialist Party of Catalonia
RRP	Radical Republican Party
SDEUB	Democratic Students' Union of the University of Barcelona
SEU	Spanish Union of University Students
UCD	Union of the Democratic Centre
UDC	Democratic Union of Catalonia
UFNR	Republican Nationalist Federal Union
UGT	General Workers' Union
UMN	National Monarchist Union
UP	Patriotic Union
UR	Republican Union
USC	Socialist Union of Catalonia

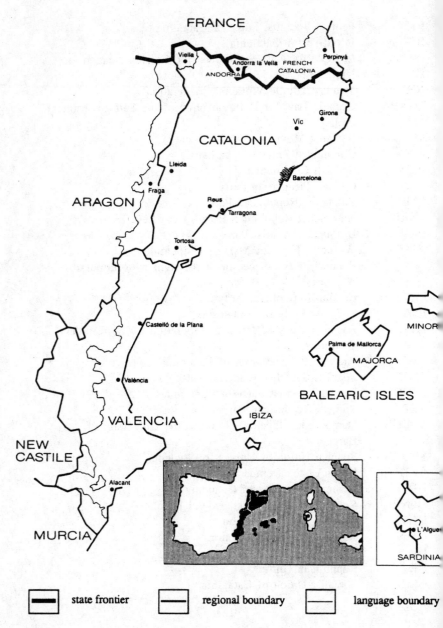

Where Catalan is Spoken

Reproduced by courtesy of Botifarra Publications, Sheffield

1 From the Origins of Catalonia to the Eighteenth Century

CATALONIA IN EUROPE

Catalonia is located at the north-eastern tip of the Iberian Peninsula, between the Pyrenees, the Mediterranean, and the Ebro basin. It covers an area slightly larger than Belgium and has 6 million inhabitants, more, for instance, than Denmark. Catalonia has a language of its own, which produced a literature from the thirteenth century onwards and fulfils all the requirements of a present-day culture. Since 1979 Catalonia has enjoyed political autonomy, exercising powers which, though far inferior to those of the member states of a federal republic such as Germany or the United States, constitute a recognition of its collective personality and are slowing down the effects of centuries of oppression of the identity of the Catalan people by the Spanish state.

Catalan identity is not confined to Catalonia proper since the Catalan language is spoken in a much larger area inhabited by a total of 11 million people and comprising Catalonia itself, the Kingdom of Valencia, the Balearic Islands, the Principality of Andorra, and the Catalan regions which were annexed to France in 1659. Today Valencia and the Balearic Islands are also self-governing communities within Spain. When the Franco dictatorship came to an end and the transition to the present Spanish constitutional system began, there were widespread hopes that these three Catalan-speaking areas would achieve some kind of political coordination. These hopes have not been fulfilled, though part of the population remains aware of the linguistic, cultural and historical community to which all the Catalan-speaking regions belong.

At the close of the twentieth century, the history of the stateless nations of Europe, far from being a mere curiosity, is a subject of great contemporary relevance. Contrary to the official versions, such nations are not a residual phenomenon of the past but a basic characteristic of a collective identity that has withstood the action of states endowed with far greater power than at any time in the past. Present events in the former Soviet Union and Yugoslavia provide a clear example of this.

1

The relationship between culture and politics is not something fortuitous but a key factor in the development of a nation. It is this relationship that guarantees the link between the exercise of power and its popular justification. An exclusively political nation is fragile because it lacks a sociocultural base: a cultural nation, on the other hand, has to become a political nation if it wishes to lay plans for its own future. Exclusively political nations strive to do away with the cultural nations they dominate and deny their national identity, while cultural nations struggle for political power, an objective that does not necessarily involve total independence, especially nowadays when the sovereignty of the great majority of old states, particularly in Europe, is steadily dwindling.

FROM DEPENDENCE ON THE CAROLINGIAN EMPIRE TO THE CATALAN–ARAGONESE MONARCHY

Twelve centuries ago, the Hispanic March, the borderland south of the Pyrenees separating Charlemagne's Frankish kingdom from Al-andalus, as Muslim Spain was then called, formed the embryo of what would later become Catalonia. In 801 the son of Emperor Charlemagne conquered Barcelona with the assistance of exiles from the area who had gone to live in Septimania in southern Gaul. The attempt to push the Frankish frontier southwards to the Ebro failed, and it was not until three hundred years later, in the twelfth century, that Tortosa and the mouth of the Ebro river were conquered by Christians, by which time Catalonia no longer belonged to the King of France.

At the beginning of the ninth century, the Hispanic March was a territory divided into nine earldoms, all of which enjoyed equal status. It played an intermediary role from the very start between the hinterland of the Iberian peninsula on the one hand, and Europe and the Mediterranean on the other. Unlike isolated strongholds in the Pyrenees, such as Aragon or the Basque Country and Navarre, which were detached from both Muslim Spain and Carolingian Europe, these eastern earldoms acted as a thoroughfare, an area where contacts could take place between Al-andalus and the Christian western world.

The resettlement of the plains and coastal regions by Pyrenean mountain dwellers gave rise in the tenth century to the establishment of small freehold family properties on frontier lands previously covered by Mediterranean scrub and woodland.

Owing to the decline of the power of the monarchy in France, the eastern earldoms became hereditary from the time of Count Wilfred the Hairy who, in 878, was able to unite under his rule the earldoms of Barcelona, Girona, Osona, Urgell, and Cerdanya, precisely on account of his loyalty to the weak kings of the Carolingian dynasty. Under the provisions of his Will the earldoms of Barcelona, Osona and Girona remained undivided, forming the backbone of the still embryonic Catalonia. This whole area, which reached no farther than the Llobregat, Cardener, and middle Segre rivers and the Tremp depression, would later be known as Old Catalonia, as opposed to the lands lying to the south and east which were conquered and settled in the eleventh and twelfth centuries and named New Catalonia.

In 985 Barcelona was sacked by the Muslims. This was the most violent of a series of attacks by the Caliphate of Cordoba, and when the Frankish monarchy proved unable to provide assistance in exchange for renewed vassalage, relations were broken off. This was the start of the severing of political ties with France, a process which culminated at the beginning of the twelfth century when the dependence of the Catalan dioceses on that of Narbonne came to an end and the ancient metropolitan see of Tarragona was re-established.

The disintegration of the Caliphate of Cordoba early in the eleventh century and its division into separate kingdoms undermined Muslim military power, though the Spanish Arabs still enjoyed considerable economic and cultural superiority. The long period of demographic and economic growth which then got underway in Europe would reach its peak in the twelfth and thirteenth centuries, the time of the great Catalan expansion. In the meantime, during the eleventh century, conquest and resettlement came to a virtual stop in Catalonia. From this time onwards it is correct to refer to 'Catalonia', since it is towards the end of the eleventh and the beginning of the twelfth centuries that we find the first documents in which the term 'Catalan' is used to designate the inhabitants of the area.

The stagnation of the process of conquest and colonization was related to the establishment of the feudal regime in the Catalan earldoms during the first half of the eleventh century, in the midst of a long period of violence. The phenomenon was an autochthonous one, not the result of the imitation of models from beyond the Pyrenees. The *vicaris*, appointed by the Counts, and local nobles seized public property and fiscal lands and set themselves up as hereditary lords, independent of the Counts. They usurped Church property and confiscated land under the direct control of the peasants, leaving them with only

Catalan Nationalism

the usufruct of the property, which was itself subject to the payment of dues, personal services, and retention of rights over hunting, fishing, the operation of mills, etc. Thus, immediately after the disappearance of the old rural slavery, part of the peasantry of Old Catalonia was reduced to serfdom and prohibited from leaving the manor without paying a ransom or *remença*. Such peasants were known in Catalan as *pagesos de remença* (ransom peasants).

The Counts were thus deprived of direct and effective power over the majority of their subjects and of a considerable part of the resources of their earldoms. In 1027 the most enlightened sector of the clergy, headed by Bishop Oliba of Vic, the Abbot of Ripoll, who was already engaged in a fight against simony, founded a movement known as the *assemblees de pau i treva de Déu* (assemblies of God's peace and truce) which sought to put a brake on the violent feudal wars. By the thirteenth century, as these assemblies began to be attended not only by the feudal nobility but also by representatives of the self-governing cities, the first steps towards the formation of the Catalan Corts or parliament had already been made.

By about 1070, thanks to the tributes paid to him by the neighbouring Muslim kingdoms, notably Lleida and Tortosa, the Count of Barcelona, Ramon Berenguer I (1035–76), had accumulated sufficient resources to put a stop to the insubordination of the nobles and impose explicit vassalage on them. In exchange, however, he had to accept the jurisdiction of the barons over the lands they had usurped. At the same time, the other Catalan Counts swore to be the first vassals of the Count of Barcelona. Thus it came about that Ramon Berenguer I created the Catalan feudal state at the same time as William, Duke of Normandy, set up the Norman state in England, soon to become the Anglo–Norman state. These two domains constitute the most highly developed examples in Europe of the institutionalization of the structure of feudal vassalage. Later, during the Lower Middle Ages, England and Catalonia would also become the most advanced models of a monarchy limited by the legislative power of a parliament representing the nobility, the clergy and the burghers.

The economic and demographic growth which marked the eleventh century laid the foundations for the widespread conquests of the mid-twelfth century and the colonization of the whole of New Catalonia – the greater part of the present-day provinces of Lleida and Tarragona – which took place during the late twelfth century.

Prior to this, however, the Counts of Barcelona had directed the energies of the fledgling nation in two directions: Languedoc and Aragon.

Catalan predominance over Languedoc and Provence was first achieved in 1112 by Ramon Berenguer III (1093–1131). The aim was to form an association with Catalonia's neighbours and potential rivals in the Mediterranean. A dynastic union with the kingdom of Aragon, secured by Ramon Berenguer IV (1131–62) in 1137, provided Catalonia with an alliance with another neighbour, further inland, which could otherwise have been a likely competitor in the conquest of new territories held by the Muslims of Lleida and Tortosa, and subsequently of the Muslim kingdom of Valencia.

Neither in the Languedoc nor in Aragon were any territories annexed by military force: links were forged through marriage or feudal vassalage. The confederal union between equals which bound Catalonia to Aragon was never to be broken. It guaranteed the independence of Aragon from Castile and that of Catalonia from France, as well as enabling the two countries to combine forces against the Muslims. Its first fruit was the Catalan conquest of Lleida and Tortosa, whereby Catalonia acquired its present-day southern and western boundaries. The dynastic union with Aragon, far from diluting the personality of Catalonia, reinforced it, as it did that of Aragon, though numerous conflicts would later arise between the two neighbours and allies. Prior to the union with Aragon, the Counts of Barcelona had not taken the title of king. Aragon, however, was a kingdom, and thereafter the title of King of Aragon preceded that of Count of Barcelona in official documents. Despite this, the members of the House of Barcelona, which was the reigning dynasty of the Crown of Aragon, were considered Catalans by outsiders, and even today the coat of arms of the Counts of Barcelona, with its four red stripes on a golden background, remains the emblem of Aragon and the flag, not only of Catalonia, but of Valencia, Majorca and the other Balearic islands, and Aragon as well.

At certain periods during the twelfth century – for instance in the times of Ramon Berenguer III (1093–1131) and Alfons I the Chaste (1162–96) – the Languedoc and Catalonia were united under a common sovereign. Alliances were also formed between related princes, when the second son of the sovereign inherited Provence and the earldoms of Languedoc, as occurred during the reigns of Ramon Berenguer IV (1131–62) and Peter the Catholic (1196–1213). During the late twelfth century, at the same time as the first literary texts in Catalan were beginning to appear, the poetry of the Provençal troubadours enjoyed considerable popularity at the court in Barcelona.

When the Cathar heresy spread through the Languedoc, a crusade was launched to eradicate it. It soon became clear, however, that behind this crusade lay the ambitions of the French crown. Peter the Catholic of Aragon and Catalonia, while condemning the heresy, decided to give support to his vassals in the Languedoc. But his intervention came too late and when he was defeated and killed at the Battle of Muret, near Toulouse, in 1213, the Languedoc policy of the House of Barcelona came to an end.

THE CATALAN EXPANSION IN THE MEDITERRANEAN

After securing peace with Castile and France, and limiting the power of the nobility with the support of the burghers, James I the Conqueror (1213–76) set about extending his territories by conquering Majorca in 1229. Following this exclusively Catalan exploit, the land belonging to the Muslims was shared out and resettled and the Muslims disappeared as a community from the Balearic Islands.

The conquest of the Muslim kingdom of Valencia, on the other hand, was a joint Catalan–Aragonese venture which lasted from 1233 to 1245. The cities and the areas of orchards and vegetable gardens around them were settled by Christians from the north, the Catalans being most numerous along the coast and the Aragonese in the hinterland. However, a large Muslim community continued to exist, retaining its own language and religion. James I made Valencia into a new self-governing kingdom, thus reinforcing the confederal nature of the Crown of Aragon (though to apply the term to the thirteenth century is clearly anachronistic). In time, Catalan cultural influence would predominate in the kingdom of Valencia, to which new territories further south around Alacant were added at the beginning of the fourteenth century.

James I divided his realms between his sons, leaving the kingdom which included Majorca, Montpellier, Perpinyà and the part of Catalonia north of the Pyrenees to his second son. The kingdom of Majorca continued to exist until 1349, when it was annexed to the Crown of Aragon.

When, in 1282, the Sicilians rose against the French, headed by Charles d'Anjou, who had become King of Naples, Peter the Great of Catalonia and Aragon (1276–85), James I's successor, seized the opportunity to conquer Sicily with the support of the majority of the inhabitants of the island. He was excommunicated by the Pope, and the King of France invaded Catalonia but was defeated. Sicily continued to be governed as an independent but allied kingdom by the second son of Peter the Great, Frederick the brother of James II of Aragon and Catalonia (1291–1327), and his successors until it was annexed to the Crown of Aragon in 1397.

The mercenaries who had taken part in the conquest of Sicily, known as the Almogàvers, were promptly dispatched under the command of Roger de Flor to assist the Emperor of Constantinople against the Turks. But once the Turks had been vanquished, there was another struggle against the Byzantines, and the Almogàvers kept the duchies of Athens and Neopatria, which remained under Catalan–Aragonese domination throughout the fourteenth century. The Catalan expansion through the Mediterranean culminated in the conquest of Sardinia, which began in 1323. With the backing of Pisa and Genoa, Barcelona's great rival in the Mediterranean, the Sardinians put up a long resistance and though Sardinia was subjected to colonial domination, in conquering it the Catalans incurred more losses than gains. The Catalan language is still spoken today in the Sardinian town of L'Alguer (Alghero).

Following the example of the Italian merchant republics, Catalan merchants carried on a flourishing trade throughout the eastern Mediterranean and North Africa. In all the chief Mediterranean ports there were Catalan consuls who looked after the interests of their compatriots and officially represented them in their dealings with the local authorities. This network was coordinated by the Consolat de Mar (Maritime Consulate) in Barcelona, which acted as a corporation of merchants, a trade exchange and a court of justice. The sentences it handed down were compiled in the *Llibre del Consolat de Mar* (*Book of the Maritime Consulate*) which was one of the earliest European trading codes. It was translated into various languages and was one of the documents from which international mercantile law was drawn up.

At times the expansionist wars interrupted the flow of trade which was the driving force behind Catalonia's economic growth. Both economic dynamism and internal political harmony reached their height in the first quarter of the fourteenth century, during the reign of James II the Just; but this was also the period of maximum fragmentation of Catalonia's territorial domains when the crown lost direct control over the kingdoms of Majorca and Sicily. By contrast, the imperialist policy which began under Peter III the Ceremonious (1336–87) and culminated with the conquest of Naples in 1443 by Alfons IV the Magnanimous (1416–58), took place at a time of economic decadence and severe political crises. Catalonia's foreign conquests were out of all propor-

tion to its resources and in the fifteenth century would ultimately lead
to a clash between the monarch's imperialist ambitions and the interests
of the bourgeoisie.

It was during the thirteenth century, the period of the rise of the
bourgeoisie, that Catalan began to replace Latin as the language of
culture and the language of the court. James the Conqueror imposed
the use of Catalan in the royal chancellery, and ordered the chronicle
of his reign to be written in Catalan. In the works of the Majorcan
writer Ramon Llull, Catalan became a fully fledged language of literature and philosophy. Catalan literature was to reach its peak in Valencia in the fifteenth century, producing works of such widespread influence
as the famous novel *Tirant lo Blanc*.

A POLITICAL SYSTEM BASED ON NEGOTIATED AGREEMENTS

In the Lower Middle Ages, Catalonia developed a complex political
system based on agreements negotiated in parliament. It would be in-
appropriate at such a period to talk of constitutionalism, given the
consuetudinary character of a system based on the privileges of the
three estates, in other words on the liberty of groups rather than egali-
tarianism. None the less, to some extent at least, the limited powers of
the monarchy and the tendency to separate legislative, executive, and
judicial powers endow the Catalan medieval political system with a
special and in some ways precocious character.

The Catalan parliament, known as the Corts, was born in the thirteenth century when the King summoned the representatives of the
self-governing boroughs to discussions, along with the nobles, bishops,
and abbots. The relationship between the Counts of Barcelona as Kings
of Aragon, and their Catalan subjects was seen as being based essentially upon negotiation, and the Corts were the central feature of this
conception. During the same period, Aragon and Valencia had their
own parliaments, different from that of Catalonia.

By the end of the thirteenth century, the King could no longer re-
voke a law approved by the Catalan Corts. When parliament met in
1283, Peter the Great had been excommunicated following the conquest
of Sicily, and the country was in imminent danger of French invasion.
This situation forced him to grant to the three estates – the nobility,
the Church hierarchy, and the burghers – joint legislative powers with

the Crown. It was at this time that the Catalan practice of political negotiation was born. In the mid-fourteenth century the Corts took a further step towards the limitation of royal power by setting up a standing committee of members of parliament who were to act while parliament itself was not in session. This committee was called the Diputació del General or Generalitat. Not only were the sums of money granted to the monarch negotiated between the latter and his subjects, but the Generalitat was also responsible for the management of the taxes raised. The rebellions of the nobility against the Crown came to an end in Catalonia, not so much because of Mediterranean expansion, as because insubordination was turned into parliamentary opposition.

At the beginning of the fifteenth century, Ferdinand I (1412–16), a member of the Castilian Trastámara dynasty, ascended the throne of Aragon. The change of dynasty helped consolidate the power of the Corts with respect to the monarch. The Generalitat, whose functions had previously been mainly fiscal, became a political organ responsible for defending the laws of Catalonian, and the King was not considered legitimate until he had sworn to respect the basic law of the land in the presence of the Corts. Despite their oligarchical character, the Corts and the Generalitat represented Catalonia before the sovereign. They thus constituted an element of cohesion, giving the country a mode of organization and an awareness of its own identity which might in some ways be described as national, though the idea of popular or national sovereignty did not yet exist.

The French historian Pierre Vilar, the author of *La Catalogne dans l'Espagne Moderne* (Paris 1962) has written: 'Between 1250 and 1350 the Principality of Catalonia may be the European country to which it would be least incorrect and least dangerous to apply the apparently anachronic terms of political and economic imperialism and nation state', and he goes on, 'This [Catalan political] creation is remarkable, therefore, especially on account of its precociousness. Language, territory, economic life, the shaping of a mentality, a cultural community – the fundamental conditions of a nation – are already fully present as early as the 13th century.'

It must be pointed out however that, as in other similar cases, the limitation of royal power in Catalonia in the Middle Ages did not entail more freedom for the majority of citizens. At a meeting of the Corts held in 1283, Peter the Great was constrained to surrender his monopoly over municipal government to the upper middle classes and a revolt in Barcelona in 1385, headed by Berenguer Oller, revealed the existence of a state of unrest among the urban lower classes. During the same session of parliament held in 1283, the feudal nobility reinforced the bonds that tied the peasantry to the land in Old Catalonia; and the support of the Church for the feudal system was such that it banned such peasants from entering the priesthood. The Jews, who had previously occupied high positions in the service of the King, were also excluded from public office from 1283 onwards.

Following an economic slump and a decline in population caused by the bad harvests of 1333 and the first wave of the Black Death, which hit Catalonia in 1348, social tension reached such a pitch that the Corts, where agreements had previously been negotiated between the King and the dominant classes, became the scene of permanent disputes between the Crown and its subjects.

THE CRISIS OF THE LOWER MIDDLE AGES

Catalonia was hit particularly hard by the economic and demographic regression which took place during the second half of the fourteenth century and the first half of the fifteenth. In 1340 Barcelona was a city of 50,000 inhabitants, but by 1477 it had dwindled to 20,000, and at the end of the fifteenth century the population of Catalonia was half what it had been one hundred and fifty years earlier.

In the midst of this upheaval the serfs, who made up one-third of the population, appealed to the King for their collective redemption, while in Barcelona the popular party known as the Busca was demanding that all the estates should take part in the city government and advocating a different economic policy from that pursued by the Biga, the party of the oligarchy.

The Corts and the Generalitat, on the other hand, demanded support from the King in putting down unrest in the countryside and in maintaining municipal power exclusively in the hands of the urban patriciate. In the mid-fifteenth century the Crown made concessions to the peasantry and to the Busca in an attempt to weaken the position of the classes who controlled the Corts and the Generalitat and who were opposed to any increase in royal power. In Barcelona the patriciate lost its monopoly of power. Henceforth, in addition to two honorary citizens – members of the upper bourgeoisie – a merchant, an 'artist' (a member of the liberal professions), and a craftsman had to be elected by the Consell de Cent (Council of One Hundred), as the City Council was known. However, the economic measures taken by the Busca in Bar-

celona failed to yield results, and the popularity of the party had declined by the time the Biga recovered control of the city.

This tension led the Generalitat to stage a rising against King John II
(1458–62 and 1472–79), thus sparking off a long civil war which divided the Catalan people between 1462 and 1472 and squandered the
country's last resources and energies. Aragon, Valencia, and Majorca
took no part in the strife. Only the island of Minorca declared its support for the Catalan Generalitat against the King. The Generalitat tried
to win over the serfs by proposing an agreement between them and
the nobility, but they remained loyal to the Crown.

The victory of John II did not have the effect of establishing an
absolute monarchy and the practice of political negotiation remained
intact. The King, however, failed to fulfil the serfs' hopes of emancipation. The *pagesos de remença* (serfs) rose again and, despite their
defeat on the battlefield, finally succeeded in 1486 in obtaining from
Ferdinand II the Catholic of Aragon/Catalonia (1479–1516) their
personal liberty and the limitation of feudal obligations in exchange
for collective compensation to the nobles. Even so, the nobility retained their jurisdiction over the greater part of the peasantry. Under
Ferdinand II the practice of *insaculació* became customary in elections to the Generalitat and the city councils. This consisted of periodically 'electing' the holders of key positions by drawing lots, and had
the effect of reducing rivalry between the parties and reinforcing the
authority of the King.

In the course of the Catalan civil war, John II had married his heir,
Ferdinand, to Isabella, the heiress to the Castilian throne, in a bid to
find outside allies. Thus the union between the dynasties of Castile
and Aragon/Catalonia took place at a time when Catalonia was weakened and prostrate. The match did not initially seem to threaten Catalan
self-government, though Catalonia lost all influence over foreign policy.
The introduction in 1487 of the new Court of the Inquisition need-
lessly sparked off resistance in Catalonia and throughout the Crown of
Aragon on account of the dangers implicit in accepting the extension
of a Castilian-based centralized judicial and police organ whose function was to control religious dissidence and keep a careful watch over
converted Jews, after exiling or expelling those who refused to be
converted.

CATALONIA WITHIN THE EMPIRE OF THE SPANISH CROWN DURING THE SIXTEENTH AND SEVENTEENTH CENTURIES

The dynastic union with Castile, which occurred in the midst of the crisis of the Catalan feudal system – a long drawn out affair, with a nobility that was entering a phase of urbanization, and an upper middle class that was becoming aristocratic – was a decisive step towards the formation of a Hispanic feudal bloc under a monarchy that was tending towards absolutism. The municipal revolt staged by the Communities of Castile was put down by Charles of Austria, King of Spain and Emperor of Germany (1517–56), with the support of the Castilian high nobility. It was followed in 1520 by an antifeudal revolt in Valencia and Majorca, initiated by the *germanies* (brotherhoods of the lower middle classes), which was also crushed through Castilian intervention.

Under the monarchy of the House of Austria, which had domains all over Europe as well as a vast new colonial empire in America, the ties that had been forged between noble families throughout Spain caused a split in the Catalan feudal nobility. A minority accepted posts in the imperial administration, formed alliances with the Castilian and Andalusian high nobility, and resided far away from Catalonia, while another group, made up of the least powerful and wealthy, remained isolated and provincial.

Though Catalonia achieved some stability towards the end of the fifteenth century, when the Catalan civil war came to an end, economic stagnation, political immobility, and loss of cultural vitality made for an unsatisfactory state of affairs which affected the greater part of the population. One expression of this feeling of dissatisfaction was the increase in banditry during the second half of the sixteenth and the first third of the seventeenth century. This phenomenon was exploited by two groups, known as *nyerros* and *cadells*, who competed for power, undermining the authority of the Viceroy, the representative in Catalonia of the permanently absent King.

During the sixteenth and seventeenth centuries Catalonia retained its own independent institutions, currency, customs, and tax system. Catalan continued to be the official language. Protected by the limitation of royal power, which prevented the Crown from raising new taxes there without the consent of the Corts, Catalonia suffered less from the overtaxation that was to drain the riches of Castile. At the same time, however, Catalonia occupied an entirely subsidiary position in the Empire, most of which – especially the American colonies – was considered to be the heritage of Castile.

The Catalan political system had seriously degenerated. The kings, who resided at the Court in Madrid, tended to summon the Catalan Corts less and less frequently. Under Charles I they met eight times, under Philip II only twice, under Philip III once, and on the two occasions when they were summoned by Philip IV, in 1626 and 1632, they ended in failure without the grievances against royal functionaries having been repaired or the grant of money requested by the Crown having been submitted to a vote. After this the parliament did not meet at all again until 1701. The King received a fixed income from Catalonia, equivalent to half the budget of the city of Barcelona and one-quarter that of the Generalitat.

Historians consider that many seventeenth-century texts reveal the existence of a defensive form of patriotism in Catalonia which makes it possible to talk about Catalan nationalism even as early as this. When Castile, weakened and exhausted, was no longer capable of supporting Spanish domination over Europe, the Court in Madrid brought more pressure to bear in order to increase the financial and military contributions of the kingdoms of the Crown of Aragon. At the same time, however, awareness of the irreparable decadence of the Empire reinforced Catalan resistance.

In the midst of the Thirty Years War, in which the kings of France and Spain struggled for hegemony in Europe, the Catalan peasantry staged a rising on the feast of Corpus Christi 1640 against the expense of maintaining Spanish troops billetted in Catalonia and also, indirectly, against feudal dues and privileges. The revolt – known as the *Corpus de Sang* (Corpus of Blood) – was headed by the Generalitat, under its president, Pau Claris. The Spanish Viceroy was assassinated, and Catalonia declared its independence from the King of Spain. However, in order to ward off a Spanish attack, Pau Claris was obliged to submit to the vassalage of the King of France. The present Catalan national anthem, the *Cant dels Segadors* (Song of the Reapers), was a popular song which appeared during this period, and the words explain the reasons for the insurrection.

French assistance, which was vital in order to hold Spanish troops at bay, soon proved more harmful to Catalan rights than the dominion of Spain. The separation of Portugal from the Spanish monarchy took place at this same period. In the mid-seventeenth century, a fall in population, caused by the war and the plague, put an end to the slow recovery which Catalonia had enjoyed during the sixteenth century.

The War of Separation (1640–51) ended in the surrender of Catalonia, and though the country's constitutional system was saved, the defeat was all too obvious. In 1659 Rosselló and Cerdanya, the Catalan regions north of the Pyrenees, were annexed by France. The King of

Spain acquired the right to exclude names from the lists of those elegible for office in the Generalitat and the Barcelona City Council. The Catalan institutions were still of use in resisting absolutism but, now the Generalitat was no longer subjected to the control of the parliament, it governed less efficiently. The Catalan Corts would never again be summoned by Charles II, the last King of the House of Austria. The situation was essentially one of transition, either towards a system of government similar to that of the Low Countries or Britain, or towards an absolutist monarchy in the French Bourbon style.

During the last third of the seventeenth century, the Catalan economy started to recover again. Catalonia began to take part in Atlantic trade since Catalan merchants wanted their share in the profits from the commerce with the American colonies, which was monopolized by Seville.

Throughout that period war was intermittent; Catalonia was invaded three times by France and in 1697 the King of France's troops even captured Barcelona. Louis XIV withdrew, however, because of pressure from the other European powers and because, in view of the imminent death of Charles II of Spain, leaving no son to succeed him, the French King needed reconciliation with the Court in Madrid in the hope that the Spanish Crown might pass to his grandson, Philip of Anjou. This outcome was made more difficult by the Francophobia of the Catalans, exacerbated by the recent wars and by their desire to recover Rosselló. The Spanish Crown failed to take advantage of the revolt that broke out in Rosselló in 1666 against the heavy taxes levied by the French monarchy, nor did it so much as consider the possibility of exchanging the Catalan regions dominated by France for territories in Flanders which sooner or later would inevitably be lost.

The billetting of Spanish troops during the war against the King of France, which occurred after the series of bad harvests, gave rise in 1688 to a situation of tension in the Catalan countryside and in a number of towns, similar to that created in 1640. On this occasion, however, the *Revolta dels Gorretes* or *dels Barretines* ('revolt of the berets', a reference to the traditional beret worn by Catalan peasants and sailors, similar in colour and shape to the Phrygian cap) did not have the support of the Generalitat, and the dominant classes sided with the repression of the peasantry.

When the Bourbon Philip V (1700–46) ascended the Spanish throne, he immediately summoned the Catalan Parliament and in 1701 swore to uphold the Catalan laws. This action enabled him to obtain a grant of money in exchange for certain concessions, but it failed to dispel the fear of Bourbon-type absolutism, and Catalan demands for participation in the government of the Empire were not satisfied either. War immediately broke out in Europe because England, Holland, and the Emperor of Germany feared that the Franco–Spanish alliance might bring to fruition the ambitions of Louis XIV to dominate Europe and America. The allies accordingly proclaimed the second son of the Emperor of Germany, Archduke Charles of Austria, as King of Spain.

In 1705 a revolt against Philip V broke out on the Plain of Vic and Catalan delegates reached an agreement with England in Genoa. The anti-Bourbon allies subsequently landed in Barcelona, and Catalonia rose against Philip V. The revolt spread to the kingdoms of Valencia, Aragon, and Majorca. The 1640 war had been a war of separation in which the Catalans had stood alone, though the independence of Portugal was achieved at the same time. The aim of the war of 1705, in contrast, was not merely to defend Catalonia's political autonomy, but to intervene in the affairs of the Hispanic monarchy, and the whole of the former Crown of Aragon was on the side of the insurgents.

Though in Catalonia the revolt was not aimed against the nobility, as it was in the Kingdom of Valencia, the greater part of the Catalan nobility supported Philip V. The allied offensive, in which troops belonging to Archduke Charles reached Madrid, was followed by the first setbacks. Valencia and Aragon were occupied by Bourbon forces and deprived of their regional privileges. By 1710 only Catalonia and the Balearic Islands remained loyal to Archduke Charles of Austria.

Then, in 1711, as a result of a series of chance circumstances, Archduke Charles succeeded the Emperor of Germany. England and Holland promptly lost interest in the continuation of the war against the Bourbons, because they had no wish to see Spain and Germany united under the same monarch either. They agreed to accept Philip V as King of Spain provided he renounced all Spain's possessions in Europe, recognized England's dominion over Gibraltar and Minorca, and granted it the right to restricted direct trade with Spanish America. The general peace in Europe was settled by the Treaty of Utrecht in 1713.

Catalonia, a mere pawn on the chess board of Europe, was abandoned by its allies. The succession being no longer at issue, the war which Catalonia now continued against Spain alone came to be seen as a defence of Catalan liberties. After withstanding a siege by French and Spanish troops for over a year, Barcelona was compelled to surrender on 11 September 1714. In the twentieth century the date of 11 September was chosen as the Catalan national day.

Philip V finally abolished all Catalan political institutions by right of conquest, and imposed Castilian laws, absolutism, and centralism.

2 The Political Provincialization and Economic Growth of Catalonia in the Eighteenth and Nineteenth Centuries

THE LOSS OF POLITICAL AUTONOMY

By the so-called Decree of Nueva Planta, issued by Philip V in 1716, Catalonia's former political system was replaced by one in which royal authority was all-encompassing. Councillors, who were normally nobles, were designated by the Crown for life to head the local councils, putting an end to the participation of the merchants, members of the liberal professions, craftsmen, and shopkeepers who had previously been appointed periodically by drawing lots. Seigniorial rights, on the other hand, were maintained intact throughout most of the country. By present-day standards, the former system had not been democratic, but the popular classes became much further removed from political institutions from 1714 onwards.

Instead of enjoying fiscal privileges as previously, Catalonia became a country overburdened by taxation in comparison with Castile. By the time the *cadastro* (a new tax on personal wealth) was lowered in 1718, to avoid reducing the country to bankruptcy, it was four times heavier than the amount the Catalan parliament had agreed to pay to Philip V in 1702. The Spanish monarchy wiped out its financial deficit through the fiscal exploitation of the countries of the former Crown of Aragon.

It was not the Spanish Bourbon administration but the fact that the property register was never updated that made Catalan economic growth possible in the eighteenth century. Catalonia's own civil law and the exemption from military service were salvaged from the defeat. As late as 1760, at a meeting of the Spanish parliament held in Madrid, deputies from Barcelona, Valencia, Saragossa, and Majorca appealed to King Charles III for the restoration of their lost political rights, but to no avail. In 1773 a revolt against the introduction of compulsory military service[1] in Catalonia forced the authorities to back down and, despite Charles III's decrees against the public use of the Catalan language, Spanish was not generally employed in primary education and notarial documents until the nineteenth century.

Catalan resistance to Napoleon Bonaparte in 1808, almost a hundred years after the War of Successsion, has been interpreted as a sign of consolidated Spanish nationalism, particularly in view of the attempt made by Napoleon to annex Catalonia to France. However, the creation of the Junta Superior del Principado de Cataluña (High Council of the Principality of Catalonia) was in fact the first attempt at self-government since 1714. Born of a revolutionary movement against the newly installed political régime following the abdication in 1808 of Charles IV and Ferdinand VII in favour of Joseph Bonaparte, the Junta de Cataluña tried to put a brake on the process of social rebellion and preserve the old régime. It did not succeed for a variety of reasons. Among them was the fact that the war itself, in which the old régime had failed to fight off the invader, obliged the Junta to undermine the foundations of the social and legal structure it sought to maintain. For instance, after defending the payment of tithes and feudal taxes, it had to seize the revenue produced by the tithes in order to finance the gigantic task of opposing Napoleon's generals without assistance from outside. In supporting the continued existence of Juntas in the former kingdoms of Spain, following the creation of a central Spanish authority for resistance against the French, the Junta de Cataluña was defining an alternative federal model – though the word federal was not used – against the liberal, centralist uniformism predominating in the rump of the Spanish parliament by now forced to retreat to Cadiz. It was this parliament that was the first to endow Spain with a liberal-type political constitution. The experience of the war against Napoleon constituted a precedent for the future Catalan federalist movement. From 1808 to 1814 the Catalans found themselves between two centralist régimes with assimilatory intentions and in such circumstances the victory of the weaker of the two, Spain, seemed for the Catalans the lesser of two evils.

INDUSTRIALIZATION

During the eighteenth century Catalonia evolved from an economy based on agricultural produce and manufactured goods for local consumption to an economy with wider commercial aspirations. The trade outlets created throughout Spain for the sale of wine and brandy were subsequently used by the new cotton mills. Spanish possessions in America constituted an additional market. The disastrous war against French domination and the loss of the greater part of Spain's colonial empire did not suffice to prevent a subsequent transition to factory production, and in the course of the nineteenth century Catalonia gradually became an economically developed country within a Spain which, even at the end of the nineteenth century, still did not fulfil the requisites of an industrial economy.

In the century of the steam engine, Catalan industrialization took place in a country without coal or iron, with very few raw materials and a market – Spain – with very low purchasing power. The poverty of the peninsular market, where Catalan goods had to compete with English-produced articles, was not offset by access to colonial outlets. Spain's American empire was lost by 1824, and Cuba and Puerto Rico did not become a reserved market until the 1890s, only a few years before gaining independence from the mother country in 1898. In 1858 as little as 3 per cent of the cotton fabrics imported by Cuba were made in Spain, that is, in Catalonia.

As a result of protectionist import policies, from 1821 onwards the Catalans were obliged to make their bread from Spanish-produced cereals that were more expensive than imported cereals, and this made the price of Catalan manpower relatively high, despite the fact that the workers' standard of living was lower than in other industrialized countries.

Catalonia's excessive dependence on outside sources of energy was made up for by hydraulic energy generated by turbines on the irregularly flowing Catalan rivers. It was, of course, not until the twentieth century that the hydroelectric potential of the Pyrenees was harnessed.

A further adverse factor was the chronic political instability of Spain during most of the nineteenth century. Instead of parties peacefully succeeding one another in power, there were military coups; and instead of changes of government there were changes in the constitution and régime. Between 1822 and 1875, opposition to liberal capitalism unleashed no fewer than five civil wars which were fought out on Catalan territory. The last three were known as the Carlist wars because the rebels were supporters of the descendents of Charles, the brother of Ferdinand VII (1813–33), against his daughter, Isabel II (1843–68), and her son, Alfonso XII (1874–85). The enormous debts of the state, despite the capital raised by the confiscation of Church and municipal property, pushed interest rates up and hindered industrial investment. Central government expenditure on public works was insufficient, and the four provincial Diputacions[2] into which Catalonia was divided in 1833 were later obliged to join together to raise new taxes in order to supplement the role of the state in highway construction.

To a Spain of farmers and artisans, and to governments in a pre-industrial city of courtiers like Madrid, the social problems generated by industrialization were something alien. They saw the labour disputes of industrial Catalonia merely as problems of public order and the Catalan labour movement as an intolerable provocation that might be imitated by the agricultural masses of the underdeveloped regions of Spain.

Because of all this, the industrialization of Catalonia was marked by numerous shortcomings: development of the metal industry came late in the day and was fraught with difficulties; light industry remained too important for too long; countless small firms sprang up, hampering technological, organizational, commercial, and financial economies of scale; the cost of manpower caused employers to maintain firm opposition to improvements in working conditions, despite the workers' low standard of living. The difficulties Catalan industry had to overcome made it uncompetitive abroad and led Catalan industrialists to press unceasingly for protectionist measures such as the generalization of high import duty as a means of developing the Spanish economy. As the Catalan industrialist and parliamentarian Josep Ferrer Vidal remarked in 1855: 'While Castilians buy ten yards of Catalan cloth once a year at a price 40% higher than English cloth, Catalans eat, and greatly enjoy, Castilian bread 30 or 40% more expensive than that from Odesa[3] three times every day.' But the protectionism demanded by the Catalans was unpopular in the agricultural regions of Spain, where it was seen, not as the Catalan protectionists claimed, as a means of safeguarding the 'national market' or of 'developing the national economy' (national in this case meaning Spanish), but as the private defence of industries concentrated in Catalonia.

The Catalan industrial bourgeoisie, constantly on the defensive and subject to the will of the great Castilian and Andalusian landowners, was a more conservative, less revolutionary class than might have been expected.

Since, in spite of the odds, Catalonia did succeed in becoming an industrialized country in the nineteenth century, it may well be asked how the effects of the adverse circumstances just enumerated were overcome. The mechanization of existing craft industries and the creation of new ones cannot be put down to the innate qualities of thrift and industriousness popularly attributed to the Catalan people. They must be related to social structures. In eighteenth-century Catalonia possession of land (not by outright ownership but through indefinite assignment in exchange for a fixed rent) was extremely widespread. This was due to the existence of long-term leases and *rabassa morta* tenancies (whereby the exploitation of vineyards was linked to the lifetime of the vines) and to the fact that Catalan law, by making the first-born the sole heir, averted the evils of 'minifundism'.

The intensive cultivation of vines on dry lands for the production of wine and brandy for export led to specialization. Once this opening to the outside world had been achieved, mills were set up to produce calico and other more traditional types of cloth. But the economic change that was to take place in the nineteenth century was brought about neither by the existence of a specialized agriculture, nor by wine exports or textile mills. The decisive factor was the importance of the middle classes in property relations and in the production system, which enabled rising incomes to generate a more than proportional rise in consumption. In Lower Andalusia, for instance, there were skilled craftsmen, capital that had been accumulated by merchants as a result of the monopoly of trade with the American colonies in the sixteenth and seventeenth centuries, first in Seville and later in Cadiz, and a prosperous wine-exporting agriculture. But property was unevenly distributed and this prevented the positive factors mentioned from leading to industrialization during the nineteenth century.

Thus in the case of Catalonia the exaltation of values such as industriousness, thrift, and the spirit of initiative was more a sign than a cause of development. Though experience in business and trade, a tradition of craftsmanship, and a thriving agriculture all constituted a very useful and, indeed, even an indispensable heritage, such factors were not sufficient to bring about the age of radical and largely traumatic upheavals which marked the emergence of industry, a process that began in the 1840s, was consolidated in the 1860s and continued to grow and change until the dawn of the twentieth century.

THE POLITICAL SUBSERVIENCE OF CATALONIA

The fact that their country was becoming industrialized within a still backward Spain inspired the Catalans with a feeling of superiority which prompted them to rebel against their political subservience and cultural dependence on Castilian, or Castilianized, Spain. It was this economic development, which set Catalonia apart from the rest of Spain, that was the solid material base on which the *Renaixença* was built, a movement which, though fostered by Romanticism, did not expire with it but continued to thrive, providing literary encouragement to political Catalanism. The Catalan thinker Jaume Balmes expressed awareness of the more modern structures of Catalonia when he wrote in 1843: 'It should not be forgotten that Catalonia is the only province that, strictly speaking, forms part of the European industrial movement. . . . On leaving Catalonia for a foreign country, one observes nothing that is not in some way a continuation of what one has seen here: it might be said that the journey is between one province and another of a single nation; but on leaving Catalonia for the Spanish hinterland, one seems really to have left the homeland behind and to have entered foreign lands.'

The creation of a liberal state in the mid-1830s facilitated industrialization, despite the deficiencies already mentioned, but it also brought with it more effective centralization and greater uniformity than under the absolute monarchy. Catalans continued to take virtually no part in the affairs of state. Of the over nine hundred ministers who served in different Spanish governments between 1833 and 1901, only 25, or 2.7 per cent, were Catalans, a figure far lower than the corresponding percentage of Catalans within the population of Spain (10 per cent).

Various factors account for this position of inferiority. Of only secondary importance was the fact that Catalan politicians had a poor command of the Spanish language in an age when parliamentary oratory seemed crucial. Other factors were more decisive. For the middle classes of the less-developed Spanish regions, social promotion could be achieved primarily through a carreer in the civil service, which still lacked professionalization and proper regulations, or in the army (both careers being confused at the time with the pursuit of politics). Moreover, the population of these regions identified with a state whose official language was, in most cases, their own mother tongue. In Catalonia, where industrialization was underway, a wider range of professional opportunities was available and for Catalans, entering the civil service meant abandoning their own identity, and first and foremost their language.

Moreover, the majority of Catalans saw politics as the representation and administration of 'moral and material interests'. This conception was quite unlike that of politics 'as a profession at the service of the state', which implied the symbiosis, and even the confusion, of party and government and led to the total subordination of the provincial heads of the Spanish oligarchical parties to the central leadership, so that instead of political integration of active citizens through representation, what occurred was the total subordination of government to its private political supporters. This state of affairs was displeasing to a society like that of Catalonia, which seemed able to create non-governmental associations in keeping with its own degree of development.

Though the Spanish governmental machinery was neither so inefficient nor so unrepresentative as its Catalan critics claimed, the ever-increasing numbers of civil and military personnel within it had a lowering effect on professional standards. In 1860 Spain had 189,000 public servants, four times more than Great Britain which had almost double the population of Spain. In 1906 only 55 per cent of the officers serving in the Spanish army had regular posts and, even so, the ratio of officers to privates was one to eight, as against one to twenty in the German and Italian armies and one to twenty-three in the French.

The political subservience of the Catalans was matched by the Catalanophobia detectable in the Madrid press, especially in times of political instability such as the War of the *Matiners* (1846–49), the *Bienio Progresista* ('Two Years of Progress') (1854–56) and the *Sexenio Democrático* ('Six Years of Democracy') (1868–74), and notably during the period of the Second Republic (1873). As the Catalan writer Mañé i Flaquer observed in 1856: 'The most serious charge against Catalonia is that its inhabitants are too Catalan; unfortunately, thanks to the misguided policy that has been applied to Catalonia, the Catalans have stopped being Catalans without becoming Spaniards.'

Seen from Madrid, Catalonia was a rebellious and disloyal province, and if the Catalans wished to take part in Spanish politics they must renounce their Catalan identity. This view was prevalent long before Catalan identity had an organized political counterpart in the form of political Catalanism. Indeed, in the nineteenth century the Catalans may well have felt more intensely Catalan than in the twentieth century, but this feeling lacked a political will.

THE DEBATE OVER THE SOCIAL ORIGINS OF CATALANISM

The question of the starting point of Catalanism as a social movement has long been debated by historians. All national movements aim to transcend class boundaries, but the various classes and social groups identify with them in different ways in different political circumstances. Class hegemonies tend to succeed one another through changes in the correlation of political forces, and social struggles influence the predominant configuration and strategy of national movements, expressing a form of solidarity which is different from class solidarity but not incompatible with it.

In the 1960s Catalan nationalism was presented as a bourgeois epiphenomenon. According to the French Marxist historian Pierre Vilar, the frustrated desire of turning Spain into a modern industrial nation led the Catalan bourgeoisie to dream of a state of their own and of a Catalan nation. The Catalan political scientist Jordi Solé Tura, in his analysis of the ideas of the early twentieth-century Catalanist politician Prat de la Riba, took this argument further than Vilar had intended by stating that Catalan nationalism was a product of the structural differences between Catalonia and the rest of Spain and of the weakness of the dominant class in Catalonia, which was incapable of carrying out the bourgeois revolution. Though Solé Tura later admitted that his book was more political than historical and its aim was to destroy myths, it contributed to the view taken by new generations of university students, at least until the widespread nationalist radicalization of the mid-1970s, that Catalanism was an exclusively bourgeois undertaking incompatible with revolutionary socialism.

To present the failure of Catalonia to intervene in the governmental affairs of Spain as the overriding factor in the emergence of Catalan nationalism was to underestimate the importance of the determination of the Catalans to resist assimilation and develop a collective identity by making Catalonia itself advance without submitting it to outside influences.

In the 1970s the Catalan historians Fèlix Cucurull and Josep Termes rejected these theses, each of them from a different point of view, by defending the notion of a political Catalanism with roots in the popular classes and claiming that it was only later that part of the Catalan bourgeoisie joined in a movement that had previously been alien to it.

Fèlix Cucurull detected a continuity in the Catalanist movement which he and other historians traced back to the Catalan revolt of 1640 and its precedents. His theory rested on a number of attempts at particularism, which other historians see as mere manifestations of inter-regional diversity in the course of the Spanish liberal revolution. Some of these attempts found expression in documents (such as *La Bandera* (1836), the proposal of Bertran i Soler (1849), studied by Joan Camps, to reestablish the Catalan Diputació del General, or J. B. Guardiola's *Libro de la Democracia* (1851) which states that 'Spain is not, in the strict and true meaning of the word, a nation but a collection of nations'). Others took the form of political action, like the anti-centralist democratic revolts of 1837, 1840, and 1843.

In Fèlix Cucurull's opinion all this was already part of political Catalanism and the name it took in each period – provincialism, *foralisme*[4], federalism, Catalanism – was of secondary importance, since the attitude of social and political rebellion adopted by the Catalans on each occasion responded to an implicit desire to obtain self-determination, with more or less extensive powers, under the banner of tradition or of socialism. Thus political Catalanism, according to Cucurull, existed long before the turn of the century.

Josep Termes stressed that part of the Catalan bourgeoisie joined in the Catalanist project very late in the day. He also attached little significance to texts emanating from political parties as indicators of Catalan national awareness and stressed the importance of the culture and aspirations of the popular classes in understanding nineteenth-century Catalanism. For Termes, the Catalan popular classes had already laid the foundations of a national awakening before conservative Catalanism – that of the Lliga Regionalista party – appeared in 1901; the democratic, federalist, and *foralista* feelings that came from the people had merged with the cultural action of professionals and intellectuals to form a multi-faceted Catalan particularism which embraced tendencies ranging from autonomist regionalism to emotional separatism via strict cultural and historicist nationalism. This particularism, according to Termes, was basically generated by the popular Left, though it was not converted into doctrine in the programmes of working-class and popular parties until the end of the 1920s. What this interpretation fails to do is account for the time lag.

The form taken by the debate about the social origins of Catalanism had more to do with ideological than historiographical interests. In recent years it has not been pursued and today attracts rather less attention than before.

THE *RENAIXENÇA*

No one disputes the role of the *Renaixença*, that is, the recovery of Catalan as a literary language, in creating the atmosphere in which Catalan nationalism was to be born. Nations have a cultural existence before acquiring a political existence and in the course of the nineteenth century Catalonia succeeded in making its own language, which had remained the only vehicle of everyday communication, into a modern literary language.

At the end of the eighteenth century a number of Catalan scholars began to sketch out the outlines of the economic, literary and political history of Catalonia from the Middle Ages onwards. These scholars' aims were towards the recovery of Catalonia's self-esteem and cultural identity, yet their work was done in Spanish. One must not forget that in a mainly illiterate society, the minority that writes and publishes tends to do so in a language with a wider readership than that of the mother tongue. The role previously played by Latin in this regard had been taken over by languages that had undergone standardization, languages supported by the power of a state, even though they were foreign languages.

As the number of potential readers grew, the mother tongue and popular language had the opportunity to become a modern literary language once more. But the process was a difficult one. For want of prestigious modern literary models in the Catalan language, the *Renaixença* tended to express itself in a medievalized, archaic language, far removed from spoken Catalan. Moreover, basic schooling was in Castilian, the official language of the Spanish State, and not in the mother tongue, with the result that the Catalans were illiterate in their own language without becoming really proficient in Spanish either. Furthermore it was no easy matter to read and write in Catalan with its lack of standard rules for spelling and usage, such as those possessed by Spanish. For all these reasons, the literary spread of Catalan occurred later in prose than in poetry. Nineteenth century histories of Catalonia, such as Víctor Balaguer's Romantic works and other more learned studies, which were an integral part of the movement of *Renaixença*, were written and published in Castilian.

Aribau's poem *Oda a la Pàtria*, written in Catalan in 1833, was a precedent whose impact was no greater than that of Joan Pau Ballot's *Gramàtica i Apològia de la Llengua Catalana* published in 1814, or the 1832 Catalan translation of the New Testament. But by identifying language and homeland, Aribau's famous poem quite unintentionally formulated one of the key ideas of Catalanism. While for other nationalities, race or religion were to constitute the main sign of a distinctive collective identity, for Catalonia this role would be played by the language.

In 1843 the publication in a single volume of the poems of Joaquim Rubió i Ors, under the pseudonym of Lo Gaiter del Llobregat, gave strength to the hitherto scattered elements of the recovery of literature in Catalan. The author's prologue, written in Catalan, states, 'Catalonia can still aspire to independence, not political independence but certainly literary independence.'

In 1859, the Barcelona Jocs Florals (Floral Games, an ancient literary contest) were restored, bringing renascent Catalan literature to a wider audience. However, other undertakings with lesser literary pretentions had a wider popular impact. These included booklets of religious apologetics by the priest and preacher Antoni Maria Claret, or the repertoire of songs collected by Anselm Clavé and sung in 1864 by the eighty-five choral societies belonging to the Euterpe movement, or the numerous short comedies of manners that were performed in Catalan.

In the 1870s, the quality of Catalan theatrical output was enhanced by the appearance of figures like Serafí Soler ('Pitarra'), who, along with other authors, defended the use of Catalan 'as it is spoken today' against the artificial language of the Jocs Florals. Finally, towards 1870, the publication of magazines in Catalan became an established fact, with the appearance of two publications that were destined to enjoy a long existence: *La Campana de Gràcia* and *L'Esquella de la Torratxa*, both of popular, republican inspiration.

But the advance of the *Renaixença* encountered more difficulties in the two forms of reading matter most widespread among the new general public that had been created by the recent spread of literacy: the daily press and serialized novels. Newspapers and novels written in Spanish but published in Catalonia did more than the schools to foster diglossia and linguistic and cultural alienation. This was so, not only because the powerful Barcelona publishing industry catered for the widest possible market and thus worked exclusively in Spanish, but because, as in the case of the daily press, as long as the Catalan language remained unstandardized it was difficult to reach the average reader, even though Catalan was both his mother tongue and the language he normally spoke.

The founders of the *Renaixença* – with the exception of Rubió i Ors – were doubtful about the viability of using Catalan in all fields. They tried to save the written use of the Catalan language but were not convinced it was possible to overcome diglossia. In this initial phase they confined themselves to defensive measures, and did not advocate a programme for restoring the Catalan language to 'normal' usage, since this would have required an autonomous Catalan public administration.

During the 1880s the *Renaixença* reached its peak and underwent a crisis of renovation. The poetical genius of Jacint Verdaguer, the plays of Àngel Guimerà and the realist novels of Narcís Oller won great popularity and succeeded in bringing the literary and spoken language together, attaining a quality that even enabled them to find readers outside Catalonia. On the other hand, the Modernist movement which followed the *Renaixença* stressed the vital urgency of overcoming orthographic anarchy, broadening the range of outside influences, and increasing the professional standards and ambitions of writers in their own language. While a Catalan literature had been created, a Catalan culture was still required, and that meant Catalanizing education and securing official-language status for Catalan. In order to achieve this, it was necessary to bring about the political autonomy without which cultural autonomy was impossible. Catalans were to discover that, in the long run, and contrary to what Rubió i Ors had said in 1843, without political independence there could be no literary independence.

Notes

1. One of every five young men fit for the army was selected at random for obligatory service.
2. Administrative and economic organs of government set up in each of the provinces of Barcelona, Girona, Lleida and Tarragona.
3. A reference to wheat imports from the Ukraine, though those from North America and Argentina were also highly competitive.
4. The tendency to call for the re-establishment of the *fors,* that is, the political privileges enjoyed by Catalonia prior to 1714. This traditionalist vision of self-government, oriented towards the past rather than the present, was characteristic of the Carlists, who were opponents of the liberal revolution.

3 Catalan Federalism and the Failure of the First Republic

THE STRENGTH AND WEAKNESS OF FEDERALISM

The experience of the *Sexenio Democrático* ('Six Years of Democracy'), which began with the dethronement of Isabel II in September 1868, had far-reaching effects on the subsequent rise of political Catalanism. In the first elections with universal male suffrage held in 1869, a new political force, Federal Republicanism, won a majority in Catalonia, though it immediately became apparent that it commanded only a minority in the rest of Spain. This was the first sign of the appearance of the distinct personality of Catalonia. Although Federal Republicanism was an organization that encompassed the whole of Spain, it presented an alternative project for a Spanish State into which Catalonia could fit without either being disloyal to Spain or giving up its distinctive features or aspirations to self-government. The rationalist, universalist formulas of Federal Republicanism served to conceal a strong undercurrent of Catalan particularism, though the regionalism of the early leader of Catalan Federal Republicanism, Pi Margall, was Spanish and not Catalanist.

For reasons of democracy, the creation of a Spanish federal State was to be based on the former kingdoms and historical and cultural regions of the Peninsula. For the Republicans, moreover, municipal autonomy was as important as regional autonomy. Later on this stand in favour of municipal rights was to be used against Regionalism. It was also the hope of the Federal Republicans that a federal solution could be found to the Cuban question, thus avoiding a break between the colony and the mother country. The break seemed inevitable, however, after the independence rising in September 1868 which sparked off the first Cuban War, or Ten Years War. Iberianism was another ideal pursued by the Federal Republicans since if Spain were to become a federation Portugal could form part of a new, radically restructured Peninsular state. Iberianism was later to be part of the Catalan nationalist ideological repertory drawn up by the Regionalist politician

Prat de la Riba, though the proposal remained inoperative.

Catalan Federal Republicanism had to contend with the fact that many Spanish Federalist leaders aimed at little more than decentralization. Moreover, since certain other Spanish regions lacked an economic metropolis and undisputed capital like Barcelona, there was a tendency towards 'cantonalism', or the defence of even smaller territorial units, which made it difficult to build an articulate form of federalism such as existed in Catalonia. But in Catalonia too, federalism came up against the rivalry between 'benevolent' and 'intransigent' factions and against a new civil war – the third in a century – that was sparked off in 1872 by the Carlists in support of the claims of a rival branch of the Bourbon dynasty to the Spanish throne. The democratic ideals and programme of social reform, which attracted the downtrodden Catalan popular classes to Federal Republicanism, at the same time drove away the local industrial bourgeoisie, who remained on the defensive throughout the *Sexenio Democrático*, and subsequently supported the Bourbon restoration which placed Alfonso XII, the son of Isabel II, on the throne.

While the 'benevolent' Federalists aimed at setting up a federal state by legal means, from above, through the use of central government machinery, and without destroying the existing institutions, the 'intransigents' were bent on building a federal state from the bottom upwards, the regions themselves freely deciding how much unity they wished and how much sovereignty they were prepared to surrender. The 'intransigents' considered the position of their 'benevolent' counterparts did not amount to federalism at all, but to decentralization, since it was not founded on the sovereigny of the regional states, but rather on that of the central State which was to grant limited regional autonomy. Even so, the 'intransigents' rejected the term 'separatists' as calumnious.

Throughout the *Sexenio* the Catalan Federalists were torn between their links with the Spanish Republicans and the objective of establishing a federal pact on the basis of an autonomous Catalan authority. At no time did they express the slightest desire for independence. The Federal Republicanists tried to set up a stable relationship with tenant farmers and industrial workers. They promised to give greater stability to land tenancies and to make *rabassa morta* leases – whose duration was determined by the lifetime of the vines – equivalent to a long-term lease that could be revoked at the farmer's request. They also promised to protect cooperatives, regulate the working day, with shorter hours for women and children, and set up a network of mixed arbitration commissions to settle labour conflicts and carry out inspections. Much of this programme became law under the First Republic (1873–74), but it remained in force for as brief a time as the Republic itself.

The inability of the Federal Republicans to gain power and reform the State either through peaceful, electoral means, or through revolution, despite the attempted insurrection that took place in the autumn of 1890, created a climate of disillusionment which was reinforced by the re-establishment of military service as a result of the Cuban War. This made the working class more receptive to the revolutionary collectivism of the First International and encouraged electoral abstentionism, a trend that was contrary to the interests of Federal Republicanism itself. Nevertheless, the ties between the Federal Republicans and the working-class Internationalists, many of whom were followers of Bakunin, were never broken off and, despite ideological conflicts, remained dormant throughout the following decades, ready to be reawakened by anyone interested in so doing. It was no coincidence that anarchism took root in the same places as Federal Republicanism and attracted a number of former militant Federalists.

In 1870, when the pages of *El Estado Catalán*, a Federalist paper directed by the intransigent but not revolutionary Valentí Almirall, were vibrating with implicitly Catalanist anti-centralism, the first Catalanist patriotic association was founded in Barcelona. Under the name of Jove Catalunya (Young Catalonia), it was made up of men of letters headed by the playwright Àngel Guimerà, Pere Aldavert, and J. Roca i Roca and aimed at heightening public awareness but not at direct political action. The following year saw the appearance of the magazine *La Renaixensa*, which became its mouthpiece. During its long life this publication was to play a key role in the Catalanist movement and would give its name, *a posteriori*, to the *Renaixença* movement whose goal was the restoration of Catalan as a literary language.

At the same time the Carlists in their own way also took up the cause of self-government. When the pretender Charles VII staged a rising in May 1872 he made a proclamation to the Catalans, Aragonese, and Valencians promising to restore the historical regional privileges (*furs* or *fueros*) abolished by Philip V. But within the Carlist ranks, as among the Federal Republicans, there were currents in favour of Catalan aspirations and others opposed to them. In 1874 the Catalan Carlists failed to pursuade their pretender to create a Diputació for the whole of Catalonia based on the ancient privileges. Whereas the Catalan Federal Republicans saw self-government for Catalonia as a matter of democratic principle, the Carlists, as enemies of liberalism, sought to achieve autonomy in the name of historical tradition by means of a Catholic, anti-revolutionary monarchy.

THE FIRST REPUBLIC

In February 1873 the then King of Spain, Amadeus of Savoy, abdicated, feeling unable to cope simultaneously with the Carlist rebellion in the Basque Country, Navarre, and Catalonia, the Cuban rising and its possible repercussions in the Caribbean, the scorn of the Castilian and Andalusian landowning aristocracy and of the greater part of the Catalan industrial bourgeoisie, and the hostility of Republican popular opinion in the cities of the Mediterranean seaboard. This led to the proclamation of the First Republic by a Monarchist parliament opposed to federalism. On 9 March 1873 the intransigent Federalists and the Internationalist anarchists called on the Barcelona provincial Diputació to proclaim the existence of a Catalan State as a first step towards federalization and demanded the demobilization of all soldiers serving in Catalonia. From Madrid, the prime minister, Estanislau Figueras, together with Pi Margall and Almirall himself, succeeded in persuading their fellow Federalists to abandon the attempt, though they did agree to replace the army in Catalonia by a volunteer corps.

The Madrid press again began to give vent to the anti-Catalan feelings that had already expressed themselves with violence on other occasions. On 15 April 1873 the Madrid paper *La Independencia de España* accused Catalonia of having betrayed Spain on various occasions in the past, and *El Eco de España* wrote, 'With the advent of the Republic, Spain has become the patrimony of Catalonia. The Prime Minister is a Catalan. The Minister of the Interior is a Catalan. The Minister of Finance is a Catalan. Of the forty-nine provincial governments, thirty-two are headed by Catalans. And still they are not satisfied. We will have to give them a homogeneous cabinet, made up entirely of Catalans, the seventeen provincial governments they still lack, and get the rest of Spain to pay them increased tributes so that they will do us the favour of not declaring their independence or considering changing their nationality. For this the Catalans themselves are not to blame, but the Castilians, Aragonese, Valencians, Andalusians, inhabitants of Extremadura, Galicians and other Spaniards who suffer and permit it.' The fact that opposition to a democratic regime could imply opposition to the participation of an exceptionally large number of Catalans in the administration of the State, that the rejection of the Republic, which was not yet federal, should involve depicting it as a Catalan undertaking, is indicative of a mentality predisposed to suspicion and antipathy towards the Catalans. And the fact that the Catalans were taking part in Spanish politics and in the reform of the Spanish State actually reinforced the negative reactions instead of attentuating them. Historically there is every indication that 'Catalanophobia' in the centre of Spain preceded the appearance of political Catalanism.

The dissolution of the regular army in Catalonia helped the Carlists, who succeeded in besieging and occupying cities that had rid themselves of their domination during the first Carlist War thirty-five years earlier. The strength of Carlism in Catalonia and the greater realism of the workers' organizations almost certainly explain why there was no attempt in Catalonia to win autonomy and impose federalism from below despite the fact that in mid-July 1873 opposition to the federalization process on the part of the new Republican constituent parliament and the state administration gave rise to such impatience and mistrust that local rebellions (the 'cantonal' revolt) broke out in some Andalusian cities, in Cartagena and Valencia; and, almost simultaneously, a workers' revolt took place in Alcoi, the home at the time of the committee of the Spanish regional federation of the International Working Men's Association (AIT).

The same generals who had been sent in with troops by the Republic to put down the local rebellions – Pavía and Martínez Campos – were to overthrow the Republic itself a few months later. The Republic never became federal because it never acquired a constitution. Even had it done so, judging by the draft that was drawn up, the seventeen federal states would, in fact, have been autonomous regions with powers granted by a decentralized State. Their powers would not have been comparable to those of the United States of America, the model frequently invoked by certain Catalan Federalists.

THE RESTORATION

When in December 1874 the second military pronunciamiento in a year led to the Restoration of the Bourbon monarchy, the Catalan bourgeoisie gave full support to the new régime set up by Cánovas del Castillo. Following the Restoration, the Catalan bourgeoisie succeeded in defeating the 1875 Carlist rising in Catalonia, in re-establishing dominion over Cuba in 1878, in pushing ahead with the dismantling of the Workers' International, and in relegating the Federalists to a position of inferiority. They also halted the movement towards free trade by suspending the fifth of the 1869 import-duty tariffs[1] and established the longed-for political stability of a two-party system in which it finally became possible for two major parties, Liberals and Conservatives, to succeed one another in power, in apparent imitation of the British model.

But the price of this political stability was the hypocrisy of a system of representation in which election results were manipulated in many districts, especially rural ones. Thus, instead of changes of government being decided by the electorate, the ruling party provided itself with a comfortable parliamentary majority so as to be able to govern without problems for a few years, before handing over the affairs of state to the other dynastic Monarchist party power when its turn came to take office. This was the system of oligarchy and *caciquismo* denounced by the Aragonese reformist Joaquín Costa, twenty-five years after the Restoration, as Spain's true form of government, and revealed much earlier (1889) by Almirall in his book *España tal como es*. While this type of political behaviour may not have been invented by the Restoration, there is no doubt that it was under the Restoration that it became systematic, giving the régime the highly convincing appearance of an advanced constitutional monarchy when male universal suffrage, which had not yet been introduced in the majority of European countries and had been replaced in Spain by limited suffrage in 1876, was restored in 1890.

Until 1899 the Catalan industrial bourgeoisie maintained a position of provincial conformity, and even displayed Spanish nationalist feelings on the outbreak of the second Cuban War and the rising in the Philippines. Under the Restoration, Conservative and Liberal governments alike imposed deputies of their own choice in Catalonia, men who knew nothing about the country and were quite alien to its interests. Despite this, and the extreme centralism introduced by the Restoration, the Catalan bourgeoisie was represented in the Spanish parliament and had the means to defend its interests.

But another series of events was to speed the advent of political Catalanism in the last quarter of the nineteenth century, that is, the emergence of the first organizations, independent of the Spanish parties, with both a programme and a theory based on the defence of Catalan aspirations to self-government, regardless of whether Spain was a monarchy or a republic. On the one hand, the Carlists had finally been defeated and the civil war that had intermittently ravaged Catalonia was over. On the other hand, the Federal Republicans had failed to satisfy Catalan aspirations to autonomy through the establishment of a democratic federal state. Furthermore, in Catalonia's already advanced stage of industrial development, relatively stable and cohesive economic structures had been set up that were conducive to internal migrations which established ties of kinship and personal relationships between Catalans from different regions, albeit at the expense of the disproportionate growth of Barcelona. The Catalan bourgeoisie was still not fully integrated into the political system, and it did not identify strongly with either of the dynastic parties that took turns in office, despite the victory of protectionism in 1891. Neither was this a triumph of the Catalan industrialists alone but also of the Basques and the Castilian cereal producers.

Note

1. When a moderately pro-free-trade customs tariff was adopted in 1869, further gradual reductions in protectionist duties were anticipated and a large new reduction was expected in 1875. Since 1869 many industrialists had been voicing opposition to the lowering of tariffs.

4 The First Catalanist Political Organizations

CENTRE CATALÀ AND THE 1885 'MEMORIAL OF GRIEVANCES'

The founder of political Catalanism and the first theoretician of Catalan aspirations to self-government was Valentí Almirall. In 1879, while still a militant Federal Republican, he founded the first Catalan-language newspaper, *El Diari Català*, and in 1880 he convened the first Catalanist Congress in an attempt to create an inter-class front in which Republicans and Monarchists, Catholics and free-thinkers could collaborate. Almirall failed at this congress to reach an agreement with the group linked to the magazine *La Renaixensa*, which styled itself 'apolitical' and turned its weekly paper into a daily to compete with his own. The Congress did however decide to appoint a commission to defend the survival of Catalan civil law against the threat of the Spanish Código Civil, which was being drawn up on the basis of Castilian law. It also decided to create an academy to unify the spelling and regulate the grammar of the Catalan language. Finally, plans were laid for the establishment of a centre to coordinate the many Catalanist organizations that were gradually springing up in various localities. The fact that the Catalanist Congress was attended by the first rambling clubs is indicative of the important role played by cultural associations with patriotic leanings in the early rise and development of Catalanism.

In 1881 Almirall and the minority Catalanist sector of the Catalan Federal Republicans left Pi Margall's party. This event, together with the fact that *El Diari Català* ceased publication leaving *La Renaixensa* as the only Catalan-language daily paper, made possible the unification of the two sectors and the foundation of Centre Català (Catalan Centre) in 1882. Initially the predominant trend within this first civil Catalanist organization was the *Renaixensa* group's rejection of political objectives. Discussion of politics and religion was banned and the only goal was to be the defence of 'the moral and material interests of Catalonia'. In 1883 Centre Català prohibited its members from belonging to Spanish political parties.

The drafting of a defensive manifesto entitled *Memoria en defensa de los intereses morales y materiales de Cataluña* (*Memorandum in defence of the moral and material interests of Catalonia*) enabled Almirall and Centre Català to succeed for the first time in bringing together a single Catalan anti-centralist front. The document, known as the *Memorial de Greuges* (*Memorial of Grievances*), was presented directly to Alfonso XII in 1885. It constituted a reaction to the threat to the Catalan textile industry posed by renewed moves towards free trade in the midst of an economic crisis and by the trade agreements with France and Great Britain; at the same time it expressed displeasure at the danger that Catalan civil law might be abolished as a result of the codification that was underway. In this first united mobilization of Catalanist forces leading men of letters and learning belonging to the *Renaixença* movement, then in its heyday, linked arms with jurists, determined to defend traditional civil law, and with the first Catalanist politicians and industrialists.

In 1886 Almirall published his doctrinal work, *Lo Catalanisme*. In it he tried to persuade the Catalan bourgeoisie to break with Spanish political parties in order to build a Catalan front over and above ideological differences, capable of transforming the Restoration régime and rallying Catalan public opinion in favour of self-government. But Almirall's renunciation of republican anticlericalism and his moderation in the area of social reform were not enough to win the confidence of the majority of the country's landed classes who were wary of his Republican origins and of a certain non-religious, progressive positivism he was unable to give up. The leader of Centre Català was against the idea, defended by the Vic-based group headed by Jaume Collell, which was responsible for the publication of *La Veu de Montserrat*, that Catalanism, like Irish and Polish nationalism, should grow from Catholic roots. He felt that a secular base and a deep commitment to ideological pluralism were necessary if Catalanism were to be a vehicle of modernity and if regionalism were to be seen as a means for regenerating Spain. But Catalonia had only just emerged from the Carlist wars, and the Catalan bourgeoisie, like the Spanish Conservative leader Cánovas del Castillo, felt that while the legitimacy of the political order no longer depended on the Church, the legitimacy of the social order still did.

When protectionism was imposed in 1891, the Catalan industrial bourgeoisie remained loyal to the Restoration system. A majority of the popular classes continued to support the Republicans, though the latter proved incapable of seizing the opportunity offered by the reintroduction of universal suffrage to offer a plausible alternative to the régime and overcome their own internal divisions. In this initial phase Catalanism failed to establish a sufficiently broad social base to become a viable political alternative.

In 1887 Centre Català broke up. The splinter group, which had *La Renaixensa* as its mouthpiece, took the name of Lliga de Catalunya (League of Catalonia). It commanded the support of the Centre Escolar Català (Catalan Centre of University Students), made up of Catalanist students headed by such future leaders of the Catalan movement as Prat de la Riba, Verdaguer i Callís, Domènech i Montaner, Puig i Cadafalch, Cambó and others. Centre Català had arisen from a convergence of views on particular goals but it lacked ideological consensus. Wide differences had continued to separate Catholics from non-Catholics, liberals from traditionalists, and political from apolitical sectors. The reasons for the split are to be sought in ideological and not strategical discrepancies, for Lliga de Catalunya, like Centre Català, was not a political party prepared to compete in elections or one with a well defined social base.

Almirall's group made the mistake of opposing Lliga de Catalunya by falsely branding it as separatist, thus resorting to the same argument as the Spanish centralists. What remained of Centre Català died out in the mid-1890s, having failed to convert Catalan Federal Republicanism into a Catalan nationalist Left. This facilitated the Conservative takeover of the Catalanist movement and delayed the establishment of a broad consensus in favour of self-government that would be capable of appealing to the greater part of the Catalan people, over and above the inevitable division between the Catalan Right and Left and their legitimate struggle for hegemony.

Almirall denounced the Universal Exhibition held in Barcelona in 1888 as a revalidation of the pact between the Catalan bourgeoisie and the Restoration through the mediation of Catalan supporters of the régime such as the Mayor of Barcelona, Rius i Taulet. The opposition of Centre Català was so strong that rival Jocs Florals (Floral Games, i.e. poetical contests) were staged to compete with the official ones, held that year under the presidency of the Queen Regent María Cristina. Lliga de Catalunya presented the Queen with a message reminiscent of the 1885 *Memorial de Greuges* which, while implicitly expressing fidelity to the Monarchy, proposed a solution similar to that adopted by the Queen's relative, the Emperor of Austria, in 1867 when he granted Hungary a very wide margin of self-government within a dual monarchy. The text, written in Catalan, asked, 'that the Catalan nation [might] recover its free and independent parliament, in which all social

classes, from the humblest to the highest, [would be] directly represented'.

THE UNIÓ CATALANISTA AND THE 1892 MANRESA BASES

In 1889 the Lliga de Catalunya and the Centre Escolar Català launched
a campaign of rallies throughout Catalonia to save Catalan civil law
from extinction. The final version of the new Spanish Código Civil
provided for the conservation of Catalan civil law, and this outcome
was described by Verdaguer i Callís as 'the first victory for Catalanism'.
The campaign gave rise to contacts which, in 1891, made possible the
establishment of a confederation of Catalanist centres called Unió
Catalanista (Catalanist Union). At its second annual assembly, held in
Manresa in 1892, Unió Catalanista approved a document known as the
Bases de Manresa (Manresa Bases), which was the first draft statute
of self-government for Catalonia and laid down the essential conditions for a Catalan Regional Constitution.

The Manresa Bases were immediately denounced as separatist. The
charge had no foundation since the opening clauses defined those matters
that were to be placed under the exclusive jurisdiction of the central
government and established the relationship between the regional and
central authorities. For a centralist, uniformist state, however, they
amounted to an intolerable provocation. They proposed that Catalan
should be the sole official language in Catalonia, that public order be
under the exclusive jurisdiction of the Catalan government, which should
also control finance and taxation, that only Catalans should be elegible
for public office in Catalonia, and that, as prior to 1714, there should
be no appeal from decisions of the Catalan high court. Finally, military service (from which the upper classes bought exemption) was to
be replaced by a volunteer corps, as had been the case up to 1845.
Over this last popular demand there was unanimity between Catalanists
and Federalists.

Evidence of the traditional standpoint of the Manresa Bases was
provided mainly by the composition of the Catalan parliament, which
was to be elected by 'all heads of family, grouped together in classes
based on manual work, technical skill or professional careers and on
property, industry and commerce, as far as possible through the corresponding guild organizations'. This type of corporative representation
looked reactionary at a time when universal, individual, direct suffrage

had just been officially re-established (though it was still subject to government manipulation). It derived from an 'organicist' conception of society, which purported to be an alternative to the individualistic character of liberalism and to the uprooting of people brought about by industrialization, and would be abandoned following the subsequent Catalanist electoral victories. It was also a manifestation of *pairalisme*, an ideology that confused patriotism with traditionalism and idealized rural precapitalist structures based on guilds.

Since liberalism served to justify the centralism and uniformity that threatened the survival of Catalonia as a nation, it is hardly surprising that Catalanism should have leant towards antiliberal traditionalism, though it was equally adamant in its rejection of Carlism and of the intransigent integrist attitudes still predominant among the clergy. A traditionalist approach like that of the Manresa Bases in any case had no future in an industrial and increasingly urbanized country like Catalonia where cultural secularization was well underway.

The men of the Catalan literary rebirth belonged to an industrialized city but they exalted an idealized rural world and a glorified medieval past. This conservative message made it possible to build an ideological bridge linking the Barcelona bourgeoisie to craftsmen and countryfolk in opposition to the urban industrial proletariat. Respect for the Church and the sanctification of Catalan civil law were channels uniting the bourgeoisie with the populations of the rural and mountainous areas, after the defeat of Carlism at the hands of the centralist liberal state.

'VIGATANISM'[1]

When confronted in the 1880s with the progressive and popular democratic line of Clavé, Pitarra and Almirall, *pairalisme* found itself to be in harmony with the 'Vigatanist' group whose ideas were expressed through the magazine *La Veu de Montserrat* (*The Voice of Montserrat*), which was published in Vic but had subscribers and contributors throughout Catalonia. *La Veu de Montserrat* invoked the ideas of the religious philosopher Jaume Balmes and would later merge with the Catholic regionalist traditionalism of Torras i Bages, who became bishop of Vic in 1899. The publication of the latter's *La Tradició Catalana* in 1892 provided this current with a corpus of doctrine which, though not integrist in character, and indeed even opposed to integrism, considered that Catalanism must be Catholic and that Catholicism had to be regionalist. The statement attributed to Torras i Bages that 'If Catalonia is to exist, it must be Christian' contained the essence of the positions of traditionalist Catholic Catalanists opposed to the predominance of Almirall's democratic liberal positions within the Catalanist movement.

In 1890 the spirit of Vigatanism was transplanted to a new Barcelona weekly entitled *La Veu de Catalunya* (*The Voice of Catalonia*) which, from the beginning of the century, in the form of a daily, was to become the mouthpiece of the first Catalanist political party, the Lliga Regionalista de Catalunya (The Catalan Regionalist League). Vigatanism was taken over by conservative nationalism, which was to gain the favour of part of the Catalan clergy without defining itself as a pro-clerical party. In 1903 the regionalist politician Enric Prat de la Riba wrote, 'A free Catalonia could be uniformist, centralizing, democratic, absolutist, Catholic, free-thinking, unitary, federalist, individualistic, pro-state, autonomist, or imperialist, and still be Catalan.' Pluralism was thus to be accepted by the Catalan national movement, though in practice conservative nationalism would continue in its attempts to monopolize it.

RADICAL THEORY AND PRAGMATIC STRATEGY

During the final decade of the nineteenth century, the Catalan industrial bourgeoisie was still far removed from Catalanism. Only ten per cent of the delegates who attended the Unió Catalanista assembly in 1892 belonged to the industrial capitalist class, a clear majority being formed by members of the liberal professions, lawyers, notaries, and rural landowners.

Two sectors began to take shape within Unió Catalanista – one regionalist and the other nationalist. The terminology of the Manresa Bases still reflected the predominance of the regionalist sector represented by the newspaper *La Renaixensa*. But from 1895 onwards, the influence of the nationalist sector gradually increased. In theory the more radical of the two, this sector was more inclined towards a pragmatic form of political action: the infiltration of institutions.

This drive to win over and Catalanize cultural and professional bodies bore its first fruit with the election in 1895 of the playwright Àngel Guimerà as President of the important cultural club known as the Ateneu Barcelonès (Barcelona Athenaeum), which from then on was to become a centre of Catalanist action. In 1896 the lawyer Permanyer i Ayats, another leader of Unió Catalanista, became President of the Academy of Jurisprudence, and in 1898, Verdaguer i Callís was appointed Secretary of the Fomento del Trabajo Nacional.[2]

Meanwhile tension between the Centre Escolar Català and the Lliga de Catalunya was growing. The former considered apoliticism unviable and wanted to convert Unió Catalanista into a party that would contest elections with the support of the cultural and civil organizations into which it was gradually spreading. The latter, on the other hand, rejected the idea of taking part in Spanish politics. They wanted Unió Catalanista to continue as a federation covering the widest possible Catalanist spectrum and feared the concessions it would have to make to win over a conservative electorate, which had so far viewed Catalanism with suspicion. Nor did they accept the division of Catalanism into Right and Left which was likely to ensue if they engaged in elections. In point of fact, the swing towards conservatism had already begun with the rejection of Almirall's group and the drafting of the Manresa Bases, but without a strategy and a political party organization, the Bases were inoperative and the *La Renaixensa* sector was muddling along under the pre-political resistance-oriented banner of a puritanical Catalanism that claimed to represent the entire country.

The publication in 1895 of Enric Prat de la Riba and Pere Muntanyola's *Compendi de Doctrina Catalanista* (*Compendium of Catalanist Doctrine*), a type of catechism of Catalanism of which over 100,000 copies were printed, contributed to the diffusion of the definition of Catalonia as a nation, though it continued to use the term 'fatherland'. A government order of seizure was issued against the work and its authors were prosecuted. The Compendium stated that Catalonia was the only fatherland of the Catalans while Spain was merely the State to which it belonged. But though nation and state were no longer considered synonymous as before, and Catalanism was now entering its nationalist phase, it still did not advocate independence.

The political situation was becoming increasingly tense: insurrections broke out in Cuba and the Philippines; severe repressive measures were taken against the anarchists at the so-called Montjuïc trials to put an end to the wave of violence in Barcelona which had begun with a bomb attack on the Liceu opera house in 1893 and had culminated in 1896 with another on the Carrer de Canvis Nous. In 1897 the Catalanists defied the government by sending a message of solidarity to the King of Greece over the conflict in Crete, which was under Turkish domination. Publication of two Catalanist periodicals

La Renaixensa and *Lo Regionalista* was suspended as a result of this action, but also, implicitly, on account of the Catalanists' opposition to the Cuban war.

The Republicans, with the exception of the Federalists, sided with the Monarchists' die-hard Spanish nationalist attitude which was to lead to the humiliating defeats of 1898, whereby Spain lost the last remnants of her American empire, and the Catalan bourgeoisie took up a similar posture through the Fomento del Trabajo Nacional. However, the Catalanists first dissociated themselves from the rampant Spanish patriotism, aimed against the Cuban rebels, by expressing regret that Cuba had not been granted self-government in time, and then, when the United States intervened, Spain had not called for immediate peace. In 1897 only the increasingly pro-Catalanist Federalists, headed by Vallès and Ribot, supported the Catalanists against the repression unleashed by the message to the King of Greece.

CATALANISM IN AN INTERNATIONAL CONTEXT

The Catalanists took considerable interest from the start in other European nationalist movements. This responded not only to a search for effective strategies, but to the will to demonstrate that Catalanism was not a form of eccentricity or of archeological nostalgia, as its enemies claimed, but part of an overall European trend in favour of the political recognition of small nationalities which had lost their independence in the process of the formation of modern European states. Though the example of the dual Austro-Hungarian monarchy had been cited in 1888, Catalonia had neither experienced a national insurrection like that which had taken place in Hungary in 1848; nor could Hungary be used as a model, since it also oppressed and attempted to Magyarize other smaller nationalities. In 1886, when it seemed that home rule for Ireland was imminent, the Catalanists declared solidarity with Parnell's movement. Interest in the case of Bohemia and the influence of the Czech example seem to have been decisive in the adoption of terms like 'nation' and 'nationalist'. The message to the King of Greece was part of this trend. In 1899 Unió Catalanista sent the Finns a message supporting them in their resistance to the Tsar's Russianization policy, and in 1900, in the midst of the Boer War, a similar message was sent to Kruger, the president of the Transvaal. Norway's bloodless transition to independence in 1905 produced great admiration in Catalonia, where the success of Ibsen's plays was seen as an example of the international publicity a small nation could attain. One consequence of Catalanist interest in the national problems of the age was the publication between 1912 and 1914 of Antoni Rovira i Virgili's *Història dels Moviments Nacionalistes* (*History of Nationalist Movements*).

THE CRISIS AT THE TURN OF THE CENTURY

The loss of the last Spanish colonies in 1898, when the age of imperialism was at its height and other European states were not only retaining their existing empires but enlarging them, had far-reaching repercussions. Until then it had been impossible to advocate self-government for Catalonia while denying it to Cuba. It had been difficult for political Catalanism to spread as long as part of Catalan society had identified with Spanish domination of Cuba and the Philippines. But by 1899 the Catalan bourgeoisie, which had supported Spanish nationalist intransigence towards the lost colonies, was more willing to listen to the regionalist and regenerationalist message of the Catalan nationalists and to break with the parties that had succeeded one another in power under the Restoration. Most of the Republicans, meanwhile, were in the same predicament as the Monarchists and one sector of the Federalists was trying to move closer to Unió Catalanista. But before breaking with the Spanish parties, Catalan conservative opinion made an attempt at regenerationalist reform from within the Restoration system itself by lending support to the Conservative government headed by Francisco Silvela, who appeared to accept the latest regionalist theses and gave ministerial posts to Duran i Bas and General Polavieja.[3] Other gestures of goodwill included the appointment of Bartomeu Robert as Mayor of Barcelona to combat municipal corruption and clean up the voting register, those of Pau Font de Rubinat and Josep Ixart as Mayors of Reus and Tarragona respectively, and the transfer of Bishop Morgadas to Barcelona from Vic, where he was replaced by Torras i Bages. In 1900 both regionalist prelates were to defend the use of the Catalan language in catechism and preaching.

But the Silvela government turned down certain requests that it had initially seemed willing to grant. These concerned a financial régime for Catalonia similar to that enjoyed by the Basque Country,[4] a single provincial Diputació embracing the whole of Catalonia and a free port for Barcelona. It also raised taxes to wipe out the deficit inherited from the colonial war. All this caused great disappointment. Duran i Bas, Polavieja and Bartomeu Robert resigned, and in 1899 tradesmen and artisans refused to pay the additional taxes. Despite the failure of this unusual movement of civil resistance, which was known as the *tancament de caixes* (closure of coffers), it was sufficiently widespread to show Catalanists belonging to this sector and who were in favour of taking part in elections that the situation might be ripe for attracting the votes of part of the Catalan bourgeoisie and reaching an agreement with the manufacturers of the Fomento del Trabajo Nacional, the founders of a political group known as Unión Regionalista (Regionalist Union).

THE FIRST CATALANIST ELECTION VICTORY

A minority headed by Prat de la Riba, Verdaguer i Callís, Cambó, Puig i Cadafalch, Domènech i Montaner, Jaume Carner, Ildefons Sunyol and others broke away from Unió Catalanista and founded the Centre Nacional Català (Catalan National Centre), which merged shortly before the 1901 general election with the Unión Regionalista of Albert Rusiñol, Pere Rahola, Ferrer i Vidal, Bertran i Serra and others, to form the Lliga Regionalista de Catalunya (Regionalist League of Catalonia), which had *La Veu de Catalunya*, now a daily paper, as its mouthpiece. It was significant that the name of the new party did not include the words 'national' or 'nationalist'. This was due to the desire to avoid alarming the central government or frightening away the Catalan conservative electorate it wanted to win over. While the group's theories were already nationalist in fact, though not separatist, its strategy was regionalist, and this was the term by which its representatives in public institutions would be known.

However the new Lliga Regionalista de Catalunya was not to emerge fully until the 1901 general election, when it achieved good results in Barcelona. The winning list of Regionalist candidates was made up of four presidents or ex-presidents: Bartomeu Robert of the Sociedad Económica de Amigos del País (Economic Society of Friends of the Country), Albert Rusiñol of the Fomento del Trabajo Nacional, Domènech i Montaner of the Ateneu Barcelonès, and Sebastià Torres of the Lliga de Defensa Comercial i Industrial (League for Commercial and Industrial Defence) which had played a leading role in the *tancament de caixes* movement. But without the joint pressure exerted by the Republican coalition, which obtained two deputies – Pi Margall, now an old man, and a young non-Catalan named Alejandro Lerroux, who was to have a long and chequered career – the Lliga Regionalista could not have overcome the scandalous efforts of the government headed by Sagasta and Segismundo Moret to manipulate the results. Contrary to later apocryphal accounts, the Liberal government tried to supplant the two victorious Republicans, while allowing the Regionalists to keep their seats. However, the manoeuvre failed. In any case, in Barcelona the newborn Lliga Regionalista had only mobilized 6.3 per cent of registered voters, closely followed by the Republican coalition with 4.4 per cent, and overall turnout had been as low as 15 per cent. Elsewhere in Catalonia, the Monarchists had retained their strength. Nevertheless, a new phase in the political history of Catalonia had begun. The conventional alternation in power of dynasties of Conservatives and Liberals was henceforth to be replaced in Barcelona by genuine rivalry between Regionalists and Republicans.

Unió Catalanista continued to exist as a historic but apolitical Catalan nationalist association and it was the Lliga Regionalista that inherited its changeable attitude towards monarchism and republicanism. At the beginning of the century, certain ex-Republicans like Jaume Carner and Joaquim Lluhí i Rissech were members of the Lliga and, at least until 1904, the Lliga claimed to represent all possible forms of Catalanism. A nationalist doctor with centre-left leanings, Domènech Martí i Julià, was elected president of Unió Catalanista, a post he held until 1916. The old Unió Catalanista presented itself as the unitary force of Catalanism and opposed the Lliga's attempt to monopolize the movement. Unió Catalanista was a breeding ground for left-wing nationalists who would militate in almost all the political organizations that grew up in the first quarter of the century, from Centre Nacionalista Republicà (Republican Nationalist Centre), created in 1906, to Francesc Macià's Estat Català (Catalan State), set up in 1922. When, around 1915, there ceased to be a left-wing alternative to the Lliga, Martí i Julià tried unsuccessfully to convert the old Unió Catalanista into a Catalan nationalist social democratic party. But by then the days of Unió Catalanista were over.

The last years of the nineteenth century and the first years of the twentieth were an age of great cultural creativity in Catalonia, embodied in the Modernist movement. Unlike that of the rest of Spain, Catalan culture not only identified with European trends of the time but made an original and creative contribution to them. The architecture of Antoni Gaudí, which has received worldwide acclaim and recognition, is only one of many examples. Modernism and Catalan nationalism went hand in hand. Nowadays Modernist art, similar to Modern Style, Art Nouveau or Liberty, is one of the chief attractions of Barcelona and other Catalan cities.

Notes

1. Translator's note: the name of this movement derives from the Catalan word 'vigatà' which designates the inhabitants of the cathedral city of Vic, some 70 km north-west of Barcelona, where it was based.
2. The Fomento del Trabajo Nacional was the main association of Catalan manufacturers, a staunch defender of protectionism at the time, which represented the employers over and above the organizations representative of specific sectors of the economy.
3. The lawyer Duran i Bas was a Conservative who had left the party led by Cánovas del Castillo on account of its centralism and because it manipulated election results. Polavieja had been the military officer in charge of the repression against the rebels in the Philippines. He was considered by part of the Catalan bourgeoisie as a possible political reformer and had expressed sympathy for decentralization.
4. The three Basque provincial Diputaciones had acquired the privilege of paying a fixed, periodically negotiable amount to the Spanish central government. This concession, which gave them greater resources and wider jurisdiction in a variety of fields, had been made following the suppression of the political autonomy that the Basques had retained till the end of the Second Carlist War in the Basque Country and the beginning of the reign of Alfonso XII in 1874.

5 Conservative Catalanism and the Republicanism of Lerroux

After the Lliga Regionalista's first victory in Barcelona in the 1901 general election, the municipal elections held in the Catalan capital in November of the same year were won by a Republican coalition which doubled the number of votes it had obtained in May. In some ten other Catalan towns and cities, the majority on the local council shifted to the Republicans. The Republican revival in Barcelona was the result of the high turnout of artisans and manual workers which was one of the indications of the climate of popular protest, already revealed by the May 1901 tram strike, an action that led to the Barcelona general strike of February 1902. As long as Catalanism failed to predominate in Barcelona, it would never achieve political hegemony in Catalonia.

The conservative direction taken by political Catalanism following the failure of Almirall and his group of ex-Federalists had reinforced the reservations of the Catalan Republicans about it. Even among the Federalists, the group closest to Catalanism, there was one sector hostile to it. Moreover, when Catalanism emerged as an electoral alternative, the Federalists were in the throes of a severe internal crisis and were losing the support of the workers. Whereas Pi Margall's Federalists saw the nation as an explicit plebiscite of individuals, the Catalan nationalists saw it as something independent of the will of man. Almirall, now isolated and ailing, made the conversion of Catalan Republicanists to Catalanism even more difficult by declaring, 'We have nothing in common with the Catalanism or regionalism now in fashion which claims to blend its aspirations and desires in a song of hate and fanaticism.'

It was at this time that the *Cant dels Segadors* (*Song of the Reapers*), based on a popular song dating back to the 1640 revolt (see Chapter 1), which was later to become the Catalan national anthem, and the commemoration of the occupation of Barcelona by the troops of Philip V on 11 September 1714, subsequently the national holiday, began to emerge as rallying symbols. The idealization of Catalan qualities and

47

the denigration of the Castilian character were an inevitable aspect of this early phase of Catalanism. As in other similar cases, they were part of an attempt to recover self-esteem on the part of a people who had been instilled with a feeling of inferiority and impotence by the dominant nation.

The apprehensions of the Catalan Republicanists of that time cannot be justified by the existence of a large Spanish immigrant population as was to be the case during the Franco régime (see Chapter 14), since in those days non-Catalan residents were very few in number and the immense majority of the working class were still native-born Catalans. The Republicanists recognized the legitimacy of autonomism but rejected nationalism, despite the fact that the party expressing it sought nothing more than self-government. During the first five years of the century Catalan Republicanism had not yet developed within it Spanish nationalist feelings hostile to the 'collective personality' of Catalonia, the existence of which was denied by nobody. Even the Republican leader Alejandro Lerroux, who was later to distinguish himself by his anti-Catalan demogogy, acknowledged on 31 March 1904 in *La Publicidad* that the Catalans were 'a people that has its own history, language, literature and art, and a personality of its own with all the ethnic characteristics of a distinct race'. Catalan Republicanism differentiated between the Catalanism of Unió Catalanista, which it considered legitimate, and the conservative Catalanism of the Lliga Regionalista, which it opposed. In point of fact, Unió Catalanista's form of Catalanism was more radical than that of the Lliga, but unlike the latter, it did not constitute an electoral challenge.

When the Republicans had to compete with the Regionalists for the petit-bourgeois electorate, which was gradually abandoning its earlier abstentionism, and when the Regionalists decided to take over the social base of the dynastic parties, a move which brought them into conflict with the Republicans instead of collaborating with them against the Monarchists, the Republicans, who had finally come together in Unió Republicana (Republican Union), allowed the bipolar dynamics of the situation to sweep them into anti-Catalanist reactions. These were only partially neutralized by the claim that they too were in favour of self-government. Anti-Catalanism, however, did not play a significant part in the relative success of Republicanism in Barcelona and other Catalan cities: the rise of Republicanism under the leadership of Lerroux owed much more to its pragmatic defense of working-class rights, to the assistance offered to imprisoned trade unionists, to the welfare, educational and recreational services provided by local Republican centres, which soon benefited from municipal grants, and to anticlericalism, which was no creation of Lerroux's.

Lerrouxist Republicanism encouraged opposition to Conservative domination of the Catalanist movement without constituting a left-wing Catalanist alternative. Successive Spanish governments, threatened by the advance of Catalanism, did not lend a wholly deaf ear to Lerroux when he presented himself in the Congress as a possible guarantor against separatism in Catalonia. But neither can Lerroux's success be explained by the personal subsidies he received from the Ministry of the Interior. The inability of the Barcelona Republicans to make up a united and disciplined force, especially in drawing up lists of election candidates, was the key to Lerroux's predominance as an arbiter. The weakness of the labour movement after the 1902 general strike also left Lerroux as the defender of the workers, the 'emperor of the Paral · lel', as he was nicknamed in reference to the Avinguda Paral · lel, the main street of a working-class district in central Barcelona. His revolutionary rhetoric was accompanied by a policy of appealing to the masses using the Republican *meriendas*,[1] militant methods and professionalized political staff, all of which, at the beginning of the century, were undoubtedly innovations.

The disorganization and decline of the labour movement from 1903 onwards accompanied by the fall in support for the anarchists, some of whom were to return to terrorist tactics, ran parallel to the rising influence of the Republicanists, but it did not affect the autonomy of the unions. If early twentieth-century political Catalanism failed to attract the workers, it was not because the latter identified with Spanish nationalist sentiment, or because they supported the stateless cosmopolitanism of the anarchists – there were very few anarchists in their ranks and even fewer socialists – but because the Lliga Regionalista's form of Catalanism did and said nothing to attract them. Lerroux took advantage of this situation but he did not create it. Signs of Catalanist feelings are to be found among Catalan workers, and even among militant anarchists. In the 1 May 1908 edition of *El Socialista*, the Spanish writer Unamuno told how a Catalan worker, when asked why socialism had failed in Catalonia, had replied, 'Because it comes to us from Madrid.' Anselmo Lorenzo, a Castilian anarchist resident in Barcelona, also criticized the conscious feelings of Catalan identity and autonomism of a great many Catalan anarchist militants. Lorenzo gave voice to passionate anti-Catalanist feelings which he was later to try to rationalize in anarchist terms by identifying the term 'Catalanist' with that of 'bourgeois'.

However, while socialism was identified with a united, centralist state, the radical federalism and opposition to the machinery of central government characteristic of anarchism held a much greater appeal for Catalan workers, who had traditionally favoured independent, apolitical unions and were extremely reluctant to support any leadership, such as that of the socialists, which emanated from Madrid. On the other hand, the space occupied by Lerrouxist Republicanism, which until 1906 was not markedly Spanish nationalist, and the functions it fulfilled, were such as could soon be expected to belong to the PSOE (Partido Socialista Obrero Español – Spanish Socialist Workers' Party), which until then had been both isolated and weak in Catalonia.[2]

THE WEAKNESS OF THE LLIGA REGIONALISTA

The disappearance of Unión Nacional (National Union), Basilio Paraíso's Castilian regenerationist organization, had left the Lliga Regionalista without potential allies elsewhere in Spain. To this isolation was added the trauma of the 1902 general strike, which reinforced the Lliga's right-wing leanings. This trend first became apparent in the electoral alliance with the Comité de Defensa Social (Social Defence Committee), a reactionary clerical group founded in 1901. Another, later sign was the attempted rapprochement with the dynastic Conservative leader Antonio Maura as revealed in a speech made by Francesc Cambó, representative of the Regionalist minority on the Barcelona City Council, to King Alfonso XIII, on the occasion of the Monarch's first official visit to Barcelona in April 1904. In this speech, Cambó appealed for municipal autonomy for Barcelona. However, it had been decided to boycott the visit made by the King in the company of Maura; and the liberal, nationalist wing of the Lliga, displeased by this swing to the right and the impotence of the party vis-à-vis Unió Republicana in Barcelona, seized the opportunity to leave the party in protest against Cambó's gesture which, in the last resort, was no more than a repetition of other Catalanist memoranda and messages addressed to the Crown in 1885, 1888 and 1898.

The dissident minority, headed by Jaume Carner, J. Lluhí i Rissech, Ildefons Sunyol, and Domènech i Montaner, founded a newspaper, *El Poble Català* (*The Catalan People*), to compete with the Lliga's mouthpiece, *La Veu de Catalunya*.

However, the group did not form a party until December 1906, the delay being due to the fact that Solidaritat Catalana (see Chapter 6) was then in its heyday. The new party, which had nine hundred members in Barcelona as against the Lliga's five hundred, took the name of Centre Nacionalista Republicà (Republican Nationalist Centre – CNR). It was made up of Catalanist former Republicans, ex-members of Unió Catalanista and Federalists. The Lliga had moved to the right, and the CNR aimed to occupy the centre-left space it had left partially vacant. But the future of the Catalan nationalist Left lay less in undermining the electoral base of conservative Catalanism than in its own ability to win Republican votes; and this was to prove more difficult than expected.

Until then, the Lliga's election defeats at the hands of Unión Republicana between 1903 and 1905 had been the price it had had to pay for winning Conservative votes through a swing to the right. In the 1903 general election, the turnout in Barcelona was 45 per cent, compared with only 15 per cent in 1901. The election was won by Unión Republicana with 30.6 per cent of the votes, while the Lliga obtained the support of only 9.8 per cent of registered voters. Four Republicans, four Conservatives, two Liberals, two Regionalists, and one independent traditionalist were elected in 1903 in constituencies belonging to the province of Barcelona. It was a major victory for the Republicans, and the new two-party system involving Republicans and Regionalists was gaining ground in the province of Barcelona. Elsewhere in Catalonia, the dynastic Liberals and Conservatives maintained their lead with only five Republican deputies and one Regionalist returned. This marked the beginning of a period of Republican domination in the city of Barcelona which was to last until 1914. It was this balance of power that the Centre Nacionalista Republicà and, four years later, the broader Unió Federal Nacionalista Republicana were to try to upset.

NATIONAL CONSENSUS AND POLITICAL RIVALRY IN THE CATALANIST MOVEMENT

It should be remembered, however, that the history of Catalan nationalism cannot be reduced to that of Catalanist political parties. A distinction must be drawn between Catalanism as a civic and cultural movement and Catalanist political parties, though the two were interdependent. Without the organizations that gave rise to the civic and cultural movement, the parties would never have existed. The social base of Catalanism consisted of choral societies, rambling clubs, *sardana* dancing groups,[3] and even independent, nationalist associations, most of them local, though some covering wider areas.

Most of these organizations were short-lived and their influence was very limited. Some, however, were destined to last for a long time, among them the Associació Protectora de l'Ensenyança Catalana (Association for the Protection of Catalan Education, 1889), the Centre Excursionista de Catalunya (Rambling Club of Catalonia, 1890), the Ateneu Enciclopèdic Popular (Popular Encyclopedic Atheneum, 1909), and the Centre Autonomista de Dependents del Comerç i de la Indústria (Autonomist Centre of Shop Assistants and Industrial Employees – CADCI, 1903). The last-named organization was the main mutual benefit organization for education and workers' rights open to clerical and shop workers. Founded initially in Barcelona, it soon spread outside the city. It was also the first large-scale Catalanist association and on its foundation defined itself as a 'workers' organization, whose goals are the moral and material betterment of persons belonging to its class and the propagation of autonomist principles'. Mention should also be made of the independent nationalist associations which emerged over the years, such as the two youth movements Joventut Nacionalista La Falç (The 'Sickle' Nationalist Youth, 1918) and Palestra (1930).

Thus the role of Catalanist organizations of a sociocultural nature was not confined to the phase that preceded the formation of political parties that sought to occupy political institutions: such organizations accompanied the parties throughout their creation and development. Obviously, during periods of dictatorship and transition towards more liberal systems, and at other times when the Catalanist parties were relatively weak, non-partisan civic and cultural associations played a more important role. One might even go so far as to say that the greater the oppression suffered by Catalonia as a nation, the greater their influence.

Catalanist civic and cultural organizations have, by definition, been unitary in nature and have taken up positions within the framework of a national front, which initially took the form of a matrix federation like Unió Catalanista. Catalanist political parties, on the other hand, even when their foundation was an attempt to represent a wide range of interests and social strata, have tended to split up in the endeavour to give Catalanism a precise political content, though they acknowledged that progress towards self-government required consensus on fundamental matters. While some continued to dream of the political unity of Catalanism, many others were opposed to the aspiration of individual Catalanist parties to monopolize the cause or present themselves as its most authentic and coherent representatives, on the grounds that the conquest of the masses required the existence of a well-defined Catalanist Left and Right which both could and should gradually dislodge ideologically similar Spanish political forces which were still present in Catalonia. This involved the establishment of a basic consensus which was extremely difficult to achieve in a conflict-ridden society such as that which existed in Catalonia in the first third of the twentieth century.

As long as consensus in favour of self-government remained the overriding consideration, political Catalanism could be confined to the centre – somewhere between centre right and centre left – but it met with insuperable difficulties in covering the entire political spectrum and eliminating organizations dependent on Spanish-based forces, as occurred up till 1923. Indeed growing success in winning the support of the conservative electorate could drastically limit the Catalanists' chances of capturing votes from the Left. The conservative hegemony of the Catalanist movement and the anti-Catalan, pro-labour message of Lerrouxism were two sides of the same coin.

But whenever Catalanism succeeded in substantially broadening its political appeal, thus minimizing the impact of Spanish parties in Catalonia, as was to happen from 1931 onwards, the polarization between the Catalanist Left and Right, due to the high level of social and ideological tension, was liable to dissolve the consensus in support of autonomy and make for a crisis within the very self-governing régime that had just been set up.

Even so, there were times when it seemed that the unitary yet pluralist nature of civic and cultural Catalanism, as revealed in the apolitical (i.e. non-partisan) patriotic associations, might extend to the political parties themselves. One instance of this was the coalition Solidaritat Catalana created in 1906. Though Unión Republicana was again victorious in the September 1905 election, the Republican vote fell in Barcelona and support for the Regionalists increased. The Republicans won in five of the other Catalan constituencies and the Regionalists in six. Monarchist *caciquismo* was still rampant, but the political forces opposed to the system were gaining ground. In the local elections held in November, Unión Republicana won fourteen seats on the Barcelona City Council and the Lliga Regionalista twelve. Despite the narrowness of its victory, Unión Republicana had succeeded in crushing dissident Republicans and making considerable progress towards the formation of a unified party, when, on 25 November 1905, three hundred officers from the Barcelona garrison assaulted two Lliga Regionalista publications, the satirical magazine *Cu-cut!* and the daily *La Veu de Catalunya*. This action, in retaliation for a series of jokes ridiculing the army's role in the 1898 defeat in the Cuban War, sparked off a series of events that was to lead to the formation of Solidaritat Catalana, to the division of Unió Republicana into pro- and anti-Solidaritat elements, to a drastic change in the balance of forces as a result of the first mass mobilization in support of Catalanism, and to the period when it finally became common to employ the term 'nationalism' to refer to political Catalanism.

Notes

1. Taking advantage of the custom of Barcelona workers, who spent Sunday afternoons in the surrounding countryside, eating (called *meriendas*) and dancing in the open air, the Lerrouxists organized festive rallies at which Lerroux himself and other Republican leaders spoke. Viewed with scorn by certain contemporaries, the Republican *meriendas* can today be compared with the celebrations organized by the Communist parties during the 1960s and 1970s.

2. The PSOE was founded secretly in Madrid in 1879 and merged in 1882 with a Barcelona Socialist group, though the leadership remained in Madrid. In 1881 the Socialists founded a trade union in Barcelona, the UGT (Unión General de Trabajadores – General Workers' Union), which had a small but mainly Catalan base. The managing committee of the UGT was located in Barcelona until 1899, when it was transferred to Madrid and pursued its activities quite independent of the PSOE which, like its Second International models, combined revolutionary theory with reformist practice.

3. At that period the *sardana* – in which the dancers form a circle and dance in the open air – became the most characteristic of Catalan dances, spreading from the region of the Empordà, in north-eastern Catalonia, where it originated, throughout the entire country.

6 From Solidaritat Catalana to the Catalan Mancomunitat

CATALANISM'S FIRST MASS MOBILIZATION

Besides reacting angrily to jokes at its expense in the Catalanist press (see Chapter 5), the Army now reappeared as a pressure group in political life, a development which was unfavourable to the progress of Catalanism since it was considered by the Army to be a disruptive force within Spain and a separatist hotbed towards which the government showed excessive tolerance. Instead of punishing the officers responsible for an attack of 28 November 1905 on the two Regionalist publications, the government of Segismundo Moret, which had succeeded that of the other Liberal faction headed by Montero Ríos, appointed General Luque, one of the field marshals who had approved the Army's action in Barcelona, as Minister of War. It also tabled a bill known as the Ley de Jurisdicciones (Law of Jurisdictions) in the Spanish Cortes whereby any offense, whether verbal or written, against the unity of the fatherland, the honour of the armed forces or the symbols that represented them, was to come under military jurisdiction. The passing of this law was a threat to political freedom, but above all it put Catalanism in danger of being outlawed. The anti-Catalan atmosphere that reigned in Madrid led Catalan Republican deputies such as Emili Junoy and Eusebi Corominas to leave political rivalry to one side and support the Lliga Regionalista. Salmerón, the president of Unión Republicana, also made overtures to the Regionalists to avoid what he perceived as the danger of a move towards separatism. In Barcelona, however, the turn events had taken and this reversal in attitudes towards those who so recently had been their adversaries caused misgivings among many Republicans.

On 9 December 1905, Lerroux broke his silence by describing the Lliga as separatist and endorsing the aggression carried out by the group of soldiers. Not a single Republican deputy elected in Barcelona, and none of the five Catalan provincial Juntas controlled by Unión Republicana, followed his lead, but half of the organizations belonging to Unión Republicana in Barcelona did.

On 11 February 1906 an electoral coalition known as Solidaritat

Catalana (Catalan Solidarity) was formed in Girona. The executive commission was made up of Francesc Cambó for the Lliga, Jaume Carner for the Republican nationalists, J. Roca i Roca for the pro-Solidaritat Republicans (see below), J. M. Vallès i Ribot for the Federalists, D. Martí i Julià for Unió Catalanista, J. M. Junyent for the Carlists, and Amadeu Hurtado, an unaffiliated Catalanist. Francesc Macià, a lieutenant colonel in the engineers and a future key figure of Catalan Republicanism, also joined Solidaritat Catalana and was subsequently obliged to give up his military career. From 1907 to 1923 he was to be the member of parliament for Les Borges Blanques.

The great popular success of a tribute paid on 20 May 1906 to the members of parliament who had opposed the Ley de Jurisdicciones and the impact of a protest meeting held in the Plaça de Les Arenes bull ring in Barcelona on 11 November strengthened the position of Solidaritat Catalana. It was the first time the Catalanist movement had succeeded in filling an area as large as a bull ring. Henceforth it was a mass movement.

None the less the situation was complex and confused. Unión Republicana split into two factions – one in favour and one against Solidaritat. Only five of the forty-two Unión Republicana centres in Barcelona gave support to the line laid down by Solidaritat while pro-Solidaritat forces had overall superiority over those opposed to the coalition in the Republican press and among Catalan Republican parliamentarians. The anti-Solidaritat Republicans felt there could be no justification for what they considered a sterile and unnatural election alliance with their former enemies, the Regionalists and Carlists. For the pro-Solidaritat faction, nothing could justify playing the game of Spanish nationalist centralism inspired by militarist and monarchist ideals, as Lerroux was doing.

But Solidaritat Catalana was created in response to a need that went deeper than tactical alliances and contradictions between parties. The Catalan nationalists had to become democrats if they were to gain the popular majority that would enable them to advance towards self-government. The Catalan Republicans had to become the Catalan national Left and establish their independence from Madrid-based forces if they were to be fully coherent with their democratic principles and achieve political hegemony in Catalonia, where Republicanism had more strength than in the whole of the rest of Spain. Indeed, it was by pursuing this policy that Catalan Republicanism was to become the dominant force in Catalonia twenty-five years later, in 1931.

But, for the time being, the division of the Republicans in Catalonia favoured the predominance of the Lliga Regionalista over Solidaritat. Conservative Catalanism was able to offset the effects of its alliance with part of the Left by the other alliance it had formed with the Carlists. This enabled it to occupy the central space and, when the Solidaritat deputies were elected to the Spanish parliament with its Conservative majority, the Lliga was to act as an intermediary and spokesman in relations with the government of Antonio Maura.

Not all pro-Solidaritat Republicans belonged to the socially moderate current: there were left-wing Republicans among them, such as Francesc Layret and Lluís Companys, just as there were many professionals and small businessmen in the Lerrouxist ranks. Even so, an image of moderation prevailed among the pro-Solidaritat Republicans. This proved beneficial to the anti-Solidaritat faction who adapted to the polarization imposed by Solidaritat without losing their previous hold over the working class, since Solidaritat Catalana was mute on the subject of social reform. While Solidaritat brought together a wide variety of elements in support of Catalan identity, the anti-Solidaritat Republicans allowed themselves to be drawn towards Spanish nationalist feelings that were now clearly anti-Catalanist in nature, and in so doing were able to gain the support of electors who had never been Republicans – members of the Army, civil servants and even dynastic Liberals. The anti-Catalan, anticlerical demagogy aimed at the working classes, which is normally termed 'Lerrouxism', was born at this time. But the Solidaritat faction also benefited from conservative, anti-Lerroux votes which were not pro-Catalanist. The *Diario de Barcelona*, the mouthpiece of dynastic Conservatism at the time, remarked: 'We will vote for Salmerón to rid ourselves of Lerroux, but once this has been achieved, then will be the time to talk.'

The first victory of Solidaritat Catalana came in the provincial elections of 1907. With a turnout of 50 per cent in Barcelona, as against only 25 per cent in 1903, the Catalanists won a majority in the Barcelona provincial Diputació which consisted of twenty-four pro-Solidaritat deputies (8 of them Republicans), eight conservatives, three dynastic Liberals and one Lerrouxist. Enric Prat de la Riba, the leader of the Lliga Regionalista, was elected president of the Barcelona Diputació. Just one year earlier he had published his most famous work, *La Nacionalitat Catalana*. The most significant early decisions of the new Diputació were the promotion of the new Universitat Industrial and the creation of the Institut d'Estudis Catalans, whose academic mandate included the establishment of the norms of written Catalan.

In the April 1907 general elections Solidaritat Catalana gained an

even more resounding victory. In the city of Barcelona turnout reached
an exceptionally high 59 per cent, and 71 per cent of the votes cast
were for Solidaritat Catalana with 29 per cent for the anti-Solidaritat
Republicans headed by Lerroux. Electoral participation throughout
Catalonia was 61 per cent with Solidaritat Catalana carrying off 67
per cent of the votes and forty-one of the forty-four Catalan constituencies in Congress. Many seats were not even contested by dynastic
Monarchist candidates. The phenomenon already observed in Barcelona had spread throughout Catalonia and dependence on Madrid-based
political forces and *caciquismo* had been defeated. Twenty-one of the
forty-one pro-Solidaritat Congressional deputies were Republicans. It
was the clearest Republican victory in Catalonia under the Monarchy,
but it was won at the price of isolating the Lerrrouxist Republicans
who, after forming the new Partido Republicano Radical (Radical Republican Party – RRP), were to demonstrate in 1909 how much strength
they still possessed. If in 1907 the Republicans had achieved the same
results in the rest of Spain as the Solidaritat Republicans did in Catalonia, the monarchy would have been in danger of falling.

NATIONALISM AND IMPERIALISM

While it was possible to consider Solidaritat Catalana as the material-
ization of the ideas of Unió Catalanista, which gave it its wholehearted
approval, Solidaritat was in fact the product of a completely different
atmosphere. At the turn of the century, the Modernist literary generation had discarded the regionalism of the *Renaixença* and its willing-
ness to enter into dialogue with Spanish culture, aspiring instead to
the creation of a Catalan culture, a national culture, with Barcelona as
its capital. This had led it to disseminate the desire for contact with
the rest of Europe and for an end to the cultural dependence of Catalonia on Spain. For the poet Joan Maragall, the only solution for Catalonia
was 'to Europeanize itself, severing more or less slowly the cord that
bound it to Death'. Cultural autonomy could not be achieved without
political autonomy. Thus Modernism and nationalism went hand in hand.
The first doctrinal model of political Catalanism, before it came to be
termed nationalism, had been positivism, two versions of which existed,
one liberal and one conservative. A few years after the foundation of
the Lliga Regionalista, three demands were formulated by a new generation of intellectuals, inspired by Nietzschean vitalism to break out

of the narrow but solid positivist channels through which Catalanism had previously flowed. The first was the recognition and reinforcement of the effective pluralism of the Catalanist political movement, that is, the legitimacy of a Left coexisting with the predominant Right. The second was the reassertion of the nationalist terminology with which, as they rightly suspected, the bourgeoisie and pro-Catalanist elements of the clergy did not identify. As already mentioned, Prat de la Riba had acknowledged the legitimacy of pluralism within the Catalanist movement in theoretical terms in 1905. This aspiration was fulfilled when the Lliga split up in 1904 and the Centre Nacionalista Republicà (Nationalist Republican Centre) was formed. At the same time the term 'nationalist' was adopted, and it came into widespread usage with the advent of Solidaritat Catalana. The third demand was that Catalan nationalism must be redefined and given as wide an influence as possible. Imperialism was one way of moving in this direction and this was proposed for the first time in 1905 by Eugeni d'Ors, a journalist who at the time was close to the Lliga. Though intellectual in nature, this imperialism identified implicitly with a policy of outside intervention and with the sense of an innate social hierarchy based on western superiority. Imperialism was not yet tainted by the negative image it acquired after the First World War and for the Latin peoples, who suffered from an inferiority complex, identifying with imperialism meant identifying with the most developed countries or, to use the terminology of the day, the most civilized. For a small nation, politically subjugated, the adoption of an imperialist ideology might lead to disruption and alienation of its people, as Martí i Julià warned in making an alternative proposal for the anti-imperialist internationalism of oppressed European nationalities. In *La Nacionalitat Catalana*, however, Prat de la Riba, while recognizing imperialism as the culmination of all nationalism, stripped it of its negative connotations by drawing a parallel with the regenerative role of Catalan intervention in the Spanish State and with a vaguer, more theoretical and inoperative version of the old Iberianist ideal. There was indeed a basic contradiction between the ideology of imperialism and the aspirations of an oppressed nationality, though it would be equally difficult to combine Catalan cooperation in the government of Spain with the struggle for Catalan autonomy, two goals that were considered antithetical in the rest of the Peninsula.

THE INTERNAL CONTRADICTIONS OF SOLIDARITAT CATALANA

Solidaritat Catalana was a highly significant phenomenon in the historical development of the Catalan national movement, yet it failed in the short term to attain any of its objectives. As a coalition, it was excessively heterogeneous. The Lliga saw it as a united platform from which to negotiate with Madrid for administrative decentralization from a position of greater strength, while making self-government a long-term objective. On the other hand, the pro-Solidaritat Republicans, who were divided into three groups – the CNR, the UR, and the Federalists headed by Vallès i Ribot – considered that the existence of an autonomous government must be recognized from the very start, and this meant a change of régime in Spain, which was not viable in the short term. By tabling a bill entitled Ley de Administración Local (Law of Local Administration) which provided for the establishment of commonwealths of provincial services, Maura succeeded in satisfying the expectations of the Lliga and in splitting Solidaritat Catalana. The project provided for the election of certain municipal councillors and provincial deputies by indirect corporative suffrage. The Republicans opposed the bill, considering that it endangered their access to the organs of local government. The Lliga supported it, but in the end it never became law. Solidaritat Catalana was worn away by the tension between its Carlist and Republican adherents and by another series of events.

Pro-self-government and Regionalist Republicans had already been cooperating on the Barcelona City Council prior to the creation of Solidaritat Catalana. From the beginning of 1905, this cooperation, christened Solidaritat Municipal by the Republican Albert Bastardas, had led to progress in the fields of education, health, and city planning.

With Solidaritat Catalana, a new majority of eighteen Regionalists and thirteen pro-Solidaritat Republicans was formed on the Barcelona City Council while the fourteen non-Solidaritat Republicans went into opposition. The pro-Solidaritat Republicans, with the support of most of the Regionalist councillors and a few Lerrouxists, succeeded in passing a special budget for culture which provided for the construction of the first four modern school complexes to remedy the inadequate education policy of the State in a city where 40 per cent of the population was illiterate. The teachers were to be selected by the Council, teaching would be mainly in Catalan, and the schools were to be coeducational and non-denominational, with religious instruction being given outside school hours. The budget was approved by twenty-seven votes to seven. But the clergy first brought pressure to bear on the Mayor appointed by the Crown, who vetoed the project and had to resign. Then they undermined the support of the Regionalists so that the budget failed to receive the approval of the Diputació. It was finally rejected by government authority which was able to prevail over municipal autonomy because of the disloyalty of the Regionalists.

Solidaritat Catalana was further weakened when Prat de la Riba and the Regionalists supported a Monarchist candidate for the vacant vice-presidency of the Diputació of the province of Barcelona in preference to a Catalanist Republican on the grounds that they needed to begin to win over the Catalan Monarchists to the autonomist cause.

The Regionalists, moreover, were looking on anxiously as the three groups of Catalanist pro-Solidaritat Republicans advanced towards unity, a process which was to culminate in 1910 in their fusion and in the formation of a new party known as Unió Federal Nacionalista Republicana (Republican Nationalist Federal Union – UFNR). When municipal elections were convened for May 1909, the left wing of Solidaritat considered that, while the alliance was still valid for Catalanist congressional deputies, it should not stand in the way of competition at local level. In May 1909, Lerroux's Partido Radical staged a comeback in Barcelona by winning sixteen seats on the City Council. The Catalanist Left won eight and the alliance between the Lliga Regionalista and the Carlists only four. Solidaritat Catalana was already doomed before it succumbed to the final blow dealt by the 'Tragic Week' of July 1909 (see below).

In 1907 a new united union federation had been born in Barcelona under the name of Solidaridad Obrera. The workers' societies, which were weak and isolated, had not responded to the efforts of socialists, anarchists and Lerrouxist Republicans to draw them into federations controlled respectively by each of them. However, some did respond to the call of Solidaridad Obrera, in which socialists, anarchists, revolutionary unionists and Republican members of the societies themselves initially collaborated. In 1908, Solidaridad Obrera became a federation covering the whole of Catalonia. Though the name seemed a challenge and an antidote to Solidaritat Catalana, it was viewed with mistrust from PSOE headquarters in Madrid as yet another manifestation of Catalan particularism. This mistrust deepened when, after the anarchists had eliminated Lerrouxist influences with the help of the socialists themselves, Solidaridad Obrera decided to organize a congress of unions that did not belong to the socialist federation UGT with a view to forming a new Spanish union federation – the CNT (Confederación Nacional del Trabajo – National Confederation of Labour).

THE TRAGIC WEEK

The *Setmana Tràgica*, or Tragic Week, was to be the last nineteenth-century-style democratic revolt in the history of Barcelona. It began with a general strike to protest against the sending of three contingents of Barcelona conscripts, one after another and including married reservists with children, to Melilla as part of the unacknowledged beginnings of what subsequently became the long Moroccan War. Opposition to this new colonial adventure was hardly surprising at a time when memories of the colonial disaster of ten years earlier were still fresh and when the burden still fell exclusively on those without the means to buy exemption from military service. The Republican press – both the Catalanist daily *El Poble Català* and the Lerrouxist *El Progreso* – had joined in the anti-war campaign. Then suddenly Solidaridad Obrera lost what was only nominal control of the hitherto peaceful strike and the protesters started burning Church property. In Barcelona forty religious schools, convents and monasteries, and twelve parish churches were destroyed. The leaderless revolt led to an attempt to convert the Republican majority on the Barcelona City Council, which was divided between Catalanist and Lerrouxist Republicans, into a Republican rebel government. In order to undermine support for the insurgents, the Minister of the Interior branded the movement as separatist. Both the Lerrouxist and the Catalanist Republican leadership remained on the sidelines, though the working-class base of the Partido Radical, whose propaganda since 1901 had paved the way for such an event, took part in the anticlerical violence.

The ensuing repressive measures included the closing down of all types of non-denominational schools, as well as working-class and Republican centres. Five death sentences were handed out and subsequently executed by the military tribunals. One was against the independent anarchist Francesc Ferrer i Guàrdia, a promoter of modern educational methods. Ferrer i Guàrdia was considered an instigator of the rebellion, though he held no office in any party or union. He was shot for what he would have liked to do but was unable to achieve. The Lliga Regionalista gave full support to the repression unleashed by the Maura government. Prat de la Riba refused to put in *La Veu de Catalunya* an article by Joan Maragall appealing for the death sentences to be commuted, and the article remained unpublished. Such was the extent of the agreement between the Regionalists and Maura that, when the Liberals joined in the campaign against Maura, the latter privately invited Cambó, a leading figure in the Lliga, to form a

Spanish party which could alternate in power with the Conservatives, thus leaving the divided Liberals on a limb.

The campaign waged all over Europe against the trial and execution of Ferrer i Guàrdia led to the constitution of the Conjunción Republicano-Socialista (Republican–Socialist Alliance). Maura fell from power and was replaced, first by a Liberal government under Moret, which lifted the state of emergency in Barcelona, and then by Canalejas, who succeeded in reuniting the dynastic Liberals.

The legislative elections of May 1910 confirmed that the Radicals, though obliged to compete with the Unió Federal Nacionalista Republicana founded just one month earlier, had kept their working-class electorate intact and were capable of maintaining their hold in Barcelona, despite anarchist accusations that they had betrayed the *Setmana Tràgica* movement, which the Lerrouxists termed the 'Glorious Week'. The Lliga suffered a severe defeat in Barcelona, but the Catalanist left succeeded in forming the opposition. Elsewhere in Catalonia, the Regionalists saw their vote drop to little more than it had been before Solidaritat Catalana. Despite their victory in Barcelona, the Radicals did not manage to win elsewhere in Catalonia, where the Republican vote went mainly to Unió Federal Nacionalista Republicana. Lerroux began his attempt to extend the Partido Radical to other parts of Spain by attracting intellectuals from the centre of Spain. These, however, soon left the party, and his bid to give it a more moderate tone brought criticism from his former working-class revolutionary base in Barcelona. Lerroux hoped to obtain the support of the Army for a change of régime like that which had taken place in Portugal in 1910. The dynastic Monarchists recovered part of the support they had lost in Catalonia with Solidaritat Catalana, winning sixteen seats, or somewhat more than a third of the Catalan parliamentary constituencies, a proportion that would remain roughly unchanged throughout the following thirteen years.

In Catalonia, voting trends continued to be quite different from the rest of Spain. Republicanism commanded much stronger electoral support in Catalonia – in 1910 half the Republican deputies elected were returned by Catalan constituencies – and on the Catalan political scene there was one important party, the Lliga Regionalista, that was opposed to the system. Even so, the defeat of the dynastic Monarchists in Catalonia and the victory of the opposition parties were to no avail, since the Catalan deputies were only a small minority in a Spanish parliament that was still dominated by the alternating dynastic parties. Despite the failure of Solidaritat Catalana, this situation was to lead to increased demands for self-government.

THE FAILURE OF THE CATALANIST LEFT AND THE DECLINE OF REPUBLICANISM

The UFNR failed to take over the leadership of the Catalanist movement from the Lliga. It had little influence among the working class
and enjoyed considerable support only among the clerical workers of
the CADCI. Hopes that the UFNR, under the leadership of Jaume Carner,
Pere Coromines and Francesc Layret, would replace the excessively
right-wing Lliga and the Spanish-nationalist Lerrouxists were not fulfilled. Membership of the united Republican party did not rise above
the total membership of the groups from which it had been formed,
nor were localism or fragmentation overcome. The initial relative suc-
cesses of the UFNR were achieved at a time of crisis for the conservative Catalanism of the Lliga and when Lerrouxist Republicanism was
at its peak. This meant that the new party could only aim for the time
being at winning new support by capturing votes from the Lliga rather
than from the left-wing Republican electorate.

The UFNR needed to build up a clientele in Barcelona and this meant
gaining control of the City Council. In municipal elections, however,
Barcelona was not a single constituency but was broken down into
districts. At the outset, the UFNR electorate, though numerous, was
widely scattered and did not form a majority in any district, while
whole areas were dominated by the Radicals and Regionalists respectively. The decline of Lerrouxism did not cause votes to shift to the UFNR.
While the Republican nationalists gave effective support to the campaign in favour of a Mancomunitat – a 'commonwealth' of the four
Catalan provinces – they derived no political benefit from this since
the strategy of pragmatism and gradual progress which eventually led
to the establishment of the Mancomunitat was proper to Regionalism,
which thus succeeded in recovering from the setback it suffered after
the Tragic Week. The strategy of the UFNR, on the other hand, aimed
theoretically at a break with the prevailing régime; and Republicanism
was so weak in the rest of Spain that it was unrealistic to expect Catalan
self-government to be produced by a change of régime.

When, as a result of the scandals that marked the Lerrouxist administration of the Barcelona City Council, the Spanish Socialists expelled
the Radical Party from the Conjunción Republicano–Socialista, the UFNR
entered it. But whereas the Conjunción was not a state-wide projec-
tion of Catalan Republican nationalism, it did give rise to the break-
away of a minority in the UFNR which in 1912 left to join the new
Partido Reformista headed by Melquíades Álvarez. The Partido

Reformista, the most moderate of the Republican parties, was prepared to collaborate with the Monarchy provided it became democratic. It was to be swallowed up by the system ten years later.

The alliance between the left-wing Catalanist UFNR and Lerroux's Partido Radical in the 1914 general election, based on what was known as the Sant Gervasi Pact, was not the cause but the consequence of the decline of the UFNR, which disintegrated rapidly after suffering a re-sounding election defeat. Since the Lliga had come to an agreement with both the dynastic wing and the Jaimist wing[1] of the Monarchist Right in an attempt to dominate these two forces, the Republican national-ists maintained that they could do the same with the Radicals without being accused of renouncing Catalanism, especially since the pact had led the Lerrouxists to take a positive attitude towards the autonomist cause. But the electorate rejected the Republican alliance, which re-ceived the support of only 16 per cent of registered voters in Barce-lona as compared with the 16 and 22 per cent that the UFNR and PPR had won separately in 1910. The victory of the Lliga Regionalista in Barcelona in March 1914 marked the beginning of its period of he-gemony, and its authority was broadened and consolidated in 1920 when it won a majority on the City Council.

When the Republican coalition stood again in the 1916 election, it obtained the support of only 13 per cent of the electorate. The dissi-dent Republicans had formed the Bloc Republicà Autonomista (Re-publican Autonomist Bloc), headed by the labour lawyer Francesc Layret, but they won only 7 per cent of the vote in Barcelona, splitting the overall Republican vote. In 1917 Layret, Marcelino Domingo and Lluís Companys, with the support of the Federalists of the Empordà region under August Pi Sunyer, of another Federalist group from Tarragona and of the Lleida branch of Joventut Republicana (Republican Youth) formed the Partit Republicà Català (Catalan Republican Party – PRC), which was further to the left than the now extinct UFNR. However, they did not succeed in winning more votes, and the former opponents of the 1914 Sant Gervasi Pact were to form an alliance with Lerroux and the PSOE in the 1918 and 1919 elections which followed the pol-itical crisis of the summer of 1917. Despite Layret's defense of the CNT, the class struggle that marked the years following the First World War prevented the Partit Republicà Català from winning working-class votes and becoming a left-wing alternative capable of dislodging the Lliga.

Once the Catalanist Left had been relegated to a position of subser-vience, the Lliga Regionalista and the Radicals set up a two-party system in Barcelona, with the latter forming the opposition. The two parties were ideal adversaries for one another, since the Lliga could claim to monopolize the Catalanist cause while the Lerrouxists could claim to monopolize the Left. On economic matters and in the area of city planning, however, they frequently reached agreement.

Despite the loss of working-class votes and the anti-Lerrouxism of the rising CNT, Lerrouxist Republicanism continued to act as the protector of manual workers until 1923, though it no longer presented itself as the party of the entire Barcelona working class.

The PSOE did not succeed in filling the space left vacant by the disappearance of the UFNR and the decline of Lerrouxism. Republicanism managed to survive without the backing of a union of its own as long as the predominant form of unionism was apolitical, as in the case of the CNT. But socialism could not grow in Catalonia as long as the UGT remained weak. Caught between the apoliticism of the anarchists and the pro-working-class republicanism of the PRR and PRC, socialism proved incapable of taking root in Catalonia, even after lending support to Catalonia's demand for self-government in 1918.

Note

1. The Jaimists supported the pretender Jaime de Borbón Parma.

7 The Mancomunitat and the Predominance of Conservative Catalanism

AN INTERPROVINCIAL FEDERATION BASED ON CONSENSUS

In May 1911, the Diputació of the province of Barcelona proposed that plans be drawn up for a commonwealth or Mancomunitat of the four Catalan provinces. Only the four Radical deputies voted against the proposal, which had the support of the Republican nationalists and the dynastic Monarchists. In October of the same year, these plans were approved by the Diputacions of all four Catalan provinces, again with the support of the dynastic Monarchists.

Canalejas endorsed the project, though the important clause it contained concerning the delegation of central government services was dropped. The proposal was defended in Congress by the dynastic Liberal deputy for Terrassa, Alfons Sala Argemí, and in October 1912 the Ley de Mancomunidades Interprovinciales (Law of Interprovincial Commonwealths) received the approval of the House. Following the assassination of Canalejas at the hands of an anarchist, the bill was held up in the Senate until promulgated by decree at the end of 1913 by the new Conservative government under Dato. After the split in the Liberal party, the Liberal administration headed by Romanones had been replaced by Dato's government and Dato himself succeeded Maura as Conservative leader, following the latter's refusal to hand over the reins of power to the Liberals.

The campaign and debate over the Mancomunitat, which took place between 1911 and 1913, acted as a catalyst in aggravating the latent divisions within the two alternating dynastic parties. The image of a Catalan regionalism linked to Maura was broken. Though Catalan demands appeared to have been channelled through the system, the dynastic parties took offence because the Catalanists had come to agreements with all the political forces which had been in government without forming a durable alliance with any. And the Catalanists were displeased by the indecisive, fickle, and disunited attitude of the dynastic groups on the subject. The campaign had made the Catalanist Left dependent on a strategy that was not its own, while the weakness of the Spanish Republicans and their failure to make a firm commitment to self-government prevented it from offering any alternative. The campaign had also affected the traditionalists, who in 1916 split into two factions, one close to Catalanism and the other opposed to it. Any study of the struggle for Catalan self-government must take into account the disintegration of the Spanish two-party monarchist system and the consequent growing political instability.

The Catalan Mancomunitat was set up on 6 April 1914 and the Regionalist leader Enric Prat de la Riba was elected President, while still retaining the presidency of the Barcelona provincial Diputació. No other regional commonwealth was created in Spain, though the law was applicable to the whole country. After the death of Prat in August 1917, another Regionalist, the architect Josep Puig i Cadafalch, was elected President of the Mancomunitat with forty-eight votes, nine more than the dynastic Liberal from Lleida, Joan Rovira i Agelet. Another Regionalist, Joan Vallès i Pujals, became President of the Barcelona Diputació.

The presidency of Prat de la Riba was a phase of projects and of adaptation, during which the organs created by the Barcelona Diputació served as a base for the interprovincial coordination that was to give way to a more consistent form of joint action. The true institutional development of the Mancomunitat and the greater part of its achievements took place under the presidency of Puig i Cadafalch. As the latter remarked in 1922, it was his role to 'translate dead paper into living things, to transform a niggardly law into the task of remaking Catalonia'. The fact that Prat's term of office has frequently been idealized and that of Puig overlooked may possibly be due to the fact that the latter had to find sometimes unsatisfactory solutions to the contradictions that had built up during the presidency of the former. The ousting of the Majorcan philologist Canon Alcover over discrepancies with Pompeu Fabra, who was in charge of standardizing the Catalan language at the Institut d'Estudis Catalans, and the discrediting of the writer Eugeni d'Ors, who until 1920 was the Regionalists' leading cultural authority,[1] were decisions with serious consequences that cannot be ascribed solely to the inflexibility of Puig i Cadafalch.

The Assembly of the Catalan Mancomunitat was made up of all the deputies of the four Catalan provincial Diputacions. The province of Barcelona was represented by thirty-six deputies, while the other three had twenty each. The Assembly elected the President and a permanent council of eight members, two from each province, which acted as the government. Though in practice the council was invariably dominated by the Regionalists, they never had an absolute majority and other parties were always represented. In the Assembly of the Mancomunitat, the Regionalists formed a minority, with around one-third of the seats, and could only govern with the conditional support of the Catalanist Left and the Monarchists.

The Diputació of the province of Lleida continued to be dominated by the dynastic Liberals while that of Tarragona remained a Republican stronghold. Initially at least, few Regionalists were elected to the former, and even fewer to the latter. From 1919, however, the Lliga Regionalista was not only represented in the Lleida provincial assembly, but won the presidency when the former Liberal Romà Sol joined the Regionalists, and by 1921 the Lliga was the largest minority group in that province. The Regionalists also commanded a majority in the wealthiest Diputació, that of Barcelona, and were the largest minority in that of Girona. In 1923, twenty-seven of the ninety-six deputies in the Assembly of the Mancomunitat were Regionalists. However, even with the support of the four deputies of the Federació Monàrquica Autonomista, the Regionalists still could not muster up 30 per cent of the votes although together the Catalanist forces, including the thirty or so nationalists and the three groups of Catalanist Republicans, commanded a wide majority.

In 1918, the four Catalan Diputacions transferred services related to roads and agriculture to the Mancomunitat and in 1920 the remaining services were also transferred. Henceforth the management of funds was to be the only function of the provincial Diputacions. The hope that State services would be decentralized and transferred to the Mancomunitat was not fulfilled, but matters under provincial jurisdiction were beginning to be concentrated at regional level.

The Lliga Regionalista's predominant position within both the Mancomunitat and the Barcelona City Council made it possible to coordinate the action of both bodies, especially in the first steps towards the creation of a Catalan education system.

THE ACHIEVEMENTS OF THE MANCOMUNITAT

Though the Mancomunitat was a purely administrative creation, its very existence marked for the first time recognition of the distinct personality of Catalonia. The Catalanists tried to give the Mancomunitat the character of a pre-state institution. The serious shortcomings of central-government services in Catalonia gave momentum to the Catalanist movement. To aspire to the creation of Catalan schools amounted to proposing to overcome illiteracy and low levels of culture and vocational training; and it meant introducing European pedagogical methods such as those of the Italian specialist Dr Montessori. Catalan jurisdiction over public works and law and order implied not merely controlling the instruments of power, but remedying grave infrastructural deficiencies and overcoming a situation in which the country was run by public servants from other parts of Spain whose ignorance of Catalonia was reinforced by prejudice. The improvement and expansion of the grossly inefficient Spanish public administration were tangible arguments in favour of the Catalanists, who were determined to give the new services a pro-nationalist significance. However, without autonomy, the Mancomunitat could be, in the long run, nothing more than an unsuccessful attempt at establishing a fully Catalan government or 'Generalitat', and indeed the name of that medieval Catalan political institution was used in texts written between 1910 and 1920 as a synonym of a truly self-governing régime.

The Catalan language did not attain normal usage under the Mancomunitat because it was not granted even co-official status. It did, however, come into public and administrative use. An important achievement promoted by the Mancomunitat was the standardization of the rules of written Catalan which enabled Catalan to break out of the narrow circle of purely poetic expression, turning it into a viable commercial and technical language. At the same time, it helped create a single cultural market covering the whole of Catalonia and made Barcelona into a cultural capital from which the language could radiate outwards towards the other Catalan-speaking countries.

The Mancomunitat planned and launched many of the projects that would be taken up by the Generalitat of the 1930s, endowed with greater resources and powers, but which survived for a shorter period. From 1914 onwards, intellectuals, professionals, and technicians who were not members of the Lliga began to participate in the work of the Mancomunitat, as did certain members and sympathizers of political forces to the left of the leading Catalan party. This joint effort was due, not only to the desire to present the Mancomunitat as the accomplishment of the whole Catalan people, but also to the presence of several different parties on the permanent council. The nationalist Left, moreover, was so weak that the participation of its members was unlikely to have any political consequences. It did nothing to alter the new concept of national culture, known as *noucentisme*, which was being developed by conservative Catalanism within the narrow degree of latitude allowed by the central government to the Mancomunitat.

In view of the meagre resources available to it, the Mancomunitat's plans were extremely ambitious and it was forced to incur debt to an extent that, by the criteria of the period, could be considered dangerous. The Mancomunitat's working budget of 20 million pesetas for 1922 was the equivalent, according to the Regionalist politician Vallès i Pujals, of the amount spent every three days on the Moroccan War. The working budget of the Barcelona City Council was more than double that of the Mancomunitat. The Mancomunitat has frequently been accused of being over-concerned with culture, yet no more than 10 per cent of its resources were spent on education and culture. In 1920 it took out a loan of 50 million pesetas for a six-year plan in which communications, including the telephone, accounted for 70 per cent of expenditure, while welfare, health and education together added up to only 22 per cent. The prime objective was to achieve balanced development for Catalonia, a goal that was threatened by the excessive growth of Barcelona. The Mancomunitat derived much of its revenue from the municipal councils via the Diputacions. Accordingly, it strove from 1914 onwards to avoid being accused of centralist policies in favour of Barcelona by creating services like the Caixa de Crèdit Comunal (Communal Credit Bank) which granted long-term loans to municipal councils for public-works projects and gave credit to agricultural cooperatives and syndicates. By 1922, the Caixa de Crèdit Comunal had handed out 4.8 million pesetas.

In addition to creating a number of model post-secondary and vocational schools, which rivalled the official state schools, the Mancomunitat drew up plans to protect and preserve the archeological, historical, and artistic heritage of Catalonia and to promote the publication of works in Catalan. Its aim was to use its very limited resources to support certain initiatives that Catalan society would later be able to maintain without public assistance.

The daily press was a particularly significant area of endeavour, since in 1915 the two Catalan-language papers in Barcelona together added up to no more than 5 per cent of the overall circulation of the fourteen Spanish-language papers also published in the Catalan capital. By 1923, little progress had been made. The poverty of the Catalan press was an impediment to the professionalization of writers in the Catalan language, for if the press is vital to professional writers in any country, this is even more true in a literature like that of Catalan in which large editions are seldom possible.

In any event, without the dynamic cultural policy pursued by the Mancomunitat between 1913 and 1923, Catalan-language publishers and periodicals could never have survived, still less multiplied, in the highly adverse political circumstances created from 1923 onwards by the Primo de Rivera dictatorship.

THE IMPACT OF WORLD WAR I

The First World War, in which Spain did not take part, created a trade situation that was favourable to Catalan industry as a result of reduced competition from other European countries in the Spanish and Latin-American markets and orders from the French army. However, the sharp decline in imports of basic foodstuffs and fuel, and the rise in the price of raw materials produced an inflationary spiral that was detrimental to wages. The ensuing social unrest led to an increase in the number of social conflicts from 1916 onwards, the year in which the UGT (the Socialist Union Federation) and the anarchist CNT signed a joint-action agreement.

The Catalan industrial bourgeoisie, with the support not only of the Lliga Regionalista but also of the Radicals, appealed in vain for tariffs that would encourage exports of manufactured goods and reduce the cost of importing raw materials, and for a free port for Barcelona. In view of the central government's hostility to this policy and its reluctance to delegate state services to the Mancomunitat, Cambó and the Regionalists headed the party alliance which in 1916 succeeded in overturning minister Santiago Alba's plan to tax extra profits accruing from the war. At the same time as the Lliga Regionalista published a manifesto entitled *Per Catalunya i l'Espanya Gran (For Catalonia and the Greatness of Spain)*, announcing its intention to intervene in the political affairs of the State, it also launched a campaign throughout the rest of Spain and decided to cooperate for the first time with the Basque nationalists. However, the newly constituted Regionalist groups in Valencia and Majorca did not succeed in upsetting the political system, as the Catalanists had done in Catalonia, and the Lliga failed to overcome its isolation or to construct a Regionalist political force throughout Spain that would enable it to oust the dynastic parties, which were now split into six different groups.

The great political crisis of 1917 began with the resignation of the

Liberal government of García Prieto over the corporative indiscipline of the Juntas Militares de Defensa (Military Defence Committees) in June. This Spanish military association, which excluded generals and non-commissioned officers, was based in Barcelona because it was inspired by the example of the working-class union movement and because the soldiers of the local garrison were conscious of their inability to control Catalanism and anarchism.

This apparent break between the Army and the régime led the entire opposition to hope that an attempt to force the Monarchy to undertake constitutional reform without it being necessary to resort to a popular revolutionary movement would meet with an attitude of benevolent neutrality on the part of the Army. The Dato government, which was formed in the midst of the civilian power crisis, suspended the constitution and closed the Spanish Cortes. The Catalan members of parliament, headed by the Lliga Regionalista, called a meeting of other Spanish deputies to be held in Barcelona in July to seek a solution to the crisis. The meeting was outlawed by the Dato government. Maura's absence deprived Cambó of a right-wing counterweight to his conjunctural alliance with the Radicals, Reformists, and Socialists in the Assembly of Parliamentarians, which called for general elections to a constituent Parliament to be organized by a multipartite government that would guarantee a fair election.

On 10 August a general strike was called by the UGT and CNT in support of the programme of reforms drawn up by the Assembly of Parliamentarians. In Catalonia, and other places where the strike call was followed, the Army crushed the movement, thus shattering any hopes that it would remain on the sidelines. But in October the Juntas Militares forced the resignation of the Dato government which had used them against the strikers in August. The Lliga Regionalista took this opportunity to abandon its circumstantial alliance with the Catalan and Spanish Left to take part in the first Government of national unity formed in November 1917. This development put an end to the Restoration two-party system. The presence of Ventosa i Calvell and Felip Rodés in a government presided over once more by García Prieto, with Juan de la Cierva as the Minister of War imposed by the Juntas Militares, did not however mean that the demands of the Assembly of Parliamentarians had been met. Whereas the Conservative Catalanists justified their about-turn as the only way of defending themselves against the false charge of separatism, the Catalan and Spanish Lefts qualified the decision as opportunistic desertion.

But in the February 1918 general election, which was followed by

TABLE 7.1   Distribution of seats in the Catalan constituencies in the Spanish Congress of Deputies

	1901	1903	1905	1907	1910	1914	1916	1918	1919	1920	1923
Dynastic Monarchists (total)	33	25	26	3	16	17	19	9	13	16	12
Regionalists	6	5	7	16	9	12	13	21	16	17	21
Traditionalists	1	–	–	6	2	1	1	2	2	1	1
Republicans (total)	4	14	11	19	17	10	9	10	11	9	8
Reformists	–	–	–	–	–	4	2	2	2	1	2

TABLE 7.2   Percentage of seats occupied between 1901 and 1923 by the main political forces in each of the Catalan provinces

Provinces	Republicans	Monarchists and FMA	Regionalists and Reformists
Barcelona	38.4	39	16.7
Girona	38	26	26.1
Lleida	53	18	23.6
Tarragona	56.8	5.6	35.2

an amnesty for those imprisoned as a result of the 1917 general strike, Conservative Catalanism succeeded in obtaining the electorate's seal of approval for its action and increased its parliamentary representation (see Tables 7.1 and 7.2).

Since no political group had a majority in the Congress, a new coalition government was formed, this time headed by Maura, with Cambó and Ventosa as ministers. The distribution of seats in the Cortes did not permit constitutional reform, and even the participation of the Lliga Regionalista in the government, where its representatives held the portfolios of Economy and Public Works, and of Supplies, did not hasten progress in the delegation of State services to the Mancomunitat. The Maura government was dissolved at the beginning of November 1918, at the same time as, elsewhere in Europe, the Armistice was signed.

The Catalan nationalists believed that an allied victory in the First World War might have had a positive effect on Catalonia's progress towards self-government since the map of Europe would have to be redrawn to take into account the rights of oppressed nationalities. The fourteen points presented by President Wilson in January 1918 only served to reinforce hopes that, years earlier, had inspired enthusiastic pro-Allied feelings in the ranks of radical Republican nationalism. As a result of this, a contingent of Catalan volunteers had joined the Foreign Legion and fought in France and the Balkans. There were not twelve thousand volunteers, as Catalanist propaganda claimed, but they did number over a thousand. However, the French Republic, which had assimilationist and uniformist tendencies identical to those of the Spanish Monarchy, if not even more overpowering, was totally indifferent to Catalan self-government. Not the slightest pressure was brought to bear on the Spanish government by the Allies once the war was over in gratitude for Catalan support, and Catalanist hopes turned out to be mere illusions. However, it was at approximately this time that a separatist form of Catalan nationalism arose, inspired by the Irish revolt of Easter 1916 and the subsequent separation of the Irish nationalists after a struggle against the British which lasted until 1921.

THE CAMPAIGN FOR SELF-GOVERNMENT AT THE END OF WORLD WAR I

The campaign in favour of self-government waged in late 1918 and early 1919 marked the climax of the Catalan national movement in the first quarter of the twentieth century. The process leading up to the campaign got underway while Cambó and Ventosa were still in the Maura government as a result of a questionnaire sent to municipal councils by the Mancomunitat's Escola de Funcionaris (School of Civil Servants). The replies were overwhelmingly in favour of Catalan self-government, which was presented as being linked to municipal autonomy.

The publication of the results of the survey coincided with the collapse of the Monarchist coalition government headed by Maura, the end of the First World War, (which brought about the fall of monarchies and the independence of hitherto dominated nations) and the impact of the Russian revolution, seen as the first step towards a socialist revolution that would sweep the continent.

On 15 November, Marcelino Domingo and other deputies belonging to the Partit Republicà Català (Catalan Republican Party – PRC), with the support of the remaining Republican deputies and of the six Socialists,[2] proposed to the Spanish Congress that Catalonia should be granted 'integral autonomy'. The movement in favour of self-government had the backing even of the Lerrouxists and the PSOE, who were trying to outdo the Lliga on its own ground. But the Catalan Left lacked the support of the rapidly growing Catalan labour movement led by the anarchist CNT.

The movement in favour of self-government drew the leadership it needed from the Lliga, but it proved difficult to control. As Cambó recalled in his memoirs, in Madrid 'there was a widespread conviction that, with the Allied victory, the fourteen points, and self-determination, Catalonia's hour had come'. The King, alarmed by the European situation and fearing the outbreak of revolution, encouraged Cambó to take control of the movement and assured him of his support: 'No one fears self-government any longer. It was you who made it possible with your good management in [the Ministry of] Public Works and the Economy.'

The council of the Mancomunitat, together with a commission of parliamentarians, drew up a proposal for a statute of self-government. The project was presented by Puig i Cadafalch to the Prime Minister, García Prieto, who was subsequently replaced by Romanones at the head of a new Liberal administration.

The Allies, however, were interested only in the emancipation of those nationalities whose independence had resulted from the defeat of the empires overthrown by the war. The only other country to gain independence was the Republic of Ireland.

On 20 November, Cambó assured the Congress that the form of self-government requested had nothing to do with separatism and he stated his opposition to complete independence for Catalonia. Even so, on 11 December the Catalan request was firmly turned down by the Chamber. The refusal was clearly expressed in the speeches made by Maura and Alcalá Zamora. The latter told Cambó, 'Your honour is trying to be the Bolívar of Catalonia and the Bismarck of Spain at one and the same time. Your aims are contradictory and you must choose between one and the other.' The intransigence of the Monarchists obliged the Lliga to join forces with the Republicans and Socialists and move towards a break with the régime, a position that was repugnant to the bourgeois base of the Regionalist party. On 16 December, following the withdrawal of the Catalan minority from the Cortes, Cambó pronounced the following words in Barcelona: 'And in this situation I ask you what we are to choose: a monarchy? a republic? No, Catalonia! Catalonia has fought for others often enough: now it is time she fought for herself. We do not tie the cause of self-government to that of the Republic, but the danger that the Monarchy may fall will not halt our advance towards self-government.'

To break the deadlock, Romanones created an extra-parliamentary commission to draw up a draft statute of self-government. The Lliga was inclined to take part in this commission, but the refusal of the

Left – Layret, Domingo, and Macià – forced it to give up the idea, especially when it was discovered that the main faction of the dynastic Conservatives, headed by Dato, had also declined to take part. A draft statute was nevertheless drawn up outside the commission, though it was a moderate proposal featuring a governor general and a singular form of self-government without constitutional reform. It aimed at the creation of a composite but not a federal state, along British lines, that would be compatible with the maintenance of the Monarchy. The Lliga had tried to avoid either breaking off its ties with the Monarchists or becoming a prisoner of its alliance with the Republicans. But it had been unable to take part in an extra-parliamentary commission in which, without the Catalanist Left, it would have been at the mercy of the Monarchists.

In Barcelona there was considerable agitation. The first Catalan separatist organization, Francesc Macià's Federació Democràtica Nacionalista (Nationalist Democratic Federation), had been formed in January 1919 and a group of Spanish nationalist extremists had created the Liga Patriótica Española (Spanish Patriotic League), which attacked the Catalanist demonstrations that took place daily in the city centre in the face of police repression. On 16 January, Romanones suspended constitutional guarantees in the province of Barcelona. He also closed down the CADCI, and took advantage of the situation to close down CNT-affiliated unions and arrest seventy-nine union leaders, despite the fact that the CNT had remained on the sidelines of the controversy over self-government. These preventive repressive measures were designed to arouse the protests of organized labour and so draw attention away from the movement in favour of self-government.

In the Spanish hinterland, especially in Old Castile, the provincial Diputaciones organized a regionalist-type front which gave expression, not so much to autonomist feelings, as to opposition to Catalanism. The desire of gaining the same privileges as might be granted to Catalonia became mingled with threatened boycotts of Catalan products. Since municipal and regional autonomy went together, the predominance of the former was often used against the latter in the fragile regionalisms that arose outside the historic nationalities (basically Catalonia and the Basque Country).

In Catalonia the campaign for autonomy led to the disintegration of the already weakened Monarchist structures. In February 1919 the majority of Monarchists, who considered the line adopted by the Lliga to be dangerous and a union offensive to be imminent, united in the Unión Monárquica Nacional (National Monarchist Union – UMN), headed by Sala Argemí, M. Rius i Rius (the Marquis of Olèrdola), the count of Fígols, and Darius Rumeu, the future Baron of Viver. The UMN was clearly anti-autonomist and it enjoyed the support of the Captain-General of the region, Joaquín Milans del Bosch. In March of the same year, a minority of pro-Catalanist Monarchist noblemen headed by the Count of Güell, Maluquer i Viladot, and Fabra i Puig, Marquis of Alella, founded the Federació Monàrquica Autonomista (Autonomist Monarchist Federation – FMA), which was to collaborate closely with the Lliga Regionalista.

On their return to the Congress, the Catalan parliamentarians proposed that a referendum on the statute of self-government be held in Catalonia. They were also considering launching a civil disobedience movement in the form of mass resignations from municipal councils. But on 27 February Romanones suspended the Cortes. The situation created in Barcelona as a result of a strike of electrical workers, which began with the employees of the main electricity company, 'La Canadiense', was giving rise to an intensified class struggle which would supersede demands for self-government as a priority issue.

A considerable number of factory owners gave up their Regionalist leanings and placed themselves under the protection of Captain-General Milans del Bosch, swelling the ranks of the Somatent,[3] which thus turned into an anti-revolutionary urban militia under military control. In 1919 Cambó himself and certain other leaders of the Lliga Regionalista went out into the street armed as militiamen. The split in the autonomist front halted the campaign which had ended in the failure of the Lliga Regionalista's strategy of gradual change. From now on its predominant position in the Catalanist movement would be challenged and it only managed to maintain it through lack of an alternative force capable of changing the situation and thanks to the rising electoral abstentionism that was particularly harmful to the Left.

A wave of strikes broke out in 1919–20, against the backdrop of the Russian revolution, triggering a reaction which led to the dismissal in March 1919 of the Civil Governor of Barcelona by Captain-General Milans del Bosch, with the support of the Juntas Militares, and the consequent resignation of the Romanones government. The events later culminated in the lock-out imposed by the Federación Patronal (employers' association) in late 1919 and early 1920. Labour unrest was accompanied by terrorist violence involving bands of anarchist gunmen, industrialists' bodyguards and, later, members of the Sindicat Lliure (Free Union) as well, which had been founded at the end of 1919 to undermine the strength of the CNT.

The last repercussions of the autonomist campaign were the events that marked the visit of the French commander Marshal Joffre to Barcelona in May 1920. On that occasion police charges, aimed not only at demonstrators but at the public who had been attending the Jocs Florals (poetry competition) led the Mancomunitat and the Barcelona City Council to break with the Civil Governor. During this same year a group of UMN deputies appealed against the transfer of the services of the four Catalan Diputacions to the Mancomunitat, but the appeal failed to stop the central government from going ahead with the transfer.

The Lliga Regionalista succeeded in defeating the UMN in the 1920 and 1921 elections and again worked with the new Monarchist coalition government under Maura, formed after the disaster at Annual in the Moroccan war, while General Martínez Anido, as Civil Governor, was ruthlessly persecuting the CNT and supporting the Sindicat Lliure. The post-war economic crisis increased both the pessimism of the employers and the social unrest caused by rising unemployment.

THE CRISIS AND RENEWAL OF CATALAN NATIONALISM

Cambó's second term as Minister, which was not beneficial to the autonomist cause, led to a split in the Lliga Regionalista in 1922. The leaders of the breakaway group, Bofill i Mates, Nicolau d'Olwer, Ramon d'Abadal, Carrasco i Formiguera, and others, joined former nationalist Republicans like Rovira i Virgili in founding Acció Catalana (Catalan Action). Of those who signed the document convening the Conferència Nacional Catalana (Catalan National Conference) of June 1922, from which Acció Catalana was to emerge, 62 per cent held office in the Mancomunitat, while 17 per cent were, or had been, provincial deputies. The Lliga lost not only its youth, but also many of the professionals and intellectuals who served in the Mancomunitat administration and defined the orientation of the *noucentiste* project for a national culture (see Table 7.3).[4]

When the Lliga Regionalista was defeated by Acció Catalana in the June 1923 provincial elections in the second district of Barcelona, and when the Partit Radical retained the third district as usual, the beginning of the end of the Regionalist hegemony had come. Cambó went into self-imposed isolation while Puig i Cadafalch, not knowing which way to turn, allowed himself to be taken in by the so-called Regionalist leanings of the Captain-General of Catalonia, Miguel Primo de Rivera.

The latter had the full support of the employers' and bourgeois organizations to whom the future of Catalanism was much less important than the dismantling of the CNT and the end, at any cost, of anarchist gangsterism.[5] Between 1918 and 1923, the Lliga Regionalista was to see its Barcelona electorate drop from 26.4 per cent to 11.6 per cent of registered voters. The Lliga Regionalista had succeeded in isolating its rival to the right, the Unión Monárquica Nacional, but at the cost of making autonomism subservient to social conservatism, a serious move which led to the formation of Acció Catalana.

Catalan nationalism was becoming increasingly radical but was unable to find the appropriate political tool. Though a certain moral separatism was becoming widespread, very few believed in the insurrectional separatism of Francesc Macià and Estat Català (Catalan State), which had been founded in 1922. Only a project that combined social change with Catalan self-government could attract artisans, white-collar workers, tenant farmers, and industrial workers, and these were the social strata to which the Catalan nationalist Left was appealing.

Two attempts to draw Catalanism towards socialism had failed. One was by Martí i Julià and the Unió Catalanista in 1916, the other by the CNT lawyer Francesc Layret and the lawyer and future Catalan President Lluís Companys with the Partit Republicà Català. In 1919 the PRC made a bid to join the Communist International, to which the CNT belonged for a very short time, but it failed in its attempt to attract CNT members before Layret was assassinated by gunmen in the pay of the Sindicat Lliure in November 1920. However, Companys succeeded in establishing links with the Unió de Rabassaires, a federation of societies for the defence of *métayers* and tenant farmers formed in the vine-growing areas during the new wave of agricultural unrest in the early 1920s. This attempt to associate the struggle of the peasantry to gain the ownership of the land they farmed with the cause of Catalan self-government was reminiscent of the then recent course of events in Ireland.

The scene of the third attempt to create a pro-Catalanist socialism was the Catalan Federation of the PSOE. Socialism has historically been characterized by the incorporation of white-collar workers, technicians, and intellectuals into a party of manual workers. The first stage in this process took place during and immediately after the First World War, when former members of the UFNR and the Unió Catalanista, including Andreu Nin, Manuel Serra i Moret, Rafael Campalans, and Joan Comorera, joined the PSOE. However, the violence unleashed by the class struggle in Catalonia and the predominance of anarcho-syndicalism undermined the prospects of socialism. Only a politically in-

TABLE 7.3   Results of the parliamentary elections held in the city of Barcelona (percentage of registered voters supporting each candidacy)

	1901	1903	1905	1907	1908	1910	1914	1916	1918	1919	1920	1923
Abstentions	79.8	54.4	71	40.1	47	42	56.8	62.6	56.6	50.5	70.5	62.2
Lliga Regionalista	6.3	9.8	10.2	–	–	11.5	18.7	16.3	24.6	22.2	15.5	11.6
Unió Republicana	4.4	30.6	18.2	–	–	–	–	–	–	–	–	–
PRR	–	–	–	–	–	22.5	–	–	–	–	8.8	10.2
UFNR	–	–	–	–	–	17.2	–	–	–	–	–	–
Renovació Republicana Autonomista (1916)	–	–	–	–	–	–	–	7.1	–	–	–	–
Coalició Republicana (1914, 1916, 1919)	–	–	–	–	–	–	15.9	13.1	–	16.5	–	–
Coalició d'Esquerres (1918)	–	–	–	–	–	–	–	–	18	–	–	–
Coalició Monàrquica	4.9	–	–	–	–	6.7	–	–	–	8	5	–
Carlists	–	3.6	–	–	–	–	–	–	–	–	–	–
Solidaritat Catalana (1907)	–	–	–	43.3	29.5	–	–	–	–	–	–	–
Anti-Solidaritat Republicans (1907)	–	–	–	17.4	23.4	–	–	–	–	–	–	–
PSOE	–	–	–	–	–	–	–	–	–	–	2.4	–	2
Acció Catalana	–	–	–	–	–	–	–	–	–	–	–	9.4

Note   From 1918 the Lliga's list of candidates included a Jaimist Traditionalist (supporter of Prince Jaime, a pretender to the throne), who was elected on each occasion until 1923. The 1918 left-wing coalition included the Partit Republicà Català, Partido Radical, and the PSOE. In 1920 and 1923 the Partido Radical presented only half the possible number of candidates in order to ensure that they would be elected, thus reluctantly accepting in advance that the Lliga Regionalista would win a majority. In 1919 and 1923 the PSOE did the same, unsuccessfully. In 1923 Rovira i Virgili, the only candidate of Acció Catalana, failed to be elected because of the manipulation of the votes.

dependent and unequivocally Catalanist form of socialism could take root in Catalonia and remedy the extremely low Catalan membership of the socialist trade union, the UGT. Of all socialist strongholds in Catalonia the UGT had in fact the most marked Spanish nationalist leanings and was the least susceptible to Catalanist transformation.

When the PSOE renounced its pro-Catalanist stand in 1923, the Catalanist Socialists set up the Unió Socialista de Catalunya (Socialist Union of Catalonia – USC). This party, however, virtually ceased operation in 1926. The failure of the PSOE to grow in Catalonia during the second half of the 1920s was also due to disapproval for its accommodating attitude towards the Dictatorship, at a time when Catalanism and the CNT were under persecution. Though the UGT grew, taking advantage of the void left by the anarchist unions, expansion of the union was not matched by that of the party, as usually occurred, and it ground to a halt in 1930.

Between 1919 and 1923 a balance was maintained between a Catalanist movement dominated by conservative forces and a labour movement led by anarcho-syndicalists. The division and decline of both in a climate marked by tension facilitated the military rising headed by General Primo de Rivera in Barcelona in September 1923, which met with neither opposition nor resistance.

In the summer of 1923 a Triple Alliance had been signed by Acció Catalana, the Partido Nacionalista Vasco and two Galician parties, Irmandade de Fala and Irmandade Nacionalista Galega. This pact also had the backing – albeit without a binding commitment – of Estat Català and Comunión Nacionalista Vasca (Basque Nationalist Communion). The Triple Alliance was basically a tactical agreement between dissident factions of Catalan and Basque nationalism, a symbolic gesture arising from a particular conjuncture, rather than an operational organization. Nevertheless, it caused alarm in the Spanish government since it was the first attempt at coordination between the Catalan, Basque, and Galician nationalists, and hence a precedent for the broader based GALEUZCA pact signed in Compostela ten years later in 1933.

Notes

1. Eugeni d'Ors had difficulty adapting to the increasingly rigid bureaucratic discipline of the Mancomunitat. He was suspected of ideological deviation when he expressed a certain sympathy for revolutionary unionism. Some years later he would move to Madrid where he ended up sympathizing with the fascism of the Spanish Falange.
2. The parliamentary representation of the PSOE was confined to these six deputies. In other Latin countries in Europe, the proportion of Socialist members of parliament was already considerably higher at this period.
3. The Somatent was a traditional civilian militia, previously confined to the countryside, which was turned into an auxiliary urban police force in 1919.
4. *Noucentisme* was the cultural movement which began to take the place of Modernism from 1906 onwards. It was to some extent opposed to the most vital and Romantic aspects of the latter movement. Both, however, were closely linked to the construction of Catalonia as a European society and to its overall modernization. The standardization of the Catalan language, a certain neoclassicism, and the desire for order and practical achievements within the framework of the Mancomunitat were the main characteristics of *noucentisme*, whose influence on Catalonia was little affected by new avant-garde trends.
5. The struggle between anarchist gunmen and others in the pay of the Sindicat Lliure led to the death in Barcelona in 1923 of a considerable number of union leaders and militants from both sides, including the CNT leader Salvador Seguí, who was opposed to terrorism, and several employers who belonged to the Somatent.

8 Catalanism under the Primo de Rivera Dictatorship

MILITARIZATION AND ANTI-CATALAN POLICY

The Lliga Regionalista as a party did not take part in the conspiracy which paved the way for the 1923 coup, but Puig i Cadafalch had given credit to the pro-Regionalist intentions of Primo de Rivera. A few days after the Military Directorate was set up in Madrid, with Martínez Anido as Subsecretary – and later Minister – of the Interior, decrees were promulgated prohibiting the public use of the Catalan language and the exhibition of the Catalan flag in public corporations, dissolving all municipal councils, and closing down the CADCI and one hundred and forty-nine more nationalist organizations. All this came as a hard blow to the authority of the governing party of the Mancomunitat. Repression fell earlier and harder on Catalanism than on the CNT, which was not banned until May 1924. Even an innocuous Catholic regionalist youth movement like the Pomells de Joventut (Garlands of Youth) was banned. The APEC (Association for the Protection of the Teaching of Catalan) which provided free Catalan classes and subsidized text books in the language was also proscribed. The representativeness of the Lliga Regionalista was in crisis, since the Catalan industrial bourgeoisie continued to support the Dictatorship, despite its persecution of the most fundamental symbols of Catalan identity.

In January 1924, when Puig i Cadafalch had resigned as President of the Mancomunitat, and the dissolution of all provincial Diputaciones in Spain, except those of the Basque Country, had been announced, the Dictatorship offered the Catalan Regionalists a subordinate role in a Mancomunitat appointed from Madrid. Though the Lliga Regionalista refused to collaborate in this denatured form of Mancomunitat, it later refrained from taking part in plots against the Dictatorship. The Mancomunitat, under the presidency of Sala Argemí, passed into the hands of the UMN (the Monarchist party), which soon became the Catalan regional wing of the new official party, the Unión Patriótica (Patriotic Union – UP). Darius Rumeu, the Baron of Viver, was appointed Mayor of Barcelona. Most of the Mancomunitat's top officials and many of its teachers either resigned or were dismissed.

Such was the need to subjugate Catalonia – because of the double danger of Catalanists and unionists – that it had become a sort of vice-royalty in which the action of the military authorities went unchecked by the weak and fleeting constitutional governments of the Monarchy. The first instance of military insubordination to civilian power (by the Juntas Militares de Defensa) had taken place in Barcelona in 1917. In 1919, the Army, under the command of Captain-General Milans del Bosch, had taken charge of the repression of the CNT and dismissed the central government representatives in the province of Barcelona. Milans del Bosch had succeeded in obtaining the collaboration of the Barcelona bourgeoisie by enlisting the support of the Sometent militia. Between 1920 and 1922 when Martínez Anido, who had collaborated with Milans del Bosch as military governor of Barcelona, was civil governor, the military authorities actually used the civil government of Barcelona as the base for their activities, and the government did nothing to halt their illicit repressive measures until Martínez Anido was dismissed by the Conservative Prime Minister Sánchez Guerra. When Primo de Rivera took over as Captain-General, the military authorities in effect usurped and eclipsed the functions of the civil governor in the spring and summer of 1923. It was in Barcelona, in the midst of this autonomous military régime, which was the precise opposite of the political self-government demanded by the Catalans, that the 1923 pronunciamento took place, and the army, after being used by the civilian authorities to maintain order, seized power for itself.

The Decrees of 18 September 1923 aimed against Catalan identity were the result not only of the transfer of Primo de Rivera to the post of Prime Minister in Madrid, but also of the attitude of the military pressure group in Barcelona, who would brook no other regional power in Catalonia than that of the Captain-General. Their aim was to subordinate and distort the Mancomunitat in order eventually to dissolve it, leaving the regional military authorities in sole command of the four newly disconnected provincial administrations, which would be entrusted to a compliant party such as the Unión Patriótica (formerly Unión Monárquica Nacional). Consequently in 1925, when Primo de Rivera, his authority reinforced by victory in Morocco and the eradication of gangsterism, replaced the Military Directorate with a Civil Directorate and withdrew the military from local government, the tandem formed by General Emilio Barrera, as Captain-General, and General Milans del Bosch, as civil governor of Barcelona, continued to wield power in Catalonia. The latter had no qualms the same year in closing down the Barcelona Football Club and the Orfeó Català choir. In 1926 he proceeded to dissolve the Governing Board of the Barcelona Col · legi d'Advocats (the Barcelona Law Society) for not having published the list of its members solely in Spanish, and he banished its members from Barcelona.

Once Alfons Sala Argemí, the new President of the Mancomunitat, had purged that institution of Catalanism, he believed he could make it fit into the framework of the new Provincial Statute and even increase its authority. The Provincial Statute stemmed from the Municipal Statute drafted by the Director General of Local Administration, José Calvo Sotelo, but neither law would ever be enforced. In the case of Catalonia, moreover, the Dictatorship proved incapable of distinguishing between a purely administrative, pro-Spanish form of autonomy and the former embryo of political autonomy. Consequently in 1925 Sala Argemí, abandoned by his own political allies, was forced to resign, and Primo de Rivera simply abolished the Mancomunitat.

NON-VIOLENT RESISTANCE

Thanks to Regionalist patronage and manned by former Mancomunitat personnel, some of the cultural services created by the former Mancomunitat managed to survive. This enforced privatization of the Catalan cultural market served merely to promote collaboration between Regionalists and radical nationalists in the production and diffusion of culture. Despite the repression of the Catalan language, both the Catalan daily press and the publication of books in Catalan were tolerated, provided they were submitted to prior censorship, and reading in Catalan increased as a form of passive resistance. Whereas in 1923 there had been seven Catalan language dailies – two of them in Barcelona – by 1927 there were ten, of which three were published in the capital. In the same year one hundred and forty-seven Catalan magazines were available. Books published in Catalan rose from two hundred and twenty-seven in 1926 – the first year for which statistics are available – to three hundred and eight in 1930. In other words, new titles in Catalan, which in 1926 had accounted for 7.7 per cent of all those published in Spain, made up 10.2 per cent of the total output in 1930. In 1928, the first festival of Catalan books was held on the feast of the Catalan patron saint, Saint George, a tradition which is still alive today.

As a result of the prohibition of the Catalan flag and language, more citizens than hitherto came to identify with them as collective symbols which were no longer associated with any particular party. The Lliga Regionalista was forgiven for its initially gullible attitude towards Primo de Rivera by its subsequent refusal to collaborate with him.

Part of the Spanish intelligentsia expressed disagreement with the Dictatorship's policy against the Catalan language, fearing that it would encourage separatism, and in March 1924 a manifesto to this effect was signed in Madrid by over a hundred writers of such diverse tendencies as Pedro Sainz Rodríguez, who was to become a minister under Franco, the future Socialist Prime Minister Manuel Azaña, the philosopher and writer José Ortega y Gasset, the historian and philologist Ramón Menéndez Pidal, and the proto-Fascist Ernesto Giménez Caballero. In 1927 this same group gave support to the exhibition of Catalan books held in the Biblioteca Nacional in Madrid and in 1930 a tribute was paid in Barcelona to the Castilian intellectuals who had signed the 1924 manifesto. On that occasion Azaña displayed understanding of Catalan demands for self-government, and some of the Spanish guests at the ceremony would later take part in the unsuccessful attempt to found the Centro Constitucional, a Spanish party supported by the Lliga Regionalista.

The attitude of peaceful resistance adopted by conservative Catalanism made the Dictatorship uneasy. Valls i Taberner, R. Abadal and Carrasco i Formiguera – all members of the Governing Board of the Barcelona Col·legi d'Advocats – were dismissed and sanctioned. A large sector of the Catalan clergy, with the backing of the Archbishop of Tarragona, Francesc Vidal i Barraquer, refused to collaborate with the Dictatorship in its plan to use only Spanish in preaching and catechism in exchange for the privileged situation offered to the Catholic Church.

Under the Dictatorship, several Catalanists, ranging from Nicolau d'Olwer, a leader of Acció Catalana, to Joan Estelrich of the Lliga Regionalista, Cambó's associate in his cultural undertakings, made appeals to the League of Nations, thereby annoying the Spanish government. They served no purpose, however, both because of the indifference of the major powers and because the rights of minority nations protected by the League of Nations had been defined on the basis of groups belonging to nation states in Eastern Europe and the Balkans that had been absorbed by other states governed by a different nationality, and they failed to take account of nations with no political recognition whatever. However, Catalan nationalism was represented at the Congress of National Minorities of Europe from 1925 onwards.

INSURRECTIONAL NATIONALISM

For radical Catalan nationalists, the Dictatorship was evidence of the failure of legal political methods of attaining self-government under the Monarchy and proved that a separatist insurrection was the only way forward. Francesc Macià, who was in exile, tried first to draw the support of Acció Catalana and then set up a revolutionary committee in Paris in 1925. The committee was made up of Ventura Gassol, for Estat Català, Rafael Vidiella, for the CNT, and the General Secretary of the tiny Partido Comunista Español, José Bullejos, as well as representatives of the most radical wing of Basque nationalism, known as Aberriano, and the Galician autonomist movement. Macià and Bullejos travelled to Moscow to ask the Communist International for help in perpetrating the armed raid being prepared by Estat Català, but no Soviet assistance was forthcoming and the only support Macià received, after breaking with the Communists, came from Catalan centres in Latin America. It was difficult to contain the impatience of the insurrectionary nationalists and in 1925 the police foiled an attempt to blow up the train in which the King and Primo de Rivera were travelling at Garraf, south-east of Barcelona. Miquel Badia, Jaume Compte and other members of the Bandera Negra group of Estat Català were found guilty. Macià disapproved of terrorism and realized that his plans for guerrilla action must be speeded up if he was to avert further dissidence.

Five months after the attempted military pronunciamento by certain Monarchist leaders, which took place in Madrid on the Eve of the feast of Saint John (23–24 June), Macià and the guerrilla squads of Estat Català tried to enter Catalonia from France in November 1926 via Prats de Molló. But the French police stopped the expeditionary force before it could cross the border. The trial of Macià and his associates in Paris gained international notoriety for Macià and drew attention to Catalan grievances all over Europe. Macià was exiled to Belgium and travelled to various Latin-American capitals to visit Catalan nationalist groups there. His tour culminated in a separatist assembly held in Havana in October 1928 at which a draft constitution was drawn up recommending no more than confederal links between Catalonia and the rest of Spain and the right to separate. A Catalan separatist flag was designed by adding a single star – inspired by the Cuban flag – to the four red stripes on a yellow background of the traditional Catalan flag.

The Estat Català adventure had no repercussions inside Catalonia,

where there was no support for insurgent methods. The major public
works projects, pursued and encouraged by the Primo de Rivera administration, went ahead in a depoliticized atmosphere. They culminated in the Barcelona International Exhibition of 1929, planned by
the Regionalists prior to 1923, which was used by the Dictatorship for
purposes of foreign propaganda. However, the exhibition did not succeed in reconciling Catalonia with the Dictatorship. In January 1930
Primo de Rivera resigned. His bid to institutionalize the emergency
powers had failed for want of a consensus between the right-wing forces
in the National Consultative Assembly, which was to draw up a new
constitution, and as a result of the Army's unwillingness to strengthen
its support explicitly. Cambó now seemed to have been right in argu-
ing that violent resistance would have been counterproductive and it
was preferable to get ready to replace the dictatorial régime so as to
avert a revolution. However, the growth in Catalan nationalist feeling
that had taken place under the Dictatorship was ill-matched to the
moderate stand of the Lliga Regionalista, as expressed in Cambó's book
Per la Concòrdia (*Towards Harmony*), which confined itself to condemning both assimilationism and separatism.

THE RESTORATION OF CONSTITUTIONAL RIGHTS

Primo de Rivera's administration was replaced by one headed by General Dámaso Berenguer, which pledged itself to the gradual restoration
of political rights. This reduced tension momentarily, but the attempt
to return to 1923 as though nothing had happened in the intervening
six years proved totally non-viable.

The Diputacions and municipal councils were immediately reinstated
with the deputies and councillors who had obtained the greatest number
of votes since 1917 and representatives of the institutions themselves.
Joan Maluquer i Viladot, of the FMA, was appointed president of the
Barcelona Diputació, while Joan Antoni Güell, of the same party, became Mayor of Barcelona. Both appointments were well received by
the Lliga Regionalista, which recovered its former positions in the institutions. Primo de Rivera's supporters, which had dominated them in
recent years, virtually disappeared and reverted to their former name
of UMN. Maluquer i Viladot successfully appealed to the new government to extend the amnesty to those sentenced for the Garraf assassination attempt. With the support of the presidents of the other Diputacions

and of the Lliga, he also asked for the re-establishment of the Mancomunitat on the basis of the Provincial Statute passed by the Dictatorship. But to the Catalan Left this was tantamount to recognizing the legality of the Dictatorship, whereas they felt that the next Cortes should have a constituent function. Though the Republican and nationalist Left constituted only a minority, its opposition led to the whole question being left in suspense. The public servants and school teachers of the former Mancomunitat returned to their posts, the Barcelona City Council school board resumed operation, rapidly building and equipping eleven schools, with room for 16,000 students, which opened after the change of régime.

The Monarchist camp was in a state of disarray. The constitutionalists considered constitutional reform to be vital, while Primo de Rivera's supporters felt resentful, and the old parties were having serious difficulties in reorganizing themselves for the coming elections. In view of this situation, the Lliga Regionalista felt the time had come to revise Prat de la Riba's doctrine of nationalism and to confine themselves within strictly regionalist limits. This ideological evolution was essential if conservative Catalanism was to resume its policy of participation in Spanish politics, but it was contrary to the radicalizing trend that had marked Catalanism since the Dictatorship. The Lliga Regionalista could not immediately take part in a Spanish government so soon after the insults to Catalan identity of which the Monarchy, through the Dictatorship, had been guilty, but it in no way desired a change of régime. Contrary to what had happened in 1906, 1917 and 1918, in this final crisis of the Monarchy the Catalanist Right and Left were not to go hand in hand, and while conservative Catalanism was driven to support the Monarchy, the still badly divided Catalanist Left was to form an alliance with the Spanish Republicans and Socialists.

THE ALLIANCE OF THE CATALAN NATIONALISTS WITH THE SPANISH REPUBLICANS

In March 1930, a pro-Republican manifesto announced that an agreement had been reached between Catalan nationalists, autonomist Republicans, and even members of the CNT. In May the CNT decided to come out of hiding and in a few months had reorganized itself in Catalonia, recovering its domination of the labour movement and ousting the officially protected Sindicat Lliure, which had dominated labour relations during the Dictatorship. On 14 April 1931, the Sindicat Lliure was closed down and banned.

In order to escape from the position of isolation in which it had found itself until 1923 and adapt to the new conjuncture, it was vital for nationalist and autonomist Republicanists of the Federalist tradition to overcome their differences and unite.

When, in August 1930, the six Spanish Republican parties and the Socialists signed the San Sebastian Pact, they invited three Catalan representatives to the meeting: Jaume Aiguader, for Estat Català, Macià Mallol, for Acció Republicana de Catalunya, and Manuel Carrasco i Formiguera for Acció Catalana (these last two being the splinter groups into which the original Acció Catalana had split and which in March 1931 were to reunite under the name of Partit Catalanista Republicà (Catalanist Republican Party)). The Catalan representatives agreed to support the Republican committee chaired by the former dynastic Liberal Alcalá Zamora, who had abandoned the Monarchist camp. In exchange they were promised that the future Republican government would grant Catalonia a statute of autonomy. The San Sebastian Pact did not recognize Catalonia's right to self-determination since the future constituent Cortes was to have the last word as to the limits of Catalan self-government. But so soon after the end of the Dictatorship, when the future was still very uncertain, the compromise seemed advantageous.

Thus, while its leader was still in exile, Macià's party had made an abrupt about-turn, abandoning the goal of independence from a Monarchist Spain in exchange for a self-governing régime granted and guaranteed by the future Spanish Republic. There would henceforth be no insurmountable obstacles to the merger of Estat Català with the non-separatist Catalanist forces, such as Partit Republicà Català, and the group linked to the weekly magazine, *L'Opinió*. Insurrectional separatism had failed under the Dictatorship, and the prospect of a new régime in Spain opened up fresh possibilities for Catalan Republican autonomism.

In September 1930 the Republican committee in Madrid, on which Nicolau d'Olwer represented the Catalan forces, began secret preparations for a military pronunciamento with the support of a general strike called by the UGT and CNT. The two union confederations, which were no longer united by an alliance as in 1917, had no desire to repeat the unfortunate experience of that year and wanted to see troops in the streets before taking any initiative. Lack of funds and the very small number of military personnel prepared to rebel left the Barcelona Republican committee dependent on that in Madrid. When the

CNT declared a general strike in Barcelona on 17 November, a messenger from the Madrid Republican committee was dispatched to persuade the CNT leaders to order a return to work, since elsewhere in Spain the plot was not yet ripe. Finally, in mid-December, Captains Fermín Galán and García Hernández of the Jaca garrison mutinied. However, the only support they obtained was from a small group of officers at the Cuatro Vientos aerodrome and they were subsequently shot, providing the Republic with its protomartyrs.

Most of the members of the Republican comittees in Madrid and Barcelona were arrested. The Republicans and Socialists announced their withdrawal from the general elections that the Berenguer government was still bent on holding immediately, so as to put an end to its interim character but still without endowing the new Cortes with a constituent role. Considering that the withdrawal of the Republicans deprived the election of validity to legitimize the monarchy of Alfonso XIII, the constitutionalist Liberals headed by Santiago Alba also decided to stand down, followed by the remaining Liberal groups and the Lliga Regionalista.

Berenguer resigned and a multi-party Monarchist government was formed under Admiral Aznar. The Lliga was forced to join this administration, Ventosa i Calvell becoming Minister of Finance. The concentration of Monarchists in the government obliged the Republicans to take up the challenge of contesting the elections, especially since municipal elections were to be held first, as they had requested, contrary to the wishes of General Berenguer, who had wanted to start with general elections. Though the municipal elections were usually administrative rather than political in character, on this occasion they were inevitably converted into a referendum on the régime.

The Lliga justified its support for the preservation of the Monarchy on the grounds that the last Monarchist government had promised 'a suitable solution to the problem of Catalonia'. The findings of an extraparliamentary commission in 1919, in which the Lliga had not taken part on account of the refusal of the Left, provided the minimum basis for such a solution. But the Monarchy had lost its reputation for constitutionality and democracy, and its autonomist credibility was practically nil. In March 1931 the Lliga, along with Maura's followers, who had not been supporters of Primo de Rivera, and various Spanish conservative regionalist groups, founded a new party; the Centro Constitucional. However, the image of the new formation was totally distorted by the fact that both Regionalists and Maurists belonged to the motley Monarchist government of unity, and the unconvincing results it obtained in the elections held on 12 April marked the end of this attempt by conservative Catalanism to create a Spanish party.

In March 1931, Acció Catalana, which at the time was seen by many as the force with the best prospects, was reunited, and Esquerra Republicana de Catalunya (Republican Left of Catalonia – ERC) was created as the result of the merger of the Partit Republicà Català of Lluís Companys and Marcelino Domingo with Estat Català (under the leadership of Macià, who by now had been able to return from exile) and the group connected to *L'Opinió*, headed by Lluhí i Vallescà. Few people believed that the still fragile ERC would become the predominant party in Catalonia for the following five years. Unió Socialista de Catalunya (Socialist Union of Catalonia – USC), which was not yet properly organized as a party, did not join the new united Catalanist Left party, but entered an agreement with it involving cooperation, not only in elections but in government, which was to be maintained throughout the five years of the Second Republic. This alliance was to enable USC to obtain results it could not have achieved on its own, but it also obscured its separate identity and made it a satellite of ERC.

THE MUNICIPAL ELECTIONS OF APRIL 1931 AND THE CATALAN REPUBLIC

In the municipal elections of 12 April 1931, the Socialist Republican coalition presented not one list of candidates in Barcelona, as in many other parts of Spain, but three. There were also two Communist lists presented by the dissidents of the Bloc Obrer i Camperol (Labour and Agricultural Workers' Bloc) and the powerless PCE respectively. Acció Catalana, renamed Partit Catalanista Republicà (Catalanist Republican Party), which had drawn up joint lists with ERC elsewhere in Catalonia, stood alone in Barcelona. Macià had offered the PCR a coalition list in which ERC would have been content with five or six candidates out of the total of thirty, but the PRC rejected the offer, fearing to lose the bourgeois electorate which it hoped to capture from the Lliga. Acció Catalana/PCR contested the elections in Barcelona with a purely administrative programme, as in any normal election.

The second Republican candidacy was that of ERC–USC, and the third the coalition of the Partit Radical with the PSOE. The outcome was entirely unpredictable: no elections had been held for seven years, many voters were exercising their rights for the first time, and part of the former electorate had disappeared. But the attitude of the CNT and its daily *Solidaridad Obrera* made it likely that many left-wing abstentionists would vote on this occasion and that their participation would be favourable to ERC, the force that had most convincingly promised a change of régime.

On 12 April, 59 per cent of those on the electoral roll in Barcelona turned out to vote, as against only 37 per cent in the 1923 general election. The various groups of Republicans and Socialists obtained 68 per cent of local councils seats throughout Catalonia, the Lliga Regionalista and its associates 20.7 per cent, declared Monarchists 5.7 per cent, Communists 1 per cent, and independents the remaining 5 per cent. In the city of Barcelona, ERC won twenty-five seats; the Radical–Socialist coalition eight; and Republicans from other formations two, while the Lliga Regionalista had only twelve and the Partit Catalanista Republicà (Acció Catalana) did not obtain a single seat. The defeat of conservative Catalanism and the decline of Lerrouxism in Barcelona heralded the beginning of the hegemony of ERC in Catalonia. A high turnout of artisans and workers – both CNT members and others – together with the rejection of the recent evolution of the Lliga Regionalista by part of the bourgeoisie brought victory for the first time to left-wing Catalan nationalists, and made Francesc Macià the charismatic national leader.

At midday on 14 April, when the news broke that the Republicans had won in all the provincial capitals throughout Spain, Companys proclaimed the Republic from the balcony of Barcelona City Hall and hoisted up the three-coloured Spanish republican flag (red, yellow, and lilac). Shortly afterwards Macià arrived, proclaimed the Catalan republic to be 'a member state of an Iberian federation', and took possession of the Diputació. This gesture helped speed up the handover of power in Madrid, where the Republic was proclaimed the same afternoon and the King went into exile. Crowds marched through the streets of Barcelona shouting 'Death to Cambó! Long live Macià!', and many of those joining in were workers from other parts of Spain.

9 The Generalitat under the Second Republic and the Statute of Self-government

THE PROVISIONAL GOVERNMENT OF THE CATALANIST LEFT

The proclamation of the Catalan Republic on 14 April 1931 was a victory for the strategy of the Catalan nationalist Left which, for a quarter of a century, had been claiming that Catalan self-government was impossible without a break with the former régime and the introduction of democracy. Macià's declaration of Catalan sovereignty was not an attempt to infringe the 1930 San Sebastian Pact but to speed up progress towards the federalization of the peoples of the Iberian Peninsula.

On 17 April, after discussions with three ministers from the provisional government of the Republic – Nicolau d'Olwer, Marcelino Domingo, and Fernando de los Ríos – Macià renounced the Catalan Republic in exchange for a regional government which adopted the historic name of 'the Generalitat'. His assumption was that, when the Spanish constituent Cortes met, they would approve a Statute of Self-government which was to be drawn up by a commission elected by an assembly of municipal council representatives and would be subsequently submitted to referendum in Catalonia. After forcing the central government to recognize a provisional autonomous Catalan government, Macià had given way, but he retained considerable moral authority, which was to gain him respect among Spanish Republican parties despite the somewhat hostile attitude of many of their members towards Catalan self-government. At no time had the atmosphere in Catalonia been that of a separatist revolt, nor had Macià aimed to trigger off an insurrection. Those who later accused him of capitulating, such as the Bloc Obrer i Camperol or the separatist splinter group of Estat Català, were neither able nor willing, in those hope-filled days of April 1931, to press him to mount an insurrection.

For the time being, Macià had achieved one important result: the four Catalan provincial Diputacions had been abolished and absorbed by the Generalitat. A provisional government of the Generalitat was set up under ERC leadership but with representatives, not only of Acció Catalana, but also of the PSOE and the Partit Radical. The Lliga, ostracized after leading the Catalanist movement for decades, was excluded.

The Statute drawn up by the commission in Núria was approved by the assembly of local council representatives and submitted to a referendum on 2 August 1931. Even the major representatives of the Barcelona conservative press acknowledged the self-restraint and moderation of the Núria Statute. None the less, it still considered a federal régime to be the only suitable framework for genuine Catalan self-government. The Spanish deputies would later use this fact to restrict the scope of the Catalan Statute, since the Republican Constitution did not establish a federation but an 'integral state', that is, one that was unitary in nature but prepared to decentralize. On 2 August 1931, 75 per cent of Catalan voters took part in the referendum, and 99 per cent of them endorsed the draft statute.

One month earlier, on 28 June, elections had taken place to the constituent Spanish Cortes. ERC and its allies repeated, and even improved on, their earlier victory, winning all five Catalan constituencies, thanks partly to the two-round majority election system. Throughout the five years of the Second Republic, the Lliga was to call in vain for proportional representation. On this occasion the Lliga obtained only four deputies in the constituent Cortes, but it subsequently recovered and soon emerged as the second party in Catalonia, especially after being restructured and taking the name Lliga Catalana (Catalan League) in February 1933. Acció Catalana, on the other hand, proved unable to overcome its isolation. Some of its members joined ERC – Rovira i Virgili, Carles Pi Sunyer – while others returned to the Lliga – Bofill i Mates – and yet another group headed by Carrasco i Formiguera, together with some dissident Carlist traditionalists, founded the Christian Democrat group, Unió Democràtica de Catalunya (Democratic Union of Catalonia – UDC).

Once the Constitution had been approved, the various forces occupied their respective political spaces and the broad coalition on which the provisional government of the Republic had been based came to an end. The Radicals left the government and took a turn to the right, while Manuel Azaña formed a government of Radical Socialists and Socialists. At the end of 1931 and the beginning of 1932, the relationship between ERC and other political forces also changed. Previously, ERC, in an attempt to avoid breaking its initial tacit agreement with the CNT, had defended the anarchist union in its struggle with the PSOE, which was very weak in Catalonia. The mixed labour tribunals set up by the Socialist Minister of Labour, Largo Caballero, to carry out mediation prior to strikes was the main bone of contention between anarchists and Socialists, the former being in favour of direct action and against state intervention in labour conflicts. Friction between Socialists and anarchists over the control of workers in the port of Barcelona led to violent incidents, whereupon ERC withdrew its support from the CNT and entered a more cordial relationship with the PSOE, though the position of the latter was anything but favourable to self-government. This development can be explained by the aggravation of the social climate and by the predominance that members of the Federación Anarquista Ibérica (Iberian Anarchist Federation – FAI) had acquired within the CNT at the expense of the unionists, who were less hostile to the Catalanist Left.[1] The unsuccessful anarchist insurrection in the Alt Llobregat region in January 1932 brought about the consummation of the breach between ERC and the CNT.

THE 1932 STATUTE OF SELF-GOVERNMENT

The final version of the Statute of Self-government was based not on the will of the Catalan people but on that of the Spanish Cortes, where the Catalans inevitably constituted a small minority. The project came under discussion in May 1932 at the same time as the agrarian reform bill. Opposition to the Catalan Statute came not only from right-wing Castilian nationalists such as Royo Villanova, but also from distinguished intellectuals like Miguel de Unamuno and José Ortega y Gasset. The debate would have gone on longer but for the unsuccessful coup of General Sanjurjo in August 1932. The reluctant Republican deputies were forced to vote for the statute in September, but the circumstances also affected the aspirations of the Catalan deputies, who accepted major cutbacks.

The statute guaranteed the Catalan language co-official status with Spanish and gave the Generalitat exclusive jurisdiction over legislation concerning Catalan civil law and local and internal administration. This enabled it to introduce and adopt new territorial divisions based on natural regions or *comarques*. In certain other fields, such as social and general insurance, labour arbitration and inspection, the Generalitat became directly responsible for executive action, though not for legislation. The State was to transfer to the Generalitat services relating to law and order, the administration of justice, labour relations, and public works. The great majority of existing civil servants remained in their posts though they were given the option of transfers. In 1934 a number of public servants in the employment of the Generalitat adopted a hostile attitude towards the Catalan administration, among them magistrates of the Barcelona regional court (Audiència de Barcelona).

The Spanish Republicans made major cuts in the draft statute approved by referendum in 1931 in two crucial areas: finance and education. Without adequate, flexible, and independent resources, there could be no true autonomy and public services could not be properly extended and reformed. The statute approved in 1931 had provided for direct taxation to be transferred to the Generalitat, with indirect taxes remaining in the hands of the central government, a typically federal arrangement. Catalonia suffered from a chronic deficit in public expenditure. In 1930 the Spanish State had raised almost 19 per cent of its revenue in Catalonia – not counting customs – but it spent only 5.5 per cent of its budget there – excluding military expenses – yet Catalonia made up 11 per cent of the total population of Spain. The 1932 Statute granted the Generalitat only certain direct taxes: local property tax (contribución territorial) and property transfer tax (derechos reales). If, and only if, these two sources were not sufficient to support the services transferred by the central government, then Catalonia would be granted 20 per cent of the revenue from industrial and commercial taxation. Not only was the system inflexible, but the Cortes could periodically revise the financial régime of the 'autonomous region' if it deemed its contribution to the overall expenses of the State inadequate.

The Joint Commission of Transfers worked slowly. Property taxes were not transferred until the middle of 1934, but the administration of justice had been handed over in October 1933, and law and order in November. Public works were not transferred until the end of 1935. The State cut back its own investments in Catalonia before handing over the corresponding jurisdiction to the Generalitat, so that between 1931 and 1935 investment in the Catalan road network was less that half what it had been in the preceding five years.

If all revenues from direct taxation had been transferred to the Generalitat they would have amounted to 233 million pesetas per year. The state had spent 138.7 million pesetas in Catalonia in 1930, whereas the Generalitat's budget for 1934 was only 128 million, and that adopted in May 1936, 143 million. The working budget of the Barcelona City Council was 127.5 million in 1935. Resorting to loans was problematic in a period of financial crisis. In May 1936, Companys, who had succeeded Macià as President of the Generalitat, asked the central government for the revenue from industrial and commercial taxation because the services transferred represented an expenditure of 15 million in excess of the funds granted.

The financial system of the Generalitat was considerably more restrictive than that enjoyed by Italian autonomous regions since the 1970 law and inferior even to the resources of the Diputación Foral of Navarre under the Franco régime.[2]

The other major cutback on the 1931 draft Statute was in the field of education. The statute approved by the Catalan people provided for the transfer of the entire education system in Catalonia to the Generalitat. Under it the teaching of Spanish would have been obligatory in all schools, but the language of instruction was to be Catalan, the mother tongue of the majority. However, in places where there had been a minimum of forty children speaking Spanish as their mother tongue for the preceding three years, there would also be classes where the teaching was through Spanish. In 1931, 19 per cent of the Catalan population had been born outside Catalonia. Immigrants from other parts of Spain were very unevenly spread, accounting for only 4–6 per cent of the population of the provinces of Girona, Lleida, and Tarragona, as against one-quarter of the population of the province of Barcelona.

But under the 1932 Statute, education remained in the hands of the Spanish State. If the Generalitat wanted to set up its own elementary and high schools where classes would be given in Catalan, it had to do so with its own meagre resources. Only at university level was a type of joint authority established under the statute of autonomy granted to the University of Barcelona. The University was to be run by a board, half of whose members were appointed by the central government and half by the Generalitat. Co-official status for the Catalan language, changes in the curriculum, the hiring of eminent personalities as guest professors outside the regular academic staff, and the participation of student delegates on academic boards, were some of the improvements made in the Autonomous University of Barcelona, where Catalan and Spanish cultures coexisted in perfect harmony, thus calming obsessive fears that the Spanish language would be banished from the schools and universities of Catalonia.

In Catalonia as elsewhere in Spain, the Republic brought undeniable progress in the regular school system. The 663 classes existing in April 1931 had risen by July 1936 to 1634, which meant that places had been created for 41,000 more children. Even so, the increase covered less than 40 per cent of the deficit detected in the province of

Barcelona in 1931. A decree passed on 29 April 1931 by the provisional government of the Spanish Republic had laid down that children up to the age of eight should be educated in their mother tongue, which for the majority in Catalonia meant Catalan. Many teachers lacked training in written Catalan and this the Generalitat tried to remedy by organizing free Catalan correspondence courses on a voluntary basis. Half the teachers in the public sector in Catalonia registered for these courses between 1931 and 1936. Those opposed to the use of Catalan invoked Article 50 of the Constitution which established the compulsory use of Spanish in teaching, in addition to its being taught as a subject.

The Spanish State, which was responsible for education in Catalonia, continued to make knowledge of Catalan no more than optional for teachers who were posted to Catalonia. The Catalanization of the school system never took place, though the decree of April 1931 was enforced in the schools of the Barcelona City Council School Board, posts were created for professors of Catalan in the teachers' training colleges run by the State in Catalonia, and the Generalitat's own college trained whole new generations of teachers who were both ready and willing to Catalanize the schools. In 1930, Catalonia had had only nine secondary schools,[3] two of them in Barcelona, but the number of these eventually rose to twenty, including seven in the capital. The Generalitat set up a secondary school that served as a pilot centre for the training of future teachers, the Institut Escola. Pedagogical innovation, coeducation, and laicism, combined always with profound respect for the Catholic faith of the majority of the pupils, were the keynotes of the Institut Escola, and all the lessons were given entirely in Catalan. Along with summer schools for teachers and summer holiday camps for Barcelona school children, it was an element in the educational experiment carried out under the Second Republic that was to leave an indelible memory in the minds of many.

Despite the failure to Catalanize the school system during the five years of the Republic, considerable progress was made towards restoring the Catalan language and culture to a more normal situation in the new mass communications medium, the radio. Moreover, Catalan underwent an unprecedented expansion in both the press and book-publishing, a fact that bears witness to the vitality of Catalan culture at the time. The ten Catalan language dailies existing in 1927 had grown to twenty-five in 1933, seven of which were Barcelona papers. The number of books published in Catalan increased from three hundred and eight titles in 1930 to 865 in 1936 despite the economic crisis. Catalan books,

TABLE 9.1   Results of legislative elections in Catalonia under the Second Republic indicating the number of deputies elected by each party and overall turnout

	23 June 1931	20 Nov. 1932	19 Nov. 1933	16 Feb. 1936
Esquerra Republicana de Catalunya	31	52	23	21
Unió Socialista de Catalunya	4	5	3	4
Acció Catalana Republicana	2	1	–	5
Partit Nacionalista Republicà d'Esquerra	–	–	–	2
Acción Republicana	–	–	1	–
Partido Republicano Radical Socialista	3	–	–	–
Izquierda Republicana	–	–	–	2
Extrema Izquierda Federal	1	–	–	–
Partido Socialista Obrero Español	1	–	–	1
Partido Obrero de Unificación Marxista	–	–	–	1
Partit Català Proletari	–	–	–	1
Partit Comunista de Catalunya	–	–	–	1
Unió de Rabassaires	–	–	–	2
Partido Republicano Radical	3	–	1	–
Lliga Regionalista/Lliga Catalana	2	16	25	11
Unió Democràtica de Catalunya	–	1	–	–
Tradicionalistes	–	–	2	1
Voter turnout	69	60.2	63.1	67.8

Notes   In 1931 one of the two ACR deputies and the three belonging to the PRSS were part of a coalition with ERC. The USC deputies were always part of the ERC lists. In 1932, the dissident autonomist Radicals elected for Tarragona on the ERC lists have not been listed separately. In 1932 the only UDC candidate elected was on the list of the Lliga Regionalista. In 1933, the two traditionalists and the single Radical deputy were part of an alliance with the Lliga. In 1936 all the deputies elected, except the eleven belonging to the Lliga Catalana and the single Traditionalist, made up the Catalan Left-wing Front.

which had accounted for 10 per cent of the Spanish total in 1930, represented 20 per cent in 1933.

In the sociocultural and educational field, the laicist policy of the Republic, which confiscated Jesuit property and decided in 1933 to prohibit religious orders from running schools – though the law was never implemented – created disquiet in Catalonia. Tension was less acute, however, than in other parts of Spain, and in Catalonia no churches, convents or monasteries were burned in May 1931 as they were in Madrid and elsewhere. Only the military rising of July 1936 was to trigger off a return to widespread arson and religious persecution.

THE ESTABLISHMENT OF THE AUTONOMOUS RÉGIME

In the elections to the first Catalan parliament of modern times, which were held in November 1932, ERC reaffirmed its overwhelming predominance, but the Lliga Regionalista had begun a recovery which, a year later, was to reach its peak. The Catalan elections revealed both the weakness of communism (since the Bloc Obrer i Camperol won only 5 per cent of the votes in Lleida where it had most support) and the impotence of separatism (radical nationalist voters continuing to vote for ERC). It also became obvious that socialism was still extremely weak, an anomalous situation in a country as highly industrialized as Catalonia. ERC, the dominant party which had no trade union of its own, and the CNT, the dominant trade union with no political representation, opposed quite as much as they complemented each other! And between the electoral predominance of ERC and the union predominance of the CNT there was no room for socialism, with its twofold party and union structure. The socialists, moreover, were split between the Catalanist USC, which collaborated closely with ERC, and the Spanish nationalist PSOE. Only a united, autonomous, Catalan national socialism, that was organically and tactically independent, could hope to create a slot for itself in Catalonia between the communism of the Bloc Obrer i Camperol, the working-class voters of ERC, and the labour hegemony of the CNT.

Surprisingly, in view of the parliamentary majority of ERC, the government of the Generalitat was shaken by three crises in less than a year as a result of internal struggles within the dominant party. These primarily involved two factions: the group associated with *L'Opinió* (now a daily), and the Estat Català group, though members of the Unió de Rabaissaires (representing the tenant vine-growers) also created problems. The disorder on the Barcelona City Council, where cases of corruption involving councillors belonging to the ERC majority group were discovered, also had repercussions on the internal stability of the party and led to the departure in September 1933 of the *L'Opinió* group and Josep Tarradellas. The splinter group rebelled against the leadership of Macià and created a new party, Partit Nacionalista Republicà d'Esquerra (Nationalist Republican Party of the Left – PNRE), led by Lluhí i Vallescà.

In 1933, labour disputes reached their height. The number of workers on strike in the province of Barcelona was double the figure for 1931, and five times higher than in 1932. Some of the longest and hardest strikes, such as that affecting the construction industry, were marked by renewed outbreaks of violence. During the two tram strikes that took place in Barcelona in 1933, there were incidents involving trams driven by volunteers, many of them from Estat Català, and the anarchists of the FAI.

By 1933 the effects of the great depression of the 1930s on the Catalan economy were beginning to be clearly felt, and though its impact was less severe than in other more developed countries, it should not be underestimated. The drop in the price of wine exacerbated tension between tenant farmers and landowners, represented respectively by the Unió de Rabassaires, one of the founding organizations of ERC, and the Institut Agrícola Català de Sant Isidre, headed initially by members of the Lliga Catalana. The rise in unemployment caused disillusionment among the working classes. At the end of 1932 the overall figure in Barcelona was 10 per cent, but in the construction industry it reached 50 per cent and one in three workers in the metal industry had been laid off. When the labour movement, under the intransigent leadership of the anarchists, went onto the offensive, the reduction in buying power and the fall in prices caused the employers to take a tougher attitude towards wage increases.

The deflationist policy of the Republican governments was unconducive to the reactivation of the economy in a situation of falling exports, and economic insecurity undermined confidence in the ability of the Republican parties to bring about reforms in an age without unemployment insurance or sickness benefits. The rise of intransigent anarchists as members of the CNT leadership seemed to be an answer, but by the end of 1933 the union had lost much of its strength, membership had declined, and it had suffered a major split with the departure from its ranks of members who followed the line of the *Treintistes*, the 'thirty signatories' of an earlier CNT manifesto.

The ease with which Hitler seized power in Germany in 1933, by destroying parliamentary democracy from within, darkened the outlook and gave rise to fears that something similar might occur in the unstable Spanish Second Republic. This helps explain the atmosphere of tension surrounding the campaign leading to the general election of November 1933, during which the Left began to threaten to stage a rising if the Confederación Española de Derechas Autónomas (Spanish Confederation of Autonomous Right-wing Forces – CEDA), the Catholic party headed by Gil Robles, was victorious – as indeed it was, thanks largely to the division of the Socialists and the Republican Left in Spain.

In 1933 the Catalan Parliament passed its internal statute, one of the main features of which was a moderate presidential-type system. The other two major laws approved were the municipal law, which called for municipal elections to be held forthwith, and the law of rural conflicts, which established provisional regulations that were to remain in force until a permanent law was approved in response to the demands of the Unió de Rabaissaires. Before the end of the year, jurisdiction over the administration of justice and public order was transferred to the Generalitat. The post of civil governor disappeared from the four Catalan provinces and even the Civil Guard was to come under the Generalitat's Department of the Interior.

The November general elections were won by the Right, but in Catalonia the victory was less sweeping than elsewhere in Spain and the results of the Left could not be described as disastrous, as it was in the case of the Spanish left-wing Republicans and Socialists. The coalition between Acció Catalana and the PNRE, which had recently broken away from ERC, received a sharp rebuff, as did that between the BOC and the PSOE. However, both deprived ERC of votes and this, together with an appreciable swing towards the Lliga Catalana and a rise in abstentions, accounted for the victory by a narrow margin of the Lliga Catalana in the city of Barcelona and the constituencies of Lleida and Tarragona. ERC retained the provinces of Barcelona and Girona. The Lliga and its allies won twenty-eight seats and ERC and its friends twenty-six. In the absence of evidence, this turn of events should not be attributed to the fact that women were voting for the first time; and it is significant that this factor is never invoked in explaining the victory of the Popular Front in 1936. The anarchist campaign in favour of abstention had little impact.

The full development of the Catalan Statute, in its final form as voted by ERC itself, was dependent on the Left continuing in power in Spain. For the Republic, and for Catalan autonomy, the problem was that the Republican Right, the Partit Radical, was weak, while the most powerful right-wing party, the CEDA, was not pro-Republican and indeed was seen by many as anti-Republican. The danger implicit in this situation led to the formation at the end of 1933 of Alianza Obrera from the numerous small socialist, communist, and labour organizations in Catalonia. The CNT saw this new organization as a mere union of labour movement minorities and kept clear of it. Alianza Obrera (Workers' Alliance) exerted pressure on the government of the Generalitat, but was unable to overpower it.

The gains made by the Right in November and the death of Macià on Christmas day 1933 also led to the formation of a left-wing coalition government by his successor as President of the Generalitat, Lluís Companys. In this ERC, Acció Catalana, the PNRE and the USC were to collaborate with leaders of the Estat Català group, including Josep Dencàs, who some months later became the Catalan Minister of Public Order.

The same group of parties that had formed the coalition simultaneously set up a common front for the municipal elections to be held in January 1934. In Barcelona and in many other large cities the Left was victorious in these elections, winning in 580 boroughs, while the Lliga Catalana and its allies triumphed in 442. Carles Pi Sunyer, who had been the chief Minister and Minister of Finance in the Catalan government the year before, was elected Mayor of Barcelona and in 1935 he became the second in command of ERC.

The Lliga Catalana was disappointed at the results of the local elections and withdrew from the Catalan Parliament after denouncing the acts of violence that had been perpetrated against some of its centres. This marked the beginning of a grave political crisis that was to lead to the events of 6 October 1934. Catalonia's newly won political autonomy was about to enter a phase of internal strife which would be followed by an eclipse.

Notes

1. The members of the FAI, founded in 1927, wanted to make the CNT more aggressive in labour conflicts and to prepare an anarchist-led insurrection against the Republic and, to some extent, against the Socialists who at the time were collaborating in the government. In 1932 members of the FAI succeeded in gaining control of the CNT at the expense of unionists opposed to revolutionary undertakings, some of whom left the CNT between 1932 and 1933. Members and sympathizers of the FAI spoke only Spanish, whereas those who had broken away from the CNT spoke mainly Catalan. Most of the followers of the FAI were immigrants from Spanish-speaking regions, whereas the majority of ex-CNT members –

many of whom would return to the fold in 1936 – were native-born Catalans and within this sector there was greater sympathy for Catalanism and less apoliticism.

2. The Diputación Foral of Navarre enjoyed a system based on an economic agreement whereby a fixed amount was paid to the central government in exchange for a degree of financial autonomy. This privilege was granted to Navarre because in that region the Carlists, or traditionalists, who rose against the Republic in July 1936, were predominant.

3. At that period in Spain, secondary education (*bachillerato*) began at the age of ten and lasted for six years, after which students could take a university entrance examination. Compulsory schooling ended at the age of ten and it was not until 1970 that the school-leaving age was raised to fourteen. It has now been decided to raise it again to sixteen.

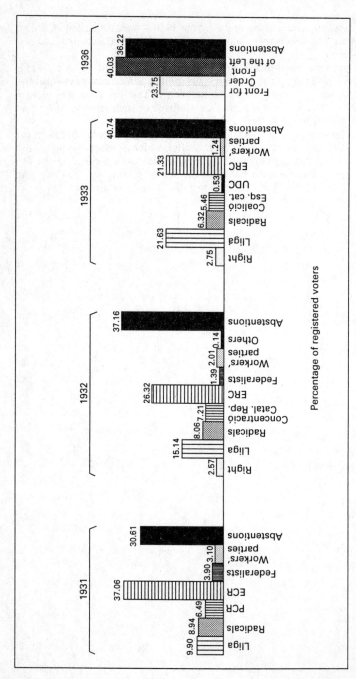

FIGURE 9.1 *Results of parliamentary elections in the City of Barcelona, 1931–6*

SOURCE: Ramon M. Canals, *Perspectiva Social*, **10** (1977).

10 The Crisis of the Catalan Self-governing System

THE CLASH OF 1934

In 1932, numerous conflicts broke out between tenant farmers and landowners in the wine-growing regions of central Catalonia. A law passed in June 1933 to settle disputes arising from agricultural contracts established that tenant farmers who had filed an application to revise the conditions of their lease could retain half the owner's part of the harvest until a verdict was handed down by the joint arbitration committees set up under the law.

The final text of the Law of Agricultural Contracts was debated in the Catalan parliament and approved in the spring of 1934, even though the Lliga Catalana had withdrawn from the Chamber and the Institut Agrícola Català de Sant Isidre had announced its total opposition. Under the Catalan Law of Agricultural Contracts (Llei de Contractes de Conreu), promulgated on 12 April 1934, the duration of the lease was to be six years, renewable unless the owner himself decided to farm the land for six years. The owner's income was limited to 4 per cent of the value of the land. Tenants who had farmed land for eighteen years were entitled to purchase it at a set price in fifteen yearly instalments while those who had planted their own vines could acquire the land at its value prior to the planting of the vines. This was the first social reform law passed by the Catalan parliament and it would have enabled an estimated 70,000 farmers to become landowners within a relatively short time.

Owing to the gradual nature of the reform and its lack of collectivist implications, it was scorned by the anarchists, though it received the backing of Alianza Obrera. The landowners of the Institut de Sant Isidre urged the Lliga Catalana to appeal against the law on the grounds of unconstitutionality. The appeal was referred by the central government, headed by the Radical Ricardo Samper, to the Tribunal de Garantías Constitucionales (Tribunal of Constitutional Guarantees), which repealed it in its entirety by a majority of thirteen votes to ten, declaring that the Catalan parliament had no jurisdiction over social agrarian policy. The minimization of Catalan self-government implicit in this verdict aroused indignation in many Catalanist sectors that had previously been indifferent to the grievances of the tenant farmers. Social reform seemed to be linked to Catalan self-government while reactionary attitudes on social and political matters seemed inseparable from anti-autonomist centralism.

Though this was not the only dispute between the Generalitat and the central government, it served to trigger off conflict between the two since Spanish landowners did not want agricultural reform to prosper in Catalonia, thanks to that region's self-governing régime, while they were working against it elsewhere in Spain; and it was after the suspension of the the Catalan autonomous régime in 1935 that the Right succeeded in effectively annulling Spanish agrarian reform.

The Catalan parliament proceeded to vote on the whole law once again and the Unió de Rabassaires launched a protest movement. ERC was in danger of losing control over its agricultural base and over the CADCI and the Federació d'Empleats i Tècnics de Catalunya (Catalan Federation of Clerical Workers and Technicians). The ERC deputies withdrew from the Spanish Cortes. The Basque nationalists, who had already realized that the Spanish Right was even more strongly opposed than the Left to Basque self-government, showed their solidarity by following suit.[1] During the summer, Lluís Companys and the Samper government worked at a compromise that would be acceptable to the Lliga Catalana. But the Lliga lost its ascendency over the Institut de Sant Isidre, and the most intransigent of the landowners became the founding group of the Catalan branch of CEDA. The diehard elements among the Catalan landowners, with the support of the Spanish Right, asked the Spanish government to resume control over services relating to the administration of justice and law and order that had already been transferred to the Generalitat.

When it looked as if a compromise had been reached and a confrontation would be averted, and when the Lliga Catalana had returned to the Catalan parliament, the Samper government in Madrid fell and was replaced by an administration headed by Lerroux, which for the first time included CEDA ministers. It now seemed likely that the threats against Catalan autonomy would finally be carried out. The Spanish Socialists were preparing to fulfil their promise of calling a revolutionary general strike if the CEDA were to enter the government.

On 6 October 1934 Lluís Companys, President of the Generalitat, declared himself in rebellion against the Lerroux government and proclaimed the existence of a Catalan State within a Spanish Federal Republic. Except in Asturias, where a ten-day insurrection broke out, the general strike called by the Socialists was not sufficiently widespread to force the Lerroux–CEDA government to negotiate. Companys' Catalan State lasted ten hours, and the government of the Generalitat surrendered to General Batet early on 7 October. The Generalitat had disarmed the old Somatent militia and organized a new one composed of supporters of the government coalition. This new militia, however, lacked the means with which to fight. The CNT remained on the sidelines and the Generalitat noted its indifference with satisfaction.

Though there was some violence outside Barcelona, the Catalan government did not seem on the verge of losing control of the situation, as was alleged. The silence in the streets of the Catalan capital after the proclamation was as significant as the ease with which the revolt was quashed. It must be acknowledged, however, that the Companys government had allowed itself to be placed in a situation so contradictory that it was unable to extricate itself with any degree of success. It had resorted formally to revolutionary procedures to defend reformist objectives. In order to protect the legitimating social content of the Republic it had contravened the Republican legality that ERC itself and the other Republican parties had built up; and in an attempt to uphold the Statute of Self-government, which was a commitment made within a unitary, non-federal state, it had declared what would be perceived of as a separatist rebellion, despite references to a non-existent federal republic.

In view of the inferiority of the means at its disposal, only a surprise attack could have given the Companys government the advantage, and in taking up a defensive attitude it was condemned to failure. The only explanation for his decision to rush into an insurrection without the means or the will to carry it through is that Companys and his supporters saw it as a new 14 April 1931 and did not expect, therefore, to have to fight.

In any event, the contradictions of ERC and its allies were no greater than those of the PSOE and Azaña himself. After all, Azaña himself, who considered that Companys had committed a major blunder on 6 October, was the chairman of the party which, the day before in Madrid, had broken with the institutions as a result of the entry of CEDA into the Lerroux government.

The victory, just seventeen months later, of the Front d'Esquerres in Catalonia, and of the Frente Popular in Spain, in no way alters the fact that the unsuccessful revolt of 6 October 1934, and the repression it unleashed, were among the main factors that undermined the viability of the fundamental political consensus the Republic needed in order to survive.

THE SUSPENSION OF THE SELF-GOVERNING RÉGIME

The Law of Agricultural Contracts was repealed; 1400 applications were filed for the eviction of tenant farmers; the government of the Generalitat was sentenced to thirty years' hard labour; most of the municipal councils in Catalonia were suspended; the majority of political centres were closed down; press censorship was introduced and a state of emergency proclaimed; some earlier labour reforms were revoked; and the University of Barcelona lost its statute. In January 1935, the Catalan Statute of Self-government was suspended, the parliament was closed and some public servants were dismissed. Though the Constitution itself was not suspended, as in 1923, Catalonia returned to practically the same situation as under the dictatorship of Primo de Rivera.

The Lliga Catalana, after stating that the suspension of the Statute of Self-government was as illegal as its suppression would have been, finally agreed to collaborate in the various councils set up by the new Governors General appointed by the central authorities to run Catalonia – Pich i Pon being the first and Villalonga the next. Within these councils the Lliga formed a minority alongside two parties with no electoral support in Catalonia: the Radicals and the CEDA (Acción Popular). The Lliga justified its collaboration by claiming that this was the price to pay in order to attenuate or abbreviate the suspension of the statute. In the midst of the total distorsion of Catalan political life, the Lliga did not succeed in re-establishing self-government in exchange for its collaboration, a fact which led to the conclusion that only a victory of the Left could restore the Statute. This conclusion went against the Lliga Catalana in the February 1936 elections convened by the central government under Portela Valladares, in which the parties formed two opposing fronts in Catalonia, as they did in most of the rest of Spain.

THE LEFT-WING FRONT AND THE REINSTATEMENT OF CATALAN AUTONOMY

In Catalonia the popular front was known as the Front d'Esquerres (the left-wing Front), a name which reflects the fact that its lists contained many more Republican and ERC candidates than did the corresponding lists of the Spanish Frente Popular (Popular Front). Socialists and Communists accounted for 41 per cent of the Frente Popular deputies elected, as against 19 per cent of those from the Catalan Front d'Esquerres. In Catalonia, moreover, labour candidates came from five different parties. The distribution of seats had been imposed by ERC on the basis of previous election results and, while it might have given the appearance of greater political moderation, it also concealed one fact – the strength of the CNT in Catalonia.

Turnout was higher than in the 1933 election and the anarchists did not campaign in favour of abstention. The Lliga was by far the major force within the Front d'Ordre (Front for Order), the right-wing coalition opposing the Front d'Esquerres, but some of its running partners were decidedly antirepublican and anti-autonomist. Lerroux, who failed to win a seat, was on the Barcelona list of the Front d'Ordre, headed by the Lliga Catalana. The Front d'Esquerres was victorious in all the Catalan constituencies, winning 59 per cent of the votes, against the Front d'Ordre's 41 per cent. The triumph of the left was more resounding in Catalonia than elsewhere in Spain, where 48 per cent of the votes went to the Frente Popular and 46.5 per cent to the right-wing alliance.

Following the elections, the hand-over of power took place quickly. Amnesty was decreed, municipal councils that had been dissolved were reinstated, purged civil servants returned to their posts, and workers sacked for political reasons were given their jobs back. The Catalan Statute of Self-government was restored in its entirety. The original government of the Generalitat was reinstated as prior to 6 October 1934, the only exclusion being that of Josep Dencàs, who, together with a whole sector of the Estat Català splinter group, had practically left ERC.

During the spring of 1936, both ERC and the Lliga tried to adopt a moderate attitude. Ridding itself of its circumstantial antirepublican allies, the Lliga Catalana acted as a loyal opposition. It supported Azaña in the presidential elections, while the CEDA abstained. Not only did the leaders of the Lliga feel that a military coup would be a disaster: they campaigned to uphold the legality of the Republic. ERC, purified of its nationalist extremists, who left to set up Estat Català as a separate party, opted for a moderate line.

In April 1936 the relative stability and order reigning in Catalonia led to its being frequently described as the 'oasis of the Republic'. It is true that Catalonia experienced far fewer assassinations and acts of violence than other parts of Spain during the months preceding the outbreak of the Civil War. On the other hand, the very high number of labour disputes was comparable to that of 1933, though there were no attempted anarchist revolts as there were during the first two years of the Republic. On 28 April 1936 came a sinister omen: the assassination, attributed to the anarchists, of the radical nationalist Miquel Badia and his brother. It was easier for ERC and the Lliga to establish an entente cordiale in the Catalan parliament than for their respective social bases to do the same, especially in villages and small towns. Tension remained high as a result of the reinstatement of evicted tenant farmers, the implementation of the controversial Law of Agricultural Contracts, the re-hiring of sacked workers and the five-year ban on holding elective office imposed on those who had accepted appointments to government posts in the place of elected representatives. *La Veu de Catalunya* stated on 5 July 1936 that it was no longer justifiable to praise the 'Catalan oasis', since Catalonia was not an oasis.

Falangism – the Spanish form of Fascism – was not at all widespread in Catalonia. The extreme Right was represented mainly by the Carlists, reunited and radicalized to face up to the Republican governments. Carlism was, nevertheless, weaker in Catalonia than, for example, in Navarre and the Basque Country. In the election of February 1936 only one Carlist won a seat under the auspices of the Front Català d'Ordre.

In 1935, a complex process aimed at forming a united workers' party in Catalonia had been set in motion but it failed. The Partit Obrer d'Unificació Marxista (Workers' Party of Marxist Unification – POUM) was set up in November 1935 when the ex-Trotskyite group headed by Andreu Nin joined Joaquín Maurín's Bloc Obrer i Camperol (Labour and Agicultural Workers' Bloc). The POUM, which aimed at covering the whole of Spain, considered the PSOE and PCE (Partido Comunista Español – Spanish Communist Party) incapable of leading a proletarian revolution and believed the two Internationals to which these parties respectively belonged had failed. Though the POUM joined the Popular Front, it had no faith in the movement underlying it and nor did it give it the support the orthodox Communists did.

On 21 July 1936 the PSUC (Partit Socialista Unificat de Catalunya – United Socialist Party of Catalonia) was set up as a result of the merger between the Unió Socialista de Catalunya, the Catalan Federation of the PSOE, the Partit Comunista de Catalunya, and Partit Català Proletari (Catalan Proletarian Party). The PSUC, headed by Joan Comorera of USC, embodied the new type of party, encouraged by the Communist International, which arose from the unification of socialists and communists. The PSUC was an exclusively Catalan, pro-Popular

Front party, but it was not recognized by the PSOE because it had joined the Communist International. It established close relations only with the PCE, and thus, though organically independent, tended to revolve in the orbit of the latter within the Communist International, which was then under the yoke of Stalinism.

Socialists, communists, and radical nationalists with varying degrees of separatist and Marxist leanings shared with ERC the same social environment consisting of non-manual workers in the growing tertiary sector and, to a lesser extent, tenant farmers. The populism impregnated with social rebellion on which ERC capitalized also had a working-class basis, in addition to its petit-bourgeois sympathies, and it proved difficult for a Marxist culture to develop in this same sector where it was by no means impossible for technical workers with medium- and low-level qualifications, shop assistants and small-time writers and journalists to set up in business on their own. Only revolution and civil war were to promote the expansion of this Marxist culture, though from May 1937 it was split into two irreconcilable factions.

Note

1. In December 1933, a referendum held in the three Basque provinces had approved the third draft Statute drawn up and debated in the Basque Country. The overall percentage in favour was 84.2 per cent, though only 46.4 per cent of voters in the province of Alava endorsed the project, and municipal councillors of the antirepublican traditionalist philosophy, which had much support in that province, asked for their province to be allowed to opt out. The Basque Nationalist Party worked towards an alliance with the dominant party in Catalonia, ERC, despite the Catholicism of the former and the anticlericalism of the latter. It was not until after the beginning of the Civil War in 1936 that an autonomous Basque government, dominated by the Basque Nationalist Party, was set up.

11 The Vicissitudes of the Catalan Autonomous Government during the Civil War

THE GENERALITAT LOSES CONTROL

From the very outset, one of the explicit objectives of the officers who staged the rising of 18 July 1936 which sparked off the Spanish Civil War was to overthrow self-government in Catalonia, or, as they put it, to eliminate separatism. The landowners in the south and centre of Spain felt threatened by agrarian reform and the peasant movement. The Catholic Church saw its influence diminishing on account of anticlerical policies. The armed forces had lost their previous power to the civil authorities. The Right, which was prepared to overthrow the Second Republic, considered that, after the socialist revolutionary strike of October 1934, an insurrection was justified. The rise of Fascism gave encouragement to the enemies of parliamentary democracy in Spain. The increasing number of assassinations and acts of violence created a pre-civil war atmosphere in Madrid and a few other places. But the social revolution was not to start until after the military rising. The Spanish Civil War would be one of the events leading up to the Second World War in Europe. In Catalonia Fascism – the Falange Española – was very weak; Carlism, which was fiercely opposed to the Republic, was a more widespread but residual force; and the Lliga Catalana, the majority right-wing party, was opposed to the military coup.

The military rising and the revolutionary reaction it triggered off demolished the society based on liberal, democratic principles that the Generalitat was striving to preserve.

Being aware of the impending plot, the Generalitat drew up a plan of resistance, having first assured itself of the loyalty of the Assault Guard, its own police force created in 1931, and at least the neutrality of the Civil Guard. The situation was unlike that which had arisen on 6 October 1934, in that this time the Generalitat was to face a military attack with the legality and legitimacy of the Republic on its side.

President Companys and his closest colleagues were determined and ready for a hard fight. The government of the Generalitat had no wish to make enemies of the anarchists, but nor did it want their intervention to cause it to lose control of the situation. It therefore refused to give them the arms they requested and then, at the last moment, in an atmosphere very different from that of October 1934, distributed a few weapons – not enough for the government to be threatened, but sufficient to establish a certain alliance between fellow combatants.

On 19 July 1936, troops from the Barcelona garrison marched to the centre of the city, encountering more resistance than they had anticipated, so that instead of the Army taking the Assault Guards by surprise, the opposite occurred. Confident in their great superiority in arms and numbers, the rebel officers were convinced the operation would go as smoothly as on 6 October 1934. But their advance was halted by the Assault Guards and, when it seemed that stalemate had been reached, the intervention of the Civil Guard in support of the Generalitat and the Republic brought victory in the centre of Barcelona.

By nightfall on 19 July 1936, only a few isolated groups were offering resistance in the Drassanes (the old shipyards), the military buildings on the Plaça Colom, and the Carmelite convent on the Diagonal where the retreating troops had taken up positions. These groups were routed on 20 July, but the incidents served to support the claim that Republican forces had been attacked from the churches, a claim that was subsequently used to justify the burning of churches and the indiscriminate persecution of the clergy which had started on the very day of the rising. In the late afternoon of Sunday 19 July, an artillery depot containing 30,000 rifles at Sant Andreu in the Barcelona suburbs was ransacked by the anarchists and other extreme left-wing organizations. Assault Guards were sent to the spot but were powerless to prevent the plunder.

By that time both Majorca and Aragon were in the hands of the rebels and it would be some time before the scales would tip clearly in favour of the Republicans in Valencia. These circumstances brought considerable pressure to bear on both President Companys and the anarchists. The latter, though very well armed, were torn between seizing power and seeking an agreement with the Generalitat. On the afternoon of 20 July, Companys proposed to the anarchist leaders the formation of what was to be known as the Comitè Central de Milícies Antifeixistes (Central Committee of Anti-Fascist Militias – CCMA), a body formally dependent on the Generalitat, but which in practice would become the real centre of power. Most of the anti-Fascist parties and unions were members of the CCMA.

By so doing, Companys saved Catalonia's Republican institutions but accepted for the time being the fragmentation of power into a multiplicity of councils at municipal, company, and militia level. A two-fold authority was created at the top, whereby the supposedly multi-party but in fact anarchist-dominated CCMA turned the Generalitat into an instrument for legalizing the revolutionary changes underway. The Lliga Catalana was dissolved, its representatives in the Catalan parliament and on municipal councils were removed, and its leaders applied for safe conducts to leave the country.

The only way the Generalitat could protect the lives of those in danger was by granting them passports to leave the country or putting them in prison, and the only way it could save the artistic heritage in the hands of the Church or private individuals was by confiscating it. But those who succeeded in crossing the border soon considered they had been exiled and many went over to the opposite camp, later to serve the side that deprived the Catalan people of all its rights. The churches that were saved from arson, but closed for services, would soon be used as proof of the religious persecution tacitly accepted by the Generalitat. But the humanitarian task of the Catalan administration during those first months of the Civil War was acknowledged even by its enemies. General Queipo de Llano, one of the insurgent officers, stated on Radio Seville on 25 August 1936 that President Companys 'has allowed over five thousand men belonging to the Right to leave Barcelona, and this will doubtless diminish the responsibility which weighs on his shoulders. May God take it into account!'

Casanovas, the Speaker of the Catalan parliament, was appointed by Companys to head a cabinet that included three ministers from the recently formed PSUC. But the veto of the anarchists, supported by the POUM, led to the failure of this first attempt to reinforce the authority of the Generalitat, which in the end consisted only of ERC, ACR (Acció Catalana Republicana – Catalan Republican Action), and the Unió de Rabassaires.

The Generalitat's second attempt to recover the initiative was an expedition launched in mid-August 1936 to try to recapture Majorca, which ended in failure. Meanwhile, columns of volunteer militiamen belonging to the various trade-union and political organizations marched towards Saragossa and Huesca.

Six weeks after the beginning of the Civil War, it was obvious that the parallel powers of the Generalitat and the CCMA were neutralizing one other. The anarchists realized they could not continue to mediatize the government and make use of legal power without assuming full governmental responsibilities. The militia of union and party members had been unable to reach Saragossa or reconquer Huesca. Madrid was threatened. The collectivization process was creating economic chaos for lack of coordination. Catalan industry had to be converted into a war industry and the public finance needed for this was a decisive trump card in the hands of the Generalitat. A stop had to be put to mob violence in the rearguard, and the judicial system had to be restored to normal operation so as to show even more clearly that such acts were both harmful and unnecessary persecution of the supposed enemies of the Republican cause in Catalonia. Of the 8360 victims of the political repression that occurred in the rearguard in Catalonia between 1936 and 1939, only four hundred or so were executed as a result of normal sentences. The remainder were assassinations, two-thirds of which took place during the first five months of the war. Between June 1937 and February 1938 there were no more deaths as a result of repression, either as the outcome of trials or by assassination.

THE GENERALITAT ADMITS THE ANARCHISTS TO THE GOVERNMENT IN AN ATTEMPT TO RECOVER POWER

On 26 September, the first steps were taken to overcome the existing two-fold system and restore the authority of the Generalitat: the anarchists, the PSUC, and the POUM entered the government, and the Comitè Central de Milícies was disbanded. The subsequent abolition of the local committees, which had replaced the borough councils, put an end to the dual power system at local level and new municipal councils were appointed, seats being shared out in a proportion similar to the composition of the government of the Generalitat itself.

Casanovas was replaced by Tarradellas, who also retained the finance portfolio. Permitting a CNT and Marxist majority in the new government might have seemed a sign of weakness on the part of President Companys and ERC, but in fact Companys had set about rebuilding the power of the Generalitat on the basis of a new legitimacy in exchange for recognizing the hegemony of anarchists and Marxists.

Under the new anti-Fascist government of unity, from which only Estat Català was absent, the assassinations of presumed enemies of the Republican cause grew less frequent but did not cease. Even Republican politicians were subjected to terror. The anarchists had already forced Dencàs to go into exile, and in October Ventura Gassol, the Catalan Minister of Culture, had to be sent to France. In November, the Speaker of the Catalan parliament and former head of government, Joan Casanovas, was also driven into exile, since the anarchists accused him of plotting with Torres Picart, Dencàs' successor as the leader of Estat Català. ERC, in fact, was in the process of splitting up, some of its members reinforcing their links with the PSUC and the UGT, others with the CNT, while a few drew closer to the extreme radical nationalists of Estat Català.

The anarchists, who occupied the key ministries in the Catalan administration, still had the support of the PSUC against any Catalan nationalist attempt to upset the balance of forces, and part of the clientele and social base of the Catalanist Republicans had drifted into the orbit of the PSUC and the UGT. In Catalonia the UGT was controlled by the PSUC. This party offered better protection to small factory owners and tradesmen and to self-employed farmers against the all-out collectivism of the anarchists and the POUM. The unity of anti-Fascist forces in economic and social policy was confirmed by the collectivization decree passed by the Generalitat on 24 October 1936 which protected small property but made effective the collectivization of larger firms.

THE LEGEND OF CATALAN SEPARATISM DURING THE CIVIL WAR

In the course of the Civil War, there were periodic rumours that the Catalanists were trying to break away from the rest of Republican Spain and sign a separate peace with Franco, thanks to the indispensable mediation and protection of France.

No foundation whatever has been found so far for these allegations. The only separatist party, Estat Català, was left out of all the organs of Catalan government throughout the war, and finally declared its support for the Generalitat and ERC. ERC can in no way be considered a crypto-separatist party, since the split that took place after 6 October 1934 consisted precisely in the exclusion of the separatists.

The only time a separatist plot would have been at all viable was in the autumn of 1936 when the government of the Republic was in no position to prevent secession. But at the time, the anarchists, the PSUC, and ERC itself were opposed to any gesture that might be interpreted as secessionist and later all possibility of Catalonia separating disappeared, especially from May 1937 onwards, when the central government took over control of the police in Catalonia.

There is documentary evidence that France was entirely opposed to Catalan independence, and Franco would never have signed a peace agreement with an independent Catalonia. Furthermore, it is frequently forgotten that Catalonia sent troops to the centre of Spain to fight for the Republic virtually from the very beginning of the war and that these troops included not only anarchists but even a contingent from Estat Català. At times there were between 30,000 and 60,000 Catalan soldiers defending Madrid and central Spain. Catalonia sent large donations of food to Madrid and welcomed a growing flood of refugees, numbering as many as a million, a figure equivalent to one-third of the population of Catalonia before the war. All this is incompatible with the allegations of Catalan indifference to the fate of the rest of Republican Spain which became very widespread in the central government bureaucracy that had by now been transferred to Valencia.

These rumours of a separate peace and Catalan independence were aimed at discrediting the Generalitat and justifying the policy of cutbacks to Catalan autonomy which was pursued by the government of the Republic as soon as it was in a position to do so.

THE CATALAN THESIS OF THE FEDERALIZATION OF REPUBLICAN SPAIN

At the beginning of the Civil War, Catalonia's self-governing powers were effectively broadened. In January 1937 President Companys made the following statement to a French newspaper: 'In reality we are already a confederation. . . . It will be impossible for the future to deny the achievements of federalism, since they will have been the foundation of resistance and the factor that led to victory.' The federal republic demanded in 1931 and 1934 seemed inevitable in the context of the Civil War and this thesis was supported by the anarchists, who saw the Generalitat's collectivization decree, which exceeded the powers attributed to Catalonia under the 1932 Statute, as the legalization of their own achievements.

The Generalitat had to set up its own war machine, create an armaments industry out of nothing, and channel, control and organize the social changes brought about by the revolutionary process that had been unleashed. It was for this reason that, following the collapse of the central government apparatus as a result of the outbreak of the Civil War and the ensuing revolutionary reaction, it overstepped the bounds of the 1932 Statute. In assuming the full powers of the State in Catalonia, the Generalitat was to some extent compensated for its loss of real power to the anti-Fascist committees. Indeed it was paradoxical that, at the same time as the Generalitat gained strength in relation to the central government, within its own territory it was extremely weak and lacked the effective capacity to restore public order. Several of what Azaña and the top civil servants of the central Republican government considered unauthorized seizures of power were designed to make up for the eclipse of the Spanish state itself.

THE FAILURE OF THE GOVERNMENT OF UNITY AND THE EVENTS OF MAY 1937

The Tarradellas cabinet suffered its first crisis in December 1936 when the PSUC demanded and obtained the exclusion of the POUM and of Andreu Nin, the minister representing it in the Catalan administration. The PSUC charged the POUM with criticizing the decisions of the government to which it belonged and denouncing the purges of the Bolshevik old guard being carried out in Moscow by Stalin, master of the only power that was helping the Republic. This struggle for superiority in the Marxist camp between the PSUC and the POUM took place against the backdrop of the Stalinism that prevailed throughout Communist ranks everywhere. The POUM accused the PSUC of being reactionary and *petit bourgeois*, and the PSUC accused the POUM of treachery.

The anarchist Diego Abad de Santillán claimed that there were 60,000 rifles in the Catalan rearguard and only 30,000 on the Aragon front. In March 1937, when the order that all arms in the rearguard be handed over and the security patrols dissolved was disobeyed, the Tarradellas government faced its second crisis. Throughout the winter of 1937 frequent clashes had taken place, especially in the farming sector, between groups bent on imposing collectivization and individual producers, while the scarcity of supplies was giving rise to popular discontent in the midst of inflation and unemployment rates that were rising despite mobilization.

When, at the beginning of May 1937, the police, under orders from leading figures of the PSUC and ERC, tried to take over full control of the Telephone Company in Barcelona, a leaderless anarchist mutiny broke out, which was immediately denounced by the anarchist ministers and the leaders of the CNT in Catalonia. The revolt was, however, backed by the POUM, and though that party had not been its instigator, it would later become the scapegoat.

Companys had to ask for central government reinforcements at the cost of allowing the Republican administration to take control of public order and censorship in Catalonia in accordance with the provisions laid down in the Statute of Self-government for highly exceptional circumstances. Five thousand guards arrived from Valencia when the fighting in Barcelona was already over, and during the following months completed the disarming of the rearguard.

THE GROWING WEAKNESS AND ISOLATION OF THE GENERALITAT

Since the government of the Generalitat had proved incapable of the united action which would have given it the strength and authority needed in times of war, it was not the Generalitat but the central government which reaped the benefits of the process leading to the recovery of political power initiated by the Tarradellas government. From May 1937 onwards, the Generalitat's real power of action began to dwindle.

Following the resignation of the anarchists from the Republican government in the aftermath of the events of May 1937, it was foreseeable that they would also leave the government of the Generalitat. Accordingly, when the anarchists opposed the entry of Bosch Gimpera, the Chancellor of the Universitat Autònoma de Barcelona and a member of Acció Catalana, into the cabinet, Companys decided to dispense with them. The appointment of Bosch Gimpera as Minister of Justice meant that the Catalan government was determined to re-establish full constitutional rights and put an end to religious persecution. The new Catalan administration was, in fact, made up solely of ERC and the PSUC. It would soon be torn by the tension between the two parties, though it succeeded in holding out till the end of the war.

The transfer of the Spanish Republican government, headed by Juan Negrín, from Valencia to Barcelona in October 1937, was carried out with the barely concealed intention of eclipsing the government of the Generalitat, to the extent that Companys learnt of the transfer when buildings were requisitioned by central government functionaries.

In 1938, the war took a distinctly unfavourable turn for the Republican cause. After recapturing Teruel at the end of February, troops hostile to the Republic broke through the Aragon front. On 3 April they occupied the Catalan city of Lleida, and on 15 April reached Vinaròs, leaving Catalonia partially occupied and cut off from the rest of the Republican zone. As though fearing French intervention, Franco then turned his troops southwards towards Valencia. A stable front was established along the Segre and Ebro rivers. On 23 July, Republican troops crossed the Ebro in a last offensive which turned into a long battle of attrition in which Catalonia, during the summer of 1938, was to expend its last reserves of men and equipment. The same summer saw the capitulation of the British and French governments to Hitler in Munich over the question of Czechoslovakia. The Catalan population, now practically without defences, was subjected to increasingly savage bombing raids, while the situation created by the lack of basic foods, the avalanche of refugees, and the loss of the hydroelectric power stations in the Pyrenees, became intolerable.

THE CONFRONTATION BETWEEN THE CATALANISTS AND THE NEGRÍN GOVERNMENT

The government of the Republic justified the take-over of public order in Catalonia by the need to eliminate secret prisons, put an end to terrorist action and re-establish constitutional rights. The disappearance and assassination of Andreu Nin – a leader of the POUM and former opponent of Stalinism and supporter of the ideas of Trotsky – turned into an international scandal which cast doubts on the Republican government's control over the police apparatus. Companys subsequently had to complain to Negrín in writing about the assassination of the political prisoners who were removed from a prison ship belonging to the central government in Barcelona, and the Generalitat's Department of Justice was obliged repeatedly to denounce the irregular methods of the Servicio de Información Militar (Military Intelligence Service), the non-respect of constitutional rights at the trials held in special courts (tribunales de guardia), and arbitrary arrests. Negrín tried to place the courts under military control to put an end to such complaints, since this was the only way of totally excluding the Generalitat from the administration of justice, an area in which it had autonomous powers.

The war industry, which was controlled by the corresponding commission of the Generalitat, was another bone of contention. The central government began to nationalize certain companies, replacing the workers' management councils set up under collectivization by directors with full authority. This move was contrary to the aims of the anarchists, who were opposed to State confiscation since it did away with self-management and the influence of the CNT, which was blamed by the PSUC for the low industrial productivity. Negrín's solution was to place the entire war industry under military authority as well.

Negrín, moreover, had refused to compensate the Generalitat for its loss of political power by including more Catalan and Catalanist political forces in the Republican government and giving them more influence. Comorera and part of the PSUC leadership shared in the displeasure of ERC and the ACR at the all-out takeover policy pursued by the central government at the Generalitat's expense.

Meanwhile, Companys, following an agreement reached with Aguirre, the leader of the Basque autonomous government, within the framework of the alliance between ERC and the Basque Nationalist Party (Partido Nacionalista Vasco – PNV), decided to make secret proposals to London and Paris for Anglo–French mediation leading to an armistice that would be followed by a referendum in both zones, providing for the preservation of Catalan and Basque self-government. The documents show that this proposal, which came too late to be of use, contained no reference to Catalan independence or to a separate peace. Azaña and Companys were in agreement over the need for an armistice, contrary to the views of Negrín and the Communists, who wanted to prolong the war at all costs. Azaña, on the other hand, supported Negrín's policy against Catalan self-government.

On 11 August 1938, a crisis broke out in the Negrín government as a result of the resignation of Jaume Aiguader, the representative of ERC, over the militarization of the war industry and the special courts for judging political crimes. The representative of the PNV, Manuel de Irujo, also resigned in solidarity. The decree to militarize the courts was never passed since President Azaña considered it unconstitutional. At the same cabinet meeting sixty-six death sentences were confirmed of the seventy-two pending approval, a move which precluded fulfilment of one of the conditions underlying any attempt at an armistice. Though the question of an armistice was not raised, it was known to be one of the factors associated with the crisis.

Companys and ERC had presented the defence of self-government as the reason for the crisis, hoping to receive the support of the PSUC, but Negrín appointed a member of the PSUC to replace the out-going ERC minister. The PSUC gambled its Catalanist image by allowing itself to be involved in a policy designed to minimize the powers of the Catalan government, thereby earning the reproof of the Republican Catalanists without gaining the confidence of Negrín, the PCE, or the delegate of the Communist International, Palmiro Togliatti, who considered Comorera and the PSUC to be affected by 'petit-bourgeois nationalism'.

Thus the Generalitat was paralyzed politically just as the final onslaught on Catalonia was about to start. Following the resignation and second exile of Casanovas, Josep Irla was elected Speaker of the Catalan parliament with Rovira i Virgili as deputy speaker. Both were members of ERC.

On 4 November 1938, the Republican army's defences along the Ebro river were destroyed, and on 23 December Franco's troops began their advance. On 15 January 1939, Tarragona was occupied and a flood of civilians and retreating soldiers began their exodus towards the French border, blocking the roads. On 23 January, Negrín ordered all government organizations and the police to leave Barcelona and head for Girona. On 5 February, the Catalan, Basque, and Spanish Republican governments crossed the border. In the midst of the disaster, everything for which generations of Catalans had struggled seemed lost.

12 Exile and Clandestinity (1939–50)

The Catalan exiles who did not return in the months immediately following the end of the Civil War numbered at least 60,000. They included the great majority of the top politicians, labour leaders, and intellectuals of Republican Catalonia in the 1930s, and it would take decades to replace them. Those who did return had to be screened and obtain guarantors before they were released from the concentration camps where they were interned.

Each party blamed the others for the defeat, and solidarity among the exiles was slight, except within small circles of political associates and friends. Most of the refugees who fled to France were put into concentration camps there, from which they gradually emerged. Both inside and outside Spain, the prestige of the political class of Republican Catalonia was very low.

The hostility between ERC and the PSUC prevented President Companys from forming a Catalan government in exile similar to that set up by the Basques. ERC members warned Companys that their ministers would resign if he maintained relations with the PSUC. The latter had by then been weakened by the departure of many former USC members – including Serra i Moret – and of those belonging to the former Catalan Federation of the PSOE. Five months after the end of the Spanish Civil War, PSUC approval of the German–Soviet pact which enabled Hitler to invade Poland and start the Second World War further reinforced the anti-Communist feelings of the Catalan nationalist Left and the Republican Catalan nationalists took a clearly pro-Allied stand.

In April 1940, Companys, who had been advised by several various key personalities to retire, set up a Consell Nacional de Catalunya (National Council of Catalonia), appointing Pompeu Fabra as chairman and Josep Pous i Pagès as the delegate of the President of the Generalitat. The other members were Antoni Rovira i Virgili, Jaume Serra Hunter, and Santiago Pi i Sunyer. The most distinguished politicians of the former era were left out for the time being. The Council never became operational because in June the Germans occupied Paris and Pétain signed the armistice which led to France being divided into two zones. Franco applied for the extradition of the Republican leaders in exile. Pétain refused, but the Gestapo handed over a number of important figures, among them President Companys, who was shot in Barcelona on 15 October 1940.

Carles Pi i Sunyer, who had been appointed by Companys as representative of the Generalitat in London, founded the Consell Nacional Català (Catalan National Council – CNC) with J. M. Batista i Roca as Secretary and four other members, including Bosch Gimpera and Josep Trueta, a distinguished surgeon who had gained much prestige in England for his services to the war-wounded. The CNC, which had the support of the Catalan communities in America, set itself up as one of several foreign governments in exile residing in Great Britain.

After the Civil War, the theory that both the 1931 Constitution and the Statute of Self-government had expired became current in Catalan nationalist circles, both inside Catalonia and in exile. In view of the anti-self-government policies pursued by the last government of the Republic and the repression of all signs of collective identity within occupied Catalonia, it was felt that the fight against Fascism must give way to the struggle for the independence of Catalonia by promoting unity and reconciliation among Catalanists. For those who were of this opinion the re-establishment of democracy implied the exercise of the right to self-determination, that is, the freedom to enter a new agreement with Spain or to decline to do so. As had occurred under the Primo de Rivera dictatorship, the impotence of autonomism led to separatism.

This was the idea behind the formation within Catalonia in 1940 of the Front Nacional de Catalunya (National Front of Catalonia – FNC) made up of former members of various nationalist parties. The FNC was initially conceived merely as a joint resistance movement without any precise programme or well-defined ideology. It succeeded in creating a clandestine organization consisting of cells, supplied information to the consulates of the allied powers, and helped fugitives from occupied France and allied airmen who had been shot down to cross the border and leave the peninsula.

When Carles Pi i Sunyer and Batista i Roca's Consell Nacional Català, together with the Catalan communities in Latin America, took up this position in favour of self-determination and independence, only a small minority of Catalan nationalists advocated the opposite stance, in support of the restoration of the Republic and of self-government. The feeling was that, since all possible formulas of coexistence had failed, nothing further could be hoped from Spain or from the Spaniards and the only alternative was to unite in the struggle for independence. This position led to the desertion of the traditional parties who were in favour of upholding the 1931 Constitution and the 1932 Statute.

THE REPRESSION OF CATALAN IDENTITY

Meanwhile, within Catalonia the public and written use of the Catalan language was totally prohibited, and Catalonia was once more split up into four provinces in complete uniformity with the rest of Spain. The University of Barcelona lost over half its teaching staff, some 25,000 civil servants were dismissed in Catalonia, many schoolteachers who were considered pro-Catalanist, though they had no political affiliation, were transferred to other regions of Spain while seven hundred teachers from Castile and Extremadura were sent to Catalonia as agents of de-Catalanization.

The military tribunals in Catalonia had 3800 people shot between 1938 and 1953. Most of them were little-known, minor officials of parties and unions who, not considering their lives to be in danger, had not gone into exile like most of their leaders and those responsible for oppression during the Civil War. Members of ERC, the CNT, and the Unió de Rabassaires predominated among these victims of Francoist repression. More people from rural areas were executed than from industrial and urban areas. Those who denounced them or who acquired goods confiscated from those sentenced to death or in exile made up a group of unconditional Catalan collaborators with the Franco régime.

The Civil War had been waged by anti-Republican Spain against self-governing Catalonia, but there were winners and losers among the Catalans because it had also been a civil war between Catalans, however much the propaganda of the resistance fighters might try to deny it. This internal division would seriously impede the struggle to re-establish democracy, despite the fact that the doctrines of Falangism – the Spanish uniformist Fascism – never took root in Catalonia and the majority of Catalan society never supported Franco.

ATTEMPTS AT UNITED ACTION BY THE OPPOSITION AFTER THE SECOND WORLD WAR

When Nazi Germany started losing ground and the Allied victory seemed inevitable, the Catalan opposition began to get organized in liberated France. The hope that the Franco dictatorship could not survive the defeat of the other Fascist régimes gave rise to two types of activities which, though generally independent, both aimed at the swift over-throw of the Dictatorship. One was the creation in exile of relatively united organizations to prepare for the change-over and appeal for the support of the Allies against Franco; the other was the maquis.

An attempted armed invasion through the Aran Valley in the Py-renees was launched in 1944 under Communist leadership but ended in total failure. From this time onwards, armed confrontation would give way to guerrilla tactics, mostly by anarchists and communists. According to figures provided by the Spanish Civil Guard, between 1943 and 1953 the maquis were responsible for thirteen assassinations, twenty-four kidnappings, seventy-five acts of sabotage, three hundred and sixty-seven hold-ups, and ninety-one armed clashes in Catalonia, in the course of which two hundred and forty-three guerrilla fighters were killed, two hundred and seventy-one wounded and 1251 arrested. They received very little cooperation from the population at large, and frequently acted without any connection with underground political and labour organizations inside Spain. This was especially true of the an-archists, who had no links whatever with the CNT in the interior. They also failed to take into account the demoralized state of the working classes as a result of the suffering inflicted by three years of Civil War, followed by post-war restrictions, rationing, low wages, unem-ployment, and police terror. The Franco régime, meanwhile, was suc-ceeding in overcoming its international isolation and the prospects of allied intervention were fading. Without support from outside the country, guerrilla movements can rarely survive.

By 1948, the Communists had admitted that guerrilla action was ineffectual and decided to put an end to it. In 1952 the anarchists fol-lowed suit. A few anarchist groups, disowned by their own movements, carried out terrorist acts in 1956 and 1957 which came to a stop after the deaths of Quico Sabaté in 1960 and Caracremada in 1963.

In 1945, following the Allied victory, the former Catalan parties in exile tried to rebuild the Catalan government institutions. Under the statute, Josep Irla, who had been elected Speaker of the Catalan parlia-ment in the autumn of 1938, was Companys' successor as President of the Generalitat. In 1945, after persuading Carles Pi i Sunyer to dissolve the CNC despite the opposition of Batista i Roca, the Catalan groups in America, and the FNC, Irla finally formed a government which included, not only personalities from ERC and ACR, but also Joan Comorera and the PSUC, who were in favour of restoring the 1931 Constitution and the 1932 Statute, as were the majority of the remaining members of ERC under the leadership of Josep Tarradellas. In 1946, the Catalan government in exile was extended to include Serra i Moret, as the representative of the recently created Moviment Socialista de Catalunya (Socialist Movement of Catalonia – MSC) and Pau Padró for the Unió de Rabassaires. Miquel Santaló of ERC and Nicolau d'Olwer of ACR joined the Spanish Republican government in exile, which had recently been set up by José Giral with Martínez Barrio as President of the Republic.

In 1945 Josep Pous i Pagès, who had returned from exile, set up in Barcelona the Consell Nacional de la Democràcia Catalana (National Council of Catalan Democracy – CNDC), which covered a wider spectrum than the Irla government, since it included the FNC, UDC, Front Universitari Català, the Front de la Llibertat set up by Joan Rovira, and members of the POUM, as well as groups from the CNT and UGT. The PSUC, however, was excluded. The Pous i Pagès committee recognized the government of Josep Irla but asked for freedom of action within Spain. It had no wish to subordinate Catalan opposition to Franco to that being carried on by Spaniards, both in exile and within the country, and was sceptical about the efficiency of the republican legalism of Irla, Tarradellas, and Comorera. The difficulties implicit in coordinating a leadership in exile and action within Catalonia were becoming obvious and would henceforth be a constant source of problems.

Despite the isolation of the Franco régime, it soon became clear that Britain, France, and the USA would not intervene to overthrow Franco and wanted nothing to do with Catalan demands, since they refused to include the Catalan national question, raised by Josep Carner Ribalta, on the agenda of the first founding conference of the United Nations. It then became generally acknowledged that the straightforward restoration of the Republic was unviable. The enmity generated by the Civil War was still very much alive. Neither the balance of forces in the interior nor the position of the victorious powers in the Second World War made change based on insurrection possible. Nobody wanted another civil war, nor did the size of the underground movement make it feasible to declare one. The pretender to the Spanish throne, Juan de Bourbón, the son of Alfonso XIII, declared abroad in 1945 that the only solution was the restoration of the Monarchy on a constitutional basis. This proposal had the support of the British. A pact between one sector of the Monarchists and the Republicans and Socialists seemed the only solution. Discussion began about the need for a transitional government which would call a referendum to decide on the type of régime. But in 1948, Juan de Borbón reached an agreement with Franco, whereby the latter was entrusted with the education of the pretender's son and heir, Juan Carlos. With the onset of the Cold War between the USA and the USSR, Franco became a trustworthy ally of the American government, and in 1953 an agreement was signed. In 1947, the Giral government in exile was dissolved and in 1948 the government of the Generalitat formed by Irla disintegrated, never to be replaced. When Pous i Pagès died in 1952, the non-operational Consell Nacional de la Democràcia Catalana was also dissolved.

THE WEAKNESS OF THE OPPOSITION TO FRANCO AROUND 1950

By around 1950, guerrilla action had failed, pacts and coalitions between opposition parties in exile had proved inoperative and an agreement with the Monarchists to overthrow Franco had proved fruitless. New methods of opposition were required and, instead of depending on exiles and outside help, these had to be based on the conditions in which Catalan society found itself under the Dictatorship which everyone now realized would be long-lasting. The propaganda constantly announcing the fall of Franco as imminent deceived no one.

The collapse of the opposition to the Franco dictatorship at the end of the 1940s and the beginning of the 1950s was due, not only to the undeniable harshness of the repression but also to the difficulty of adapting approaches and strategies to new circumstances. The old quarrels inherited from the Civil War were aggravated by new ones arising from the Cold War, which separated Communists and non-Communists, and by a policy based on two opposing blocs, making it impossible to launch a truly united offensive. The fragmentation and weakness of the opposition was still further accentuated by the internal divisions of nearly all the organizations involved.

The FNC had been founded as a unitary force but the continued existence of ERC, despite the latter's extremely low membership within

Catalonia, reduced it to just one more party and prevented it from giving Catalan nationalism a new direction beyond mere resistance – hence the difficulties experienced by the FNC in rebuilding after the repression which crushed its risky activism in 1947.

The main organization in the underground opposition within Spain itself, after the Second World War was the CNT. By 1945 not only had it succeeded in rebuilding its structure within Catalonia but its former mouthpiece, *Solidaridad Obrera*, had resumed publication, printing 6000-copy editions which included the novelty of a few pages in the Catalan language. However, in 1945 a deep split divided the CNT itself into a political wing and an apolitical one of the more traditional libertarian kind. The political wing, which was predominant within Spain, gave priority to union action, something extremely difficult to achieve at the time, and was in favour of collaborating with Republicans and Socialists. The apolitical faction rejected coalitions with other anti-Franco forces and laid emphasis on the armed struggle. It was predominant outside the country and within the anarchist youth organization, Juventudes Libertarias, inside Spain, which broke away from the CNT. At all events, its traditional rejection of state intervention in labour relations was to prevent the CNT from working within the framework of the Francoist official 'vertical union' (whose membership included both employers and workers) even in collective bargaining and at company level. This was the strategy which enabled the Communists to establish contact with unaffiliated but militant workers.

The POUM also split up. The majority of its members in the interior were determined to rebuild the party, only to see it promptly destroyed by repression, while the majority of those in exile, led by Josep Rovira, set up in France the Moviment Socialista de Catalunya (Socialist Movement of Catalonia – MSC), together with former PSUC members who had left the party since 1939. The creation of a broad Catalan and Catalanist socialist force, independent of the PSOE and offering an alternative to the Stalinist Communism of the PSUC, was an encouraging proposal at the time. But the MSC wasted too much energy trying to rebuild an underground UGT and the shadow of anti-communism hanging over the European social democrat movement in the 1950s would prevent it later from becoming the sole representative of Catalan socialism.

Unió Democràtica de Catalunya (Democratic Union of Catalonia – UDC) and the PSUC had the best prospects of all the former opposition forces because of their connections with large-scale organizations outside the country, but they also faced problems, some of which were

due to these same international links. UDC had a democratic and nationalist past. Both its loyalty to the Generalitat during the Civil War,
despite religious persecution and the assassination of some of its members, and its links to the European Christian Democrat movement which
governed Italy and Germany, could be seen as attractive during a period
when Catholicism was omnipresent in Catalonia. However, these features also had the disadvantage of identifying it with conservative forces
outside Spain, which would not always meet the expectations of young
Christians attracted by the personality of Emmanuel Mounier and his
call for a critical dialogue with Marxism.

The PSUC had remained a Catalan national party and continued to
publish *Treball* (*Work*) in Catalan. In 1939 it split up, as mentioned
above, and many of its former Socialist members eventually followed
the example of Manuel Serra i Moret by joining the MSC. Since becoming Stalinized, the PSUC was no longer one of the new-style parties resulting from the merger of socialists and communists, as in 1936,
and this deprived it of the basis of its unusual independence from the
PCE. Following the dissolution of the Communist International, it was
no longer even recognized by Moscow. Comorera succeeded in pre-
serving the personality of the party in exile until he was accused of
nationalism and Titoism because of his opposition to the absorption of
the PSUC by the PCE and was ousted in 1948. The take-over never in
fact took place, but steps were taken to ensure that the PSUC could
not deviate from the line fixed by the PCE and/or establish external
relations of its own without going through the Spanish party.

The issue that led to the expulsion of Comorera and forty other
militants from the PSUC shows how difficult it is for a party which
aspires to the leadership of the Catalan national movement and to political supremacy in Catalonia to be dependent on a Spanish-based party.
In 1954 Comorera was arrested in Barcelona and sentenced to thirty
years imprisonment.

Gregorio López Raimundo was sent to head the PSUC inside Catalonia. The Catalan communists had suffered as severely from political
repression as had the anarchists and the FNC. The arrival in the 1950s
of immigrants from other parts of Spain had led to the appearance in
Catalonia of PCE cells which were quite ignorant of the PSUC. The
process proved difficult to reverse, but the notion that the PSUC was
a Catalan and Catalanist party, but not a nationalist one, incorporating
members from all geographical origins, finally prevailed. Towards the
middle of the 1950s the PSUC began to establish itself in the University but its influence at the time was no stronger than that of the MSC

or UDC. Though its leadership was made up of key figures from the Civil War generation, the PSUC none the less succeeded in attracting members of the new generations that had not taken part in the war, thus removing some obvious limitations and contradictions. Thanks to its ability to infiltrate the base of the 'vertical union' at company level, it gradually and painfully gained an influence over the working class that other movements with deeper pre-war roots would lose.

CATALANISM AND CATHOLICISM

First Catalan identity and then Catalanism were forced to seek refuge and a basis for recovery in the Roman Catholic Church. No protection whatever was afforded by the hierarchy, which identified with Franco's ideal of National Catholicism and collaborated in the de-Catalanization process. Even so, the Church was the least Fascist of the various forces that lent legitimacy to the Dictatorship and was so powerful throughout society that only from within it was it viable to go beyond the action of tiny underground groups, salvage the remains of an identity that the régime was bent on destroying, and defend human rights. The Catalanist Catholicism that had existed prior to 1931 offered a traditional basis from which to do this, but it soon proved outdated. A clear example is provided by a group of Catholic students who belonged to an organization named after Torras i Bages. Originally devoted to religious training, it soon developed civic objectives too and its leaders included both the future Catalan nationalist leader Jordi Pujol and the future socialist leader Joan Raventós. The continued exile of the Archbishop of Tarragona, Vidal i Barraquer, who had refused to take the side of General Franco during the Civil War, and the works attacking the subordination of the Church to the Franco régime published by another expatriate, Canon Carles Cardó, provided further indication that the Catalan clergy's support for Franco's National Catholicism was not unanimous.

The first sign of the ambivalence of part of the Catalan clergy appeared at the celebrations held in 1947 to mark the enthronement of the Virgin of Montserrat, an event which, though nominally religious in nature, may be considered the first mass mobilization of Catalanism after the Civil War. The event was marked by the public use of the Catalan language in the presence of the crowd of 70,000 which had congregated at Montserrat. Even more important, however, was the fact that the Comissió Abat Oliba, responsible for the event, comprised men who had supported or fought on both sides during the Civil War, thus prefiguring the unitary organizations that were required if Catalonia was to emerge from its silence and immobility. The four red stripes of Catalonia's forbidden flag fluttered illegally over the celebrations from an inaccessible peak, and one of Franco's ministers and the Papal Legate were obliged to take part in a ceremony in which Catalonia's identity was revealed anew, despite its numerous contradictions.

Many years later, the Church was to be used as a shield for the opposition, though much more than this had formerly – and vainly – been expected of it, namely that its entire structure, headed by the hierarchy, should react against a State that failed to respect basic human rights, also violating those of Catholics, some of whom were opponents of the régime. The activities of the Juventud Obrera Católica (Young Catholic Workers' Association – JOC), who were to establish links with the new labour movement and follow the example of the working-class apostolate and the worker priests in Belgium and France, provided a particularly clear example of this. But it was not until the 1960s, after the Second Vatican Council had denied the legitimacy of Franco's National Catholicism, that the bishops would begin to disassociate themselves from the Dictatorship, and by then the redemptory social mission of the progressive sector of the Church was undergoing a crisis, and the secularization of society was well underway.

13 From the 1951 Strike to the Catalanist Challenge of 1960

1951–2: FROM THE TRAM BOYCOTT TO THE EUCHARISTIC CONGRESS

The spontaneous popular movement which began with a boycott of the Barcelona trams and continued with a general strike in March 1951 was the most important and widespread to occur during the first twenty years of the Franco régime. The rise in fares on the Barcelona trams, while those in Madrid remained unchanged, was perceived of as a flagrant piece of injustice and sparked off so much protest that the authorities withdrew the increase. The ensuing twenty-four hour general strike was mercilessly crushed, but it brought to light the unease of the working classes after over ten years of electricity restrictions, high prices, housing shortages, rationing of basic foods, and black-market racketeering. It also showed that workers opposed to the régime had infiltrated the base of the 'vertical union' and all but taken over the Falangist movement since the call for a general strike had come from an assembly of 2000 official union delegates. The experience of the 1951 tram boycott, which had forced a return to the previous fare scale and caused the fall of a mayor and a civil governor, lived on in the memory of the Catalans. This explains the attempt to stage a new boycott in January 1957, though the second one did not succeed in making the authorities give in.

A new era had begun, yet the early 1950s were anything but propitious to the democratic opposition, which had to put up with the pomp with which the Franco régime and National Catholicism celebrated the International Eucharistic Congress in Barcelona in 1952. To some extent the Congress was turned into a mass religious festival with connotations very different from those of the enthronement of the Virgin of Montserrat in 1947. Nevertheless, the opposition forces, particularly UDC, strove to draw attention to the true political and social situation of the country by means of documents in a variety of languages and interviews with certain foreign delegates. During the multitudinous closing ceremony, a group of activists flew a giant Catalan flag from a nearby hilltop.

Before the Eucharistic Congress, the government had put an end to the rationing of bread, sugar, and other foods and to restrictions on electricity consumption. During the same year, Spanish foreign trade for the first time reached pre-war levels. But it was not until the end of the decade that the State began to loosen its control over the economy.

In 1952 Spain was admitted to UNESCO; in 1953 the Spanish government signed the Concordat with the Vatican and an economic and military agreement with the United States; in 1955 Spain joined the United Nations, all of which amounted to the international community absolving Franco of the crimes for which it had condemned him ten years earlier.

During the 1950s, the new postwar generations were not yet old enough to take over leadership of the opposition, and for those who had lived through the Civil War the memories were still too painful. The influence of the underground organizations that were the successors of those of the 1930s grew less and less. Outward support for the régime, however, began to dwindle in Catalonia during the 1950s, though its sociological impact remained as strong as ever. The Dictatorship never lacked for Catalan mayors, presidents of provincial Diputacions, municipal councillors, parliamentary deputies, and even ministers, when they were needed. Between 1957 and 1973, the Barcelona City Council, like many others, was headed by a former member of the Lliga Catalana, Josep M. de Porcioles, who also acted as intermediary between the régime and that part of the bourgeoisie that was engaged in real estate and the construction industry. Gual Villalbí, who was more representative of the Catalan industrial bourgeoisie, was Minister without Portfolio from 1957 to 1965. López Rodó, an eminent member of the Opus Dei, was Secretary to the Prime Minister in 1956, Commissioner for the development plan in 1962, and became the right-hand man of Franco's Deputy Prime Minister and chosen successor Carrero Blanco. He did not, however, represent the Catalan bourgeoisie, and in 1967 less than 3 per cent of the top civil servants, from which the government elite was recruited, had been born in Catalonia. The great majority of the Catalan bourgeoisie adopted a conformist position and became increasingly dependent on the Spanish financial oligarchy. This explains the plausibility of claims made by socialists and communists during the 1960s that they represented the only genuine, popular Catalanism and were acting as intermediaries between the Catalanist movement and working-class immigrants from southern Spain so as to

avoid the danger of Catalonia splitting into two opposing communities. The partially Castilianized local bourgeoisie was little concerned
about this danger because it was in the popular classes that Catalanist
feelings had survived.

Following the decline of Falangism, however, which was more patent
in Catalonia than elsewhere, a new-style dictatorship managed to succeed the old one. During the 1960s, economic development gave rise
to a social mobility that was beneficial to the system, enabling the
régime to obtain passive collaboration, not necessarily matched by explicit
declarations of support, and thus to continue in power despite the fact
that economic progress was not matched by political liberalization.

THE INCREASING DISTANCE OF THOSE IN EXILE

From 1950 onwards, Catalan politicians in exile were increasingly far
removed from the underground organizations within the country, though
expatriates continued to organize Jocs Florals (poetry competitions) in
Europe and America and to denounce the situation in Catalonia. One
example was the memorial addressed to UNESCO in 1952, invoking
the persecution of the Catalan language and culture in an attempt to
block the admission of Franco's Spain, but such actions failed to prevent the Franco régime from consolidating its position abroad.

In 1954 Josep Irla, the President of the Generalitat in exile, resigned
on the grounds of serious health problems. There were two possible
successors. Under the Statute of Self-government, Serra i Moret, who
had become Speaker of the Catalan parliament on the death of Rovira
i Virgili, should have automatically succeeded to the post, just as
Companys had previously been replaced by Irla. However, Josep
Tarradellas, a member of the ERC leadership, maintained that the new
President should be chosen by the members of the Catalan parliament.
Thus Tarradellas himself was elected President in Mexico in August
1954 by twenty-four votes out of twenty-six. Nine deputies were present
at the meeting and a further seventeen sent in written votes. The remaining members of the former Catalan parliament then met for the
first and last time after the war. Tarradellas declined to form a government
in exile and remained in France waiting for the situation to change.
He was viewed with mistrust by some groups of exiles and ignored by
the opposition within Catalonia.

In 1953, the Conferència Nacional Catalana met in Mexico. It was attended by representatives of seventy organizations based in thirty countries who decided to appoint a new Consell Nacional Català under the chairmanship of the deputy Salvador Armendares. Years later the Consell Nacional Català, now headed by Batista i Roca, undertook numerous campaigns to denounce the cultural and political repression suffered by the Catalan people to various international organizations.

Another organization opposed to Tarradellas was the Comitè de Coordinació de les Forces Polítiques de Catalunya (Coordination Committee of Political Forces of Catalonia) comprising representatives of ERC, ACR, UDC, MSC, and FNC under the chairmanship of Claudi Ametlla. This committee, which existed in Barcelona from 1958 to 1968, exerted a negligible influence on the activities of the opposition to the Franco régime during a period when agitation and mobilization in university and labour circles were becoming increasingly widespread. Ametlla's committee sought an understanding with the liberal monarchist supporters of Juan de Borbón and sent a delegation to a meeting held in Munich in June 1962 within the framework of a conference of the European Movement at which there was passed a motion granting 'recognition to the personality of the different natural communities'. For the first time at this conference, Spaniards from inside and outside the country, both monarchists and socialists – but not communists, since the latter were opposed to the European movement at the time – discussed the prospect of a peaceful transition to democracy of the kind that would take place fifteen years later and called for Spain to be excluded from the European Community as long as it remained under a dictatorship. Ametlla's committee, however, was never more than a political discussion group and disintegrated on the death of its founder.

THE APPEARANCE OF A STUDENT OPPOSITION MOVEMENT

In January 1957, a new popular movement of passive resistance broke out in the form of the second tram boycott triggered off by an increase in fares. This time students took a more active part in the events than in 1951. The police entered the University, and the Vice-Chancellor resigned to avoid having to take repressive measures. Responsibility for such measures had by now been given to the academic authorities rather than to the Falange as it had been in 1946 when certain earlier protests had arisen. On this occasion the students defying the régime were no longer a small minority but extremely numerous. In February 1957 the first free students' meeting took place in the assembly hall of the University of Barcelona. It called for the abolition of the official Sindicato Español de Universitarios (Spanish Union of University Students – SEU), membership of which was compulsory, and the resignation of the Minister. Trapped in the assembly hall, the 800 participants were sanctioned and given police records, and the events sparked off a two-week general strike of university students. This marked the end of the conformist attitude of a student population which still came from a narrow upper-class social background.

For the new generation of students the ideas inherited from the Civil War held no appeal. Nor, indeed, did they for the new generation of workers, who suffered repression after the 1958 wave of strikes but were able thereafter to seize the opportunities afforded by a new law of collective bargaining, which put an end to the regulation of wages by decree and allowed periodic bargaining within individual firms. This limited liberalization was vital if productivity was to increase prior to the adoption of a stabilization plan that was to allow the Spanish economy to aspire to membership in the European Community set up under the Treaty of Rome in 1957. Though the 'vertical unions' continued to control the situation, collective bargaining at company level would henceforth make it possible for a true labour movement to be born towards 1964, when militant communist, Christian, and socialist workers decided to unite and create the Comissió Obrera Central de Barcelona (Barcelona Central Workers' Commission).

THE NEW CATALANISM

In the mid-1950s a new Catalanism was born. It was strongly influenced by Catholicism and rejected the Catalanism of the Republic, holding it partly responsible for the Civil War on account of its anti-clericalism. It also considered the Catalanism of the Lliga Catalana to be outdated because of its conservative stand on social issues, though it respected such 'classical' figures as Prat de la Riba. The magazine *Quaderns de l'Exili* (*Notebooks in Exile*), published in Mexico between 1943 and 1947, with its anti-intellectual orientation, its defence of the military values of loyalty and discipline, and its pursuit of national reconciliation, provided the initial group with its inspiration. The spirit of the magazine was brought to Catalonia by its publisher Joan Sales

and Raimon Galí, one of the founders of the new Catalan Scout Movement and its main ideologist at the time. Other members of the group
were young people educated at the Virtèlia schools, activists from the
Acadèmia de la Llengua Catalana, one of the student sections of the
Jesuit Marian Congregations, and the Catholic Scout Movement headed
by Father Antoni Batlle, while Abbot Escarré, the superior of the
Benedictine abbey of Montserrat, was its *point d'appui*. In 1954 an
organization known by the initials CC – Crist i Catalunya (Christ and
Catalonia) or Cristians Catalans (Catalan Christians) – was founded. A
pre-political movement which served to heighten awareness and train
future militants, it was led from 1955 to 1957 by Frederic Roda and
from 1957 to 1962 by Xavier Muñoz.

In 1959, the most militant sector, headed by Jordi Pujol, organized
a campaign against Luís Martínez de Galinsoga, the pro-Franco editor
of the Barcelona daily newspaper, *La Vanguardia*. While attending a
mass at which the celebrant, as usual, preached in Catalan, Galinsoga
had protested by remarking that 'Todos los catalanes son una mierda'
(All Catalans are shit). The ensuing campaign against the paper cost it
many subscriptions and much advertising revenue, and showed that
Catalan society rejected all forms of domination which rashly recalled
armed occupation. The Government was finally forced to dismiss
Galinsoga.

A few months later the same group of activists brought about the
failure of one of the régime's most ambitious schemes to improve its
image and ingratiate itself with a sector of Catalan public opinion.
This consisted of granting a 'municipal charter' to Barcelona – a substitute for true municipal autonomy – handing over the ancient fortress
of Montjuïc to the city authorities, compiling Catalan civil law, and
holding official celebrations to mark the centenary of the Catalan poet
Joan Maragall, all of which took place while Franco was on an official
visit to Barcelona. When the singing of *El Cant de la Senyera* (The
Song of the Catalan Flag), a patriotic song with words by Maragall
which was traditionally used by the Orfeó Català choir to round off its
concerts, was prohibited at a concert held in the Palau de la Música
Catalana, the apparently benevolent Dictatorship, aided and abetted by
the Mayor of Barcelona, Josep M. de Porcioles, was shown in its true
colours. The audience began to sing the song in the presence of several
of Franco's ministers. Twenty people were arrested, and Jordi Pujol
and Francesc Pizón were tried by court-martial and sentenced to seven
and three years' imprisonment respectively for their part in the events
and in the diffusion of a pamphlet entitled *Us Presentem el General*

Franco (*Let us introduce General Franco to you*).

During the same year, 1960, a hundred intellectuals, among them Josep M. de Sagarra, Josep Pla, Jaume Vicenç Vives, and Joan Oliver, and members of the younger generation like Josep M. Espinàs, Josep M. Castellet, and Antoni Comas, signed a manifesto calling for the Catalan language to be included in the curriculum at all levels of the education system.

From the time of the imprisonment of Jordi Pujol in 1960, CC split into two. The majority, headed by Xavier Muñoz, adopted an approach based on the doctrinal orientation laid down by Antoni Pérez, a worker from Extremadura. This consisted of replacing Raimon Galí's nationalism by a pro-labour ideology, laying aside Catholic denominationalism, without, however, rejecting Christianity, and giving priority to the class structure over Catalan national identity. In the spring of 1962 this group decided to become a political party, known as Comunitat Catalana (Catalan Community). Its unofficial mouthpiece, from 1963 and 1966, was to be *Promos*, a legal journal dealing with economics, in which socialists affiliated to other organizations, such as the Front Obrer de Catalunya (Workers' Front of Catalonia – FOC) also collaborated. In 1964 the group changed its name to Força Socialista Federal de Catalunya (Federal Socialist Force of Catalonia – FSFC). It disappeared at the end of the 1960s.

The smaller group from the original CC, made up of Jordi Pujol's followers, was opposed to this evolution and gave up underground political action to pursue the slogan of '*fer país*' (making a country). Henceforth, they and their leader devoted their efforts to building a cultural infrastructure to prevent the denationalization of Catalonia.

THE NEW SOCIALISM

Another new political force born at the end of the 1950s was the Associació Democràtica Popular de Catalunya (Popular Democratic Association of Catalonia – ADPC). Founded in 1959, it too pursued the explicit objective of going beyond the now outdated ideas of the generation of the 1930s. The founders of the ADPC, like those of CC, were Christians opposed to the Dictatorship. Some were associated with the magazine *El Ciervo* while others came from the JOC or the Catholic Scout Movement. The main goal of the ADPC, and later of the FOC, was not Catalan nationalism but socialism, a socialism which rejected social democracy and Stalinism alike and was influenced by the anti-imperialist movements of the day, such as the Algerian FLN and the Castroist movement in Cuba. Nevertheless, the position of the ADPC in favour of Catalan self-government was obvious, since it was on an equal footing with its counterpart in Madrid, the Frente de Liberación Popular (Popular Liberation Front – FLP), and proposed a Yugoslavian-style federal structure for Spain.

The ADPC sought to demonstrate the compatibility between Marxism and Christianity, but it was against denominationalism in politics. The MSC was unable to absorb this new socialist current because of the weakening effect of the imprisonment of its leaders within Catalonia, such as Joan Raventós, who was arrested in 1958, and because of the anti-communist moderation of its leadership in exile, headed by Josep Pallach. The two leaderships clashed in 1964 and the MSC split up in 1966.

In 1961 the ADPC itself divided into two. One sector, which was in favour of setting up a political party forthwith, founded the Front Obrer de Catalunya (Workers' Front of Catalonia – FOC). The other, which felt the time was not ripe for making a small training group like the ADPC into a party, promoted joint action between university students belonging to the group and others from the MSC within the so-called Moviment Febrer 62 (February 62 Movement). This movement was a forerunner of the united socialist party, Convergència Socialista de Catalunya, that was formed in 1974 by members of the two organizations.

On the occasion of the 1962 strikes, the FOC was mobilized to provide industrial action with political content. Nearly all its members were arrested, as were those who had remained in the ADPC. Both inside and outside prison, the failure of this move facilitated the reunification in 1963 of the two groups within the new FOC, which had federal links with the Frente de Liberación Popular and ESBA, a Basque organization with similar leanings. The FOC, however, was more firmly established, and had greater influence in Catalonia than the FLP in the centre of Spain. Some of the foremost leaders and officials of the present Partit dels Socialistes de Catalunya were members of the original FOC.

14 The Catalanist Cultural Movement under the Franco Régime

FROM SURVIVAL TO RECOVERY

The defeat of the Republican side in the Civil War had brought with it the annihilation of the Catalan publishing industry within the country. Some writers, however, remained active in exile, publishing some of the finest works of Catalan twentieth-century literature. During the ten years following the war, one hundred and eighty books and smaller works appeared in Catalan abroad. Between 1939 and 1975, one hundred and eighty periodicals and some 650 books in the Catalan language were published in exile. The poetry readings held by small private groups within the country during the long post-war period had the added attraction of being something semi-clandestine, a way of asserting Catalan identity itself in spite of the official ban.

Though the hopes for political change it had awakened failed to materialize, the Allied victory in World War II did lead to the Franco régime making a few minor concessions to Catalan culture, which had previously been reduced to total silence. The censors tolerated new editions of certain classical works in Catalan but continued to prohibit the publication of new works or translations in the hope of reducing Catalan literature to a form of local folklore with no future. Two publishing houses specializing in Catalan books were founded, Selecta and Aymà. In 1946 authorization was given for a theatrical performance in Catalan and a concert by the Orfeó Català choir.

The literary prizes created in 1947 played an important part in the difficult task of bringing writers in the Catalan language closer to the reading public. In order to draw more attention to the prizes, from 1951 onwards they were awarded simultaneously on the eve of the feast of Saint Lucy (13 December), the same date on which the Generalitat had formerly awarded the Joan Crexells prize for novels. Private initiative was replacing the action of the former Catalan government authorities; and the return of certain intellectuals made it possible to establish links between the pre-war cultural heritage and the small elite of young university students. From 1942 onwards this same group of people had been attending secret courses in Catalan history, literature, and language at the re-established Estudis Universitaris Catalans, since these subjects were banned in the University itself. Catalan classes reached a wider public from 1953 onwards thanks to the newly founded Centro de Información Católica Femenina (Catholic Women's Information Centre), known nowadays as the CIC. The Institut d'Estudis Catalans had secretly resumed its activities in 1944, but for many years its insecurity and lack of resources made its activities more symbolic than effective. In 1953, on the occasion of the Seventh International Congress of Romance Linguistics, papers were presented and scientific debates were held in Catalan at the University of Barcelona for the first time since the war. But official teaching continued to be exclusively in Spanish.

In 1946 only twelve books were published in Catalan inside Catalonia. In 1948 the total was sixty and in 1954 it reached ninety-six. By the beginning of the 1960s over two hundred books per year were coming out in Catalan, a figure well below that for 1936, but encouraging in comparison with the alarming situation of the 1940s.

The Dictatorship was confident that by excluding the Catalan language from the radio, the daily press, the cinema, the schools and, later, from television, it would succeed in cutting off the great majority of the population from the difficult rebirth of Catalan national awareness. And indeed by the time it was obliged to tolerate certain cultural activities in Catalan – albeit with many restrictions – the new generation, which had to take over from those who had fought in the Civil War, was illiterate in its own mother tongue and had become accustomed to considering the official language as the sole language of culture. Thus diglossia had established a foothold even in the educated classes and the quality of the spoken language was steadily deteriorating. The post-war generations were unfamiliar with the rich pre-war Catalan cultural heritage and ignorant of Catalan history, which was likewise banned from the schools, and they had to rediscover them imperfectly and at the cost of considerable effort.

Catalonia did not emerge unscathed from the Franco Dictatorship, though the régime never stopped considering it an unsolved problem. The only way of keeping the Basques and Catalans under a centralized, uniformist régime was by subjecting the whole of Spain to a dictatorship. Conversely, the progress of both peoples towards self-government required the democratization of Spain. It was for this reason that the Spanish opposition to Franco would ultimately be obliged to include in its projects a binding commitment to the distasteful but unavoidable goal of self-government for the Basque Country and Catalonia. This enabled it to rid itself of the uneasy conscience that plagued Spanish nationalism as a result of Franco's attempt to do away with the Catalan and Basque cultures, an attempt which, in fact, was no more than the continuation, with vastly reinforced means, of the policies of assimilation pursued by successive Spanish governments over the centuries.

Whereas in the Spanish-speaking regions of Spain the Franco régime could at least aspire to monopolizing and instrumentalizing Castilian-based Spanish national feeling, in Catalonia the Dictatorship appeared as the pure and simple negation of collective identity, coming as it did after a brief but intense period of political self-government and assertion of national identity on all fronts. From the 1950s onwards a network of civic, cultural, and educational associations began to develop in Catalonia. Though formally apolitical, these organizations made it possible to offer legal resistance to the attempt to assimilate and de-Catalanize the country. The existence of a relatively large, educated middle class provided a social basis which lent itself, first to cultural resistance, and later to reconstruction. In this process the ability of Catalan society to organize itself was essential, not only in order to make up for the grave deficiencies of the State set up by Franco, but so as to enable Catalans to recover political faith in themselves and realize that they were capable of governing themselves. Thus the study of legal anti-Francoist organizations such as the Scout Movement and bodies devoted to fostering Catalan culture becomes as important as that of the clandestine political parties, and possibly more so. Catalan cultural opposition had an existence and dynamics all of its own, though militants of political groups were active within it. It was not merely the façade of clandestine political opposition or a training ground for future militants.

The Catalan Scout Movement has played a prime role in the training of youth and has always been associated with Catalanist feelings. The movement underwent considerable growth at the beginning of the 1950s, following the clandestine reconstruction of a coordinating body which aimed to carry on the work of the Catalanist Scout Movement begun by Batista i Roca in 1927. Hounded by the Falange, which still purported to monopolize extra-curricular youth training, the Scout Movement – at least the Catholic branch, which was the largest – achieved legal status by being recognized by the Church hierarchy. In 1966 nearly half the delegates who made up the Sindicat Democràtic d'Estudiants de la Universitat de Barcelona (Democratic Students' Union of the

University of Barcelona) – the first post-war democratic students' union – were former scouts and both the Chief Scout, J. M. Martorell, and the ecclesiastic councillor of the Catholic branch, R. Pedrals, were present at the founding meeting. The Scout Movement trained future educators and parents who wanted to apply the methods of the movement itself and the principles of active education by setting up a series of private schools. In 1965 these initiatives led to the foundation of the Institució Pedagògica Rosa Sensat (Rosa Sensat Pedagogical Institution), which ran courses for teachers and summer schools that greatly influenced educational revival in Catalonia and even in Spain as a whole. Some of the present-day Catalan political leaders – members of the governing nationalist coalition, Convergència i Unió, and of the Socialist and Communist parties alike – were educated in the Scout Movement, as were many top public servants in the Catalan and municipal administrations.

At the end of the 1950s and the beginning of the 1960s, the creation of a series of cultural organs marked the transition of Catalan culture from mere survival to a stage of recovery and renovation. In 1959, *Serra d'Or* (*Golden Mountain*), the first Catalan language magazine to survive for any length of time during the Franco period, commenced publication under the protection of the Benedictine Abbey of Montserrat. For many years it displayed all the virtues and faults attributable to its being the only Catalan cultural magazine in existence. The first children's magazines in the Catalan language also appeared during the same period.

The year 1961 saw the beginning of the Nova Cançó (new song) movement, with the appearance of a group of Catalan singers and songwriters known as Els Setze Jutges (The Sixteen Judges). From performing Catalan versions of works by singers like Georges Brassens, they soon went on to create original works which incorporated and recreated contemporary trends in song, lent new prestige to traditional songs, and finally made the works of Catalan poets, both ancient and modern, better known. Their activities brought unusual popularity to the endeavour of restoring the Catalan language to a normal cultural situation. The success enjoyed in Catalonia by the Valencian singer Raimon and the Majorcan Maria del Mar Bonet, both faithful representatives of the speech and traditions of their native lands, and exponents of modern general cultural trends, went far towards heightening awareness of the community formed by the three different Catalan-speaking countries, Catalonia, Valencia, and the Balearic Islands. This same concept was timidly emerging at the begining of the 1960s thanks to the efforts of intellectuals such as the writer Joan Fuster and the publisher Eliseu Climent, both in Valencia, and Max Cahner in Barcelona. Such developments were but the beginning of a long process of closening the ties between the three areas, a relationship which would not, on the other hand, be successful in establishing links with political connotations on account of the different degrees of national awareness existing in the different countries where Catalan is spoken. The desire for a political federation between Catalonia, the Balearic Islands, and Valencia had been expressed in the 1940s and 1950s in clandestine documents emanating from radical Catalan nationalist organizations such as the Front Universitari de Catalunya (Catalan University Front) and the FNC. Within Catalonia, however, awareness of the links with the other Catalan-speaking countries had been all but wiped out.

A noteworthy advance took place in the field of books in Catalan with the establishment in the early 1960s of new publishing houses such as Edicions 62. The annual output of two hundred new titles in Catalan in 1952, rose to over four hundred in 1966 and reached 548 the following year. In 1968, however, Catalan book publishing entered a crisis from which it did not begin to emerge until 1973 and the figure for 1967 was not exceeded until 1975. The factors underlying this crisis were political, since it was impossible to maintain the expansion of a sector like publishing as long as the Catalan language was banned from the education system, the communications media and official public life. Nor could a popular news weekly become established if it was prevented from publishing information and opinions about the most burning current issues. An example of this was the disappointing experience of *Tele/Estel* (*Tele/Star*), which began publication in 1966 and disappeared in 1970. It is no coincidence that the recovery and expansion of book production in Catalan got underway in 1973, at the same time as the movement in support of democracy and self-government was relaunched. Finally in 1976 the number of new titles published in Catalan equalled that of 1936. Taking into account the great increase in the percentage of the population attending school and university that had taken place in the meantime, and the consequent rise in the average level of education, it was clear that making up lost ground was proving extremely difficult.

An important step towards the restoration of a normal cultural situation was the creation of a chair of Catalan language and literature at the University of Barcelona in 1961 in response to demands by both students and the intellectual elite. In 1964 the literary prizes awarded on Saint Lucy's eve made the front page of as important a newspaper as *La Vanguardia*. From 1958 onwards it became possible to publish translations of foreign works in Catalan, a development that enabled Catalan publishing houses to keep abreast of the latest trends, to such an extent that foreign works sometimes came out earlier in Catalan than in Spanish. The 1966 Press Law abolished prior censorship of printed materials, but publishers and periodicals which failed to apply self-censorship were threatened with severe sanctions. It soon became apparent how the régime intended to use the 1966 law. In 1967 penalties began to hail down on the magazine *Destino*, which had given up its previously conformist attitude, until publication was suspended for two months, the magazine was fined half a million pesetas, and in 1968 its director Néstor Luján was dismissed. The press was further intimidated by the 1969 state of emergency. An arbitrary hardening of cultural repression between 1969 and 1974 put an end to the previous trend towards limited liberalization in the field of publishing. The same ideas when expressed in Catalan aroused greater wrath on the part of the administration than if they had been expressed in Spanish. And abstract, universal ideas, though hostile to the Franco régime, were more easily tolerated in Spanish than more moderate ideas related to precise changes in Catalan society.

To make matters worse, Fascist groups carried out with impunity over twenty terrorist attacks between 1971 and 1975 against book shops, publishers, distributors, magazines, cinemas, and other cultural organizations in Barcelona. During 1973 this wave of bibliophobic violence reached its peak with twelve acts of Fascist aggression in Barcelona and four in Valencia.

THE PROMOTION OF CATALAN CULTURE

During the 1960s, a series of events took place, all of which, though with variable repercussions, gradually reinforced the national awareness of the Catalan people and their opposition to the Franco régime. Statements against the Dictatorship made by the Abbot of Montserrat, Aureli M. Escarré, to the French daily *Le Monde* in 1963 were one such event. The next was the first attempt, on 11 September 1964, to commemorate the Catalan national day on the site where the statue of Rafael de Casanova, a hero of the siege of Barcelona by Philip V in 1714, had stood before being removed by the régime. Then in 1966 the appointment of the Castilian Marcelo González Martín as the successor to the outgoing pro-Franco Archbishop of Barcelona, Gregorio Modrego, triggered off a mobilization of Catalanist forces as part of a campaign which had as its slogan *Volem bisbes catalans* (We want Catalan bishops). It also led to the publication of a book entitled *Le Vatican et la Catalogne* which highlighted the contradiction between the agreements reached at the Second Vatican Council and the privilege of proposing the names of future bishops that was still enjoyed by the Spanish government. This movement succeeded in ensuring that, at least from that time onwards, only Catalan-speaking bishops would be appointed to Catalan dioceses and that Marcelo González's successor as Archbishop of Barcelona in 1971 would be Narcís Jubany. In 1969 another campaign was launched, this time under the slogan *Català a l'escola* (Catalan at school). It had the support of 2500 organizations and took place while the Ley General de Educación (General Law of Education) was being debated in the Cortes. Finally in 1969 the new Abbot of Montserrat, Cassià Just, criticized the Dictatorship on Bavarian radio and television.

The 1960s also saw the creation of a number of new private organizations devoted to the diffusion of culture. The activities of these organizations compensated to some extent for the lack of government bodies able to carry out such a task. The best known was Omnium Cultural, which was founded in 1961 by a group of leading industrialists to bring together isolated forms of patronage, promote literary awards, and provide grants for the teaching of Catalan. Omnium Cultural also took charge of the Institut d'Estudis Catalans. At the end of 1963, following the campaign of petitions in favour of the public use of Catalan in education and the communications media, and a month after the statements made by Abbot Escarré of Montserrat against the Franco régime to the French daily *Le Monde*, Omnium Cultural was closed down. It was not permitted to resume operations legally until 1967, but in the interim it was far from idle. In 1970 it had 8000 members and by 1975 the number had grown to 20,000. In 1971, Omnium Cultural was giving Catalan classes to three hundred and fifty groups totalling 10,000 students. By 1974 the number of groups had reached 1886 and the students numbered 80,000. Some of the classes were held outside regular hours in state schools in urban areas inhabited primarily by Spanish-speaking immigrants. Omnium Cultural was the result of cooperation between a very small Catalanist group within the Catalan industrial bourgeoisie and a wide circle of intellectuals, many of whom were influenced to a greater or lesser extent by Marxism.

The activities pursued between 1965 and 1971 by the Centre d'Informació, Recerca i Promoció (Centre of Information, Research and Promotion) headed by Jordi Pujol were parallel and complementary to those of Omnium Cultural, though they came in for less public attention. Rather than creating a new underground nationalist party, which would have competed with those already in existence, Pujol felt, on his release from jail, that it would be more viable to devote his energies to legal undertakings. Some of these, such as Banca Catalana, founded in 1961, were designed to create new infrastructures; others aimed at promoting areas of cooperation in which, however, confrontation and even failure were not always avoided. There is no doubt that the career of Pujol who, in 1980, would be elected President of the re-established Catalan Generalitat, was influenced by the role he played during this period in the promotion of Catalan culture in a wide variety of fields.

Another organization which, though not directly Catalanist, exerted considerable influence was the Círculo de Economía (Circle of Economy). The foundation of this organization in 1958 marked the appearance of a new generation of businessmen and neo-capitalist executives who brought new vitality to savings banks and chambers of commerce, set up technical and commercial services in particular sectors, such as the Centro de Estudios y Asesoramiento Metalúrgico (Metallurgical Consultancy and Study Centre – CEAM) and the Servicio Comercial de la Industria Algodonera (Commercial Service of the Cotton Industry – SECEA), and even began to rejuvenate the old Fomento del Trabajo Nacional, which had remained dormant. A wide range of options were to emerge from the Círculo de Economía: its first chairman was Carles Ferrer Salat, later to become the founder and leader of the Spanish employers' association, CEOE; its first secretary was the future Socialist Minister of Health Ernest Lluch; while both Jordi Pujol and Narcís Serra (who became successively Socialist Mayor of Barcelona, Minister of Defense and Deputy Prime Minister) were members of the board.

The Círculo de Economía was tireless in its efforts to influence the economic policy of the Franco régime. No other group of businessmen at the time argued so coherently and forcefully in favour of Spanish membership of the Common Market, with all its economic and political implications, as did the Círculo de Economía in 1972 in collaboration with twelve other organizations.

It should be stressed, however, that the true reins of economic power in Catalonia were not in the hands of this particular sector, a fact that was later revealed in a seminar on the Catalan bourgeoisie held at the Universitat Autònoma de Barcelona (1981). That seminar, based on a study of the Catalan firms with the largest turnover, reached the following conclusions: that very few of these firms are among the top hundred Spanish companies; those that are in this category are controlled by non-Catalan capital; and that of the fifty-four Catalan families with greatest economic power, very few can be considered either a modernizing bourgeoisie or a Catalanist bourgeoisie, since the majority are seen to have conservative and mildly Spanish nationalist tendencies. All of this helps to account for the course of action taken by the group headed by Pujol in the 1960s. It also explains the misgivings of the employers towards Catalan self-government during the transition to democracy and the lack of enthusiasm shown by the bourgeoisie, not only towards a Generalitat which might fall into the hands of the Left, but, at least until 1980, towards the party headed by Jordi Pujol, Convergència Democràtica de Catalunya.

In 1974, Radio Barcelona began to broadcast the first regular programme in Catalan and the popularity and social impact of the intensely politicized Nova Cançó Catalana reached its peak. A survey conducted in Catalonia by FOESSA (Fomento de Estudios Sociales y de Sociología Aplicada – Organization for the Promotion of Social Studies and Applied Sociology) in 1970 showed that 97 per cent of those interviewed wanted their children to be able to speak Catalan, though Catalan was the first language of only 56 per cent. In March 1975, a municipal councillor proposed that the Barcelona City Council should assign 50 million pesetas to the promotion of the Catalan language and culture and asked in vain to be allowed to speak Catalan at council meetings. The proposal was rejected by eighteen votes to nine, sparking off such widespread protest that it had to be revoked. The same year thousands of organizations supported the proposal of the Col · legi d'Advocats de Barcelona (the Barcelona Law Society) to hold a congress of Catalan culture. This congress was extremely successful in heightening public awareness and laid down the bases for a programme of political action in a wide range of areas in preparation for the future granting of self-government, for it was now obvious that political autonomy was the only way of achieving effective cultural normalization and true democracy.

IMMIGRATION AND CATALAN IDENTITY

The economic development of Catalonia triggered off a wave of immigration from the less developed Spanish-speaking regions of Spain, notably Andalusia, which reached unprecedented proportions during the 1960s. Between 1951 and 1981 the excess of immigrants over emigrants in Catalonia was 1,464,000, over half this figure being concentrated in the 1960s. In 1970 only 62.3 per cent of the total population of Catalonia had been born there. A study published in 1976 on the language of school children in Catalan boroughs with over 10,000 inhabitants indicated that Catalan-speaking children accounted for only 47.7 per cent of the total in the city of Barcelona. In Greater Barcelona the figure was as low as 29.2 per cent and elsewhere in Catalonia it was 62.2 per cent. In 1970, when the wave of immigration reached its peak, 37.6 per cent of the Catalan population had been born outside the country. In order to compare this phenomenon with those which occurred in other countries, suffice it to say that the immigrant population of the United States and Argentina was never more than 30 per cent at the time of the greatest influx and that the newcomers were from much more varied origins than those who settled in Catalonia.

During the 1940s and 1950s, immigrant ghettoes on the outskirts of the large cities were still few in number. In their home neighbourhoods and at work the immigrants constantly heard Catalan spoken. Though banned from schools, the radio, and the press, the Catalan language was understood and even spoken by the immigrants themselves and especially by their children, who also assimilated Catalan customs and popular culture. As a result of sheer numbers, the immigrants who arrived in the 1960s were massed together in outlying areas, in deplorable living conditions, to such an extent that the entire population of certain districts came from the same place of origin. These circumstances, combined with the exclusive use of Spanish in the communications media and the schools, made it extremely difficult for the newcomers to become 'Catalans by adoption'.

It was the hope of the Franco régime that the immigrants would be a fortuitous means of putting an end, once and for all, to the Catalan working-class tradition of protest and associationism, that they would carry out 'a slow but steady Castilianization from below, consistent with the industrial growth rate and speeded up by different birth rates', as was stated in January 1968 in the *Boletín de Orientación Bibliográfica del Ministerio de Información y Turismo* in a commentary on the book *Spanien heute*.

The impact of immigration on the national future of Catalonia gave rise to a long debate. A book published in 1964 aroused considerable interest. Its title was *Els Altres Catalans* (*The Other Catalans*) and it was written by Francisco Candel (himself a Spanish-speaking immigrant of the 1930s). Based on a positive attitude towards Catalan identity, it proposed an interbreeding of cultures and advocated respect for the immigrants' own values. Candel warned that the living conditions of the immigrant workers were making it difficult for them to identify with a society which they wanted to join, and finally expressed confidence that the second or third generation might well become defenders of Catalan identity.

Candel's book was praised by Jordi Pujol who, in 1958, had written that all those who lived and worked in Catalonia, and became part of the country and were not hostile towards it, were Catalans. Integration was defined as persuasive assimilation, mainly of a linguistic and cultural nature.

Manuel Cruells criticized Candel's book from a more traditional nationalist viewpoint, considering that it underrated the importance of the adoption of the Catalan language and, in his view, amounted to accepting as a permanent resident a type of immigrant who, having been uprooted from his native land, failed to make new roots in Catalonia.

Antoni Pérez, analyzing the problem in the light of the socialist positions of left-wing Christians of the time, stated in the mid-1960s that overriding importance should not be attached to the adoption of the Catalan language as part of the immigrants' incorporation into Catalan society. Pérez considered that the concept of integration was related to the desire to see the working class accept Catalan capitalist society; the true integration of immigrant workers, in his view, was dependent on progress towards an egalitarian society in which collective promotion would be possible. In 1972 Pérez went on to criticize those who stressed the cultural aspects of integration and overlooked its social dimensions, claiming that what they were proposing was individual promotion through a change of language and cultural integration.

The collective work entitled *La Immigració a Catalunya* (*Immigration in Catalonia*) (1968) reinforced the notion that integration could not be understood as straightforward assimilation into pre-existing organizations but as a process in which the host society is only one part of a whole yet to be built, a whole which cannot be identical to that which existed previously. Integration was dependent on social progress.

At this same period an attitude of widespread indifference towards the question of the Catalan language emerged. This attitude, which made virtue of necessity, accepted a situation of bilingualism, ignoring the fact that in situations where languages are in contact it is usual for one to replace the other, and that in view of the political weakness of Catalonia, the outcome was easily foreseeable. Integrationist paternalism and xenophobia disappeared and with them the habit of referring to immigrant workers by the offensive epithet *xarnego*. However, the critics of Catalan nationalism were prone to overlook the existence of many Spanish civil servants, professionals, and businessmen who came to settle in Catalonia with an arrogant, hostile attitude towards Catalan identity, and with the backing of a State that was determined to prevent the Catalan language, as the main indicator of Catalan national identity, from gaining an equal footing with the official language of Spain. Though the degree of outright violence had abated since the early years of the Franco régime, the same destructive policy towards Catalonia was maintained. Those who viewed the integration thesis as a bourgeois ploy were ignoring the fact that the Catalan bourgeoisie as a class was indifferent to the cultural integration of immigrants.

The PSUC strove in this context to avert the danger of the rise of neo-Lerrouxism. But in Marxist circles, the parallel between the Catalan language and culture and the bourgeoisie was not always avoided. The booklet *El Problema Nacional Català* (*The Problem of Catalan Nationality*), published by the Communist magazine *Nous Horitzons* (*New Horizons*) in 1961, was an attempt to make a positive assessment of the Catalan national movement from the viewpoint of the new generations of the PSUC. The idea of the 'Catalan Countries', however, was rejected as an imperialist aspiration of Catalan nationalism. Nor were the internal contradictions over the Catalan national question which had been evident in the socialist camp during the Civil War and the postwar period acknowledged; and though the work adopted with some modifications the theory of the three historical phases of Catalanism formulated by the pre-war Communist leader Joaquín Maurín, they accused its author of having led the workers of Catalonia to 'positions of a nationalist nature'.

Jordi Solé Tura's book *Catalanisme i Revolució Burgesa. La Síntesi de Prat de la Riba* (*Catalanism and the Bourgois Revolution. Prat de la Riba's Synthesis*), published in 1967, was instrumental in creating the view, at the end of the 1960s, that Catalanism was a bourgeois undertaking.[1] This prejudice sought further endorsement from the new composition of the working class in Catalonia as a result of the major wave of immigration that had taken place during the same decade. In an academic world influenced by a leftism born of May 1968, the ideas which have been referred to as 'Marxism–Lerrouxism'[2] acquired widespread currency. Some of those who expressed them would have no compunction a short time later in reacting to Catalan demands by taking up a stance in favour of self-determination.

Once the young generations had recovered from the initial impact of the discovery of Leninist theses on movements of national emancipation, the most lucid and Catalanist of the Catalan Marxists acknowledged, in the 1970s, the insufficiency and stagnation of Marxist thought on phenomena such as Catalan nationalism. Rafael Ribó, for instance, has noted the purely strategical and superficial nature of most Marxist analyses of nationalism, something which explains the vacillating and contradictory positions adopted at different conjunctures, and the tendency to consider such phenomena and the contradictions they engender as something outside the revolutionary movement, to which national emancipation is unilaterally subordinated. The solidity of the ideological background with which the Catalan communists and socialists were to face the second half of the 1970s and the transition to democracy and Catalan self-government was more apparent than real.

THE MORAL UPHEAVAL OF THE LATE 1960s

Only faint echoes of the youth revolt of 1968 reached Catalonia, which was then in the throes of a state of emergency. The situation there bore little resemblance to the events which were shaking Western countries possessed of a distinctly higher degree of political freedom and cultural and economic development. But the change in moral patterns had repercussions on a whole series of anti-Franco cultural and political institutions and organizations which, while continuing to suffer the effects of the immobilism of the régime, found themselves being challenged by their own membership. Pedagogical renewal, both in schools and in the Scout Movement, suffered the impact of non-directive education. Permissiveness clashed head-on with the conceptions of self-discipline and moral asceticism that had previously underlain Catalanist civic reconstruction. Radical communalism and feminism rejected outright the traditional family model which Catholic-inspired Catalanism saw as the basis for the regeneration of the country.

The situation of Communism was no better, with left-wing splits, the 1968 occupation of Czechoslovakia, which brought Soviet socialism into final disrepute, the mythification of the Chinese model established by Maoism, and the reappearance of Trotskyism. Adult members of the Catalan opposition to Franco found their objectives and models being questioned by the young before the régime had allowed them even to approach fulfilment. What with the Dictatorship's refusal to change and the leftist challenge born of 1968, a lasting disorder was created which would be very difficult to overcome. But numerous features of today's society also belong to the heritage of those years: the ecologist movement, built on awareness of the grave deterioration and pollution of the environment; widespread pacifism; less authoritarian relationships between adults and the young; the lowering of the age of legal majority and the voting age; the condemnation of racial segregation; the legitimation of women's liberation; less repressive sexual morality; and the acceptance of homosexuality. On the other hand, self-management, communalism, and other proposals of the time have fallen into oblivion, drowned in the conservative wave of the 1980s. And two phenomena of the 1970s were born of the frustration of the hopes of 1968: the unprecedented spread of drug addiction and the action of terrorist groups, which, both in Europe and in Catalonia, would have been unthinkable during the 1960s.

Notes

1. In 1991 Jordi Solé Tura became Minister of Culture in the Spanish government.
2. See Chapter 5.

15 The Catalan Opposition to the Franco Régime between 1962 and 1975

THE PHASES OF THE NEW PERIOD

The development of Catalan society in the 1960s and 1970s posed a serious challenge to the Franco régime. Its aim was to ensure not merely the survival of Catalan culture but its reconstruction and modernization. The opposition was successful, furthermore, in establishing areas in which collaboration between parties was possible and in creating the first large-scale organizations within the new labour and student movements. Apart from isolated events, such as the 1950 general strike, a few local or sectorial disputes, and the student meeting held in the university assembly hall in 1957, there had been no movement of sufficient scope or duration to allow the transition from clandestinity to illegality to occur. The process began in the mid-1960s and gathered strength during the declining years of the dictator and his régime.

Though all chronological breakdowns are conventional in nature, fitting certain milieux and sectors better than others, the political and cultural evolution of the opposition to Franco in Catalonia between 1962 and 1975 can be divided into three phases. The first, from 1962 to 1967, was characterized by the advent of mass movements – which, despite their size, still in fact involved only a minority of the population – in addition to rapid advances in the cultural use of the Catalan language and by growing signs of a new awareness of national oppression. During the second period, from 1967 to 1971, a new wave of oppression, the determination of the régime to continue in power, and the impossibility of forcing political liberalization all caused progress to slow down in the fields of culture and politics, both in the university and on the labour front. During these years Catalan society was also in the throes of a value crisis similar to that expressed by the 1968 generation in more developed capitalist countries. Finally, the third period, from 1971 to 1975, was marked by the gradual resumption of large-scale opposition as a result of the united impetus created by the newly-formed Assemblea de Catalunya (Assembly of Catalonia). During this period Catalonia's demands for self-government received unanimous support. Labour disputes were also increasing since, prior to the onset of the economic crisis, unemployment rates were still low and the end of the Dictatorship seemed in sight.

THE STUDENT MOVEMENT

The University of Barcelona, which had expanded slowly until 1962, doubled its student population between 1962 and 1968. The overcrowding which occurred during those six years only worsened the situation in a University which was already out of step with economic and social needs. The 1960s saw the formation of a credible student movement, endowed with considerable strength, which succeeded in setting up an independent organization, the Sindicat Democràtic d'Estudiants de la Universitat de Barcelona (Democratic Students' Union of the University of Barcelona – SDEUB), founded in the monastery of the Capuchin monks in the Sarrià district of Barcelona in March 1966. The democratization of the official SEU, in the wake of the process initiated in 1958, could be carried no further. The creation of the SDEUB meant the disappearance of the SEU. It also meant that the students, with the support of much of the teaching staff and the intelligentsia, were determined to make responsible proposals for urgent structural changes in the University. The SDEUB was founded through joint action by students belonging to various parties: the FOC, MSC, FNC, and PSUC. The last of these was the predominant force, since the influence of the Christian Democrats was steadily declining.

When the police surrounded and entered the Capuchin monastery, in a raid subsequently nicknamed 'La Caputxinada', the Catalanist cultural personalities invited by the students – among them the President of the Institut d'Estudis Catalans, Jordi Rubió, and the poets Salvador Espriu and Joan Oliver – were arrested. Predictably, the University staff who had sided with the students were also dismissed, all of which sparked off an unprecedented movement of solidarity involving not only academic circles but also the population at large and generating new forms of moral and material help to those punished.

One of the upshots of the repression of the SDEUB was a demonstration by one hundred and thirty priests and the religious in front of Police Headquarters in Barcelona in protest against the ill-treatment of a student leader who was a Communist. Policemen swinging truncheons dispersed the cassock-clad demonstrators and the scene caused such an impression that it went down in collective memories as one of the foremost events of the opposition to Franco. This demonstration, together with the 'Caputxinada' itself, are also key examples of the support given by the clergy to the fight for democracy, though in 1963 the Abbot of Montserrat, Aureli M. Escarré, had already opened fire with his statements to *Le Monde* against the Franco régime two years before he had been obliged to leave the country.

The expulsion of the sixty-nine university professors took place before the 1966 referendum on Franco's new Organic Law providing for limited political reform and the eventual transition to a monarchy. But when the referendum was over, repression became ever harsher. García Valdecasas, the Vice-Chancellor of the University, punished the whole student body by obliging them to pay their registration fees over again or miss the entire year. The Tribunal de Orden Público – a special tribunal for judging political crimes which had replaced the military courts – outlawed the SDEUB and sentenced its committee of faculty delegates to six months' house arrest. The SDEUB survived for one more year. However, like Comisiones Obreras (Workers' Commissions – CCOO) in the labour field, its strength was clearly being undermined by repression and by the situation of illegality in which it was forced to exist. It was becoming increasingly difficult to maintain a mass organization in an antidemocratic context.

In 1967, the Madrid student movement took over from that of Barcelona. When, in 1968, the Minister of Education, Lora Tamayo, fell from office after the Cortes refused a grant for the Opus Dei-controlled University of Navarre, he was succeeded by another member of the Opus Dei, Villar Palasí, who took a more liberal line. Two new so-called autonomous universities were set up, one in Madrid and one in Barcelona, and a bill to update the education system, the Ley General de Educación (General Law of Education), was tabled. The newly appointed Vice-Chancellor of the University of Barcelona and his advisers announced changes in the curriculum, cancelled the sanctions, and readmitted a faculty which had been expelled. Had these measures been taken two or three years earlier, many conflicts would have been averted. As it was, they came too late. In the interim the SDEUB had disappeared, the PSUC had suffered its most serious split of the entire Franco period, and in the 1967 student elections it had lost its majority to a coalition made up of break-away Communists, the FOC, and the university section of the group Força Socialista Federal (Federal Socialist

Force). All three organizations would subsequently be taken over by extremist elements.

An attempt was made, both in the university and in the labour field, to resolve the contradiction between the formation of mass movements and the situation of illegality in which they were obliged to move, by taking up extreme positions designed to provoke head-on clashes. The response to the new Vice-Chancellor's proposals was an assault on the University Offices in January 1969. Soon after this, the government declared a state of emergency. As a result of the defeat of the SDEUB, all forms of representative democracy and of participation in organizations representing the teaching staff had been rejected and replaced by a policy based on mass meetings and direct action. Though the new trend was reinforced by the atmosphere created by the events of May 1968 in France, the original cause was the defeat of the SDEUB, a classic students' union which had been eliminated before it had had the opportunity to compel the régime to accept it.

From 1968 onwards the student movement not only broke up into numerous extremist groups, but simply failed to understand the progressive character of the struggle against national oppression in Catalonia. At the same time, while paying lip service to the cause of labour, it became increasingly isolated from political reality and the working class. It is significant that during the early 1970s, the student movement was absent from the Assemblea de Catalunya (see below). Unlike the SDEUB, which had sought the support of Catalanist intellectuals, later left-wing student agitators were indifferent to the Catalan national problem.

In 1975, the university situation reached its lowest ebb. Following a long strike of assistant lecturers on temporary contracts, all students were awarded token 'passes' in the examinations of that year. However, the strikers had failed to achieve the changes they demanded in the selection of university teaching staff, and the régime did not dare to deduct the long strike period from their pay.

THE NEW LABOUR MOVEMENT

The fact that by 1965 Comisiones Obreras already possessed a coordinatory body at State level has led many observers to overlook the fact that the rise and consolidation of the new labour movement during the 1960s was not a uniform process throughout Spain, but took on special characteristics in Catalonia. Though some strikes had occurred, such as that in Barcelona in 1951, there was no true labour movement before the 1960s, and industrial action was initiated solely by minute underground parties. The creation of a Comisión Obrera Central de Barcelona (Barcelona Central Workers' Commission) in the parish church of Sant Medir in the district of Sants in 1964 was the result of joint action by Communist, Christian, and Socialist labour leaders. Some were elected delegates and members of works councils in the 'vertical union' – the single, compulsory union – while others held no official post. The meeting at Sant Medir was sparked off by developments in Asturias and Madrid and by local experience and events. However, the use of specific individual party initials to transmit union orders to *all* members of the association eventually brought about the collapse of the Comisión Obrera Central, which in any case only really began to operate as such in 1966, in preparation for the union elections held during those years.[1]

In Barcelona, the overall structure did not emerge as a result of Commissions existing at lower levels, as in Asturias, where there was a trend towards the formation of an alternative union opposed to the CNS (Central Nacional Sindicalista, National Union Confederation – the official name of the 'vertical union'). Nor was it the outcome of a process generated by debates over sector-based collective bargaining, as in Madrid, where there was a tendency at the time to underestimate the importance of creating an organization outside the structures of the official 'vertical union'.

The creation of the Comisión Obrera Central in Barcelona in 1964 was brought about by a joint decision which was of an eminently political nature. This was to have its advantages and disadvantages. On the one hand, there was a fuller realization of the different problems inherent in the labour situation as a whole, among them the Catalan national question, but on the other hand, ideological and strategic debates acquired undue importance. Because of this the unity of the labour movement was endangered more quickly in Catalonia, and it also led to the departure of Christian labour militants after 1965 and to a power struggle between the PSUC and the FOC.

It is worthwhile recalling at this point that the mid-1960s were not merely the time of the CCOO victory in the union elections of 1966: this was also the period of maximum growth for the JOC and ACO (Acción Católica Obrera – Catholic Workers' Action) before both organizations entered a phase of rapid decadence at the end of the decade as a result of confrontations with the Church hierarchy. It was also in the late 1960s that the boom in religious books in Catalonia came to an end, attendance at Sunday mass dropped sharply, basic communities sprung up outside the official parishes, the seminaries emptied, and many members of the clergy, starting with the most progressive among them, began to leave the priesthood. This phenomenon also occurred in other countries where State and Church were separate, but in Catalonia its sociocultural significance was greater.

The fact is that in Catalonia in the 1960s, street action predominated over activities related to collective bargaining at company level within the CCOO. Two facts prove CCOO's support for Catalonia's national demands: its participation in 1967 in events to mark the Catalan national day, 11 September (which in 1964 had been celebrated in public for the first time since 1938), and the creation of the Comissió Obrera Nacional de Catalunya (National Workers' Commission of Catalonia). This important decision helped to avert a split in the working class in Catalonia over the national question and may have been one of the reasons why no Catalan nationalist union movement was formed, in contrast to what happened in the Basque Country. The move was more pedagogical in nature, however, rather than being the expression of any well-developed Catalanist feelings among labour militants. The support given to Catalan demands should also be seen against the background of two other factors. One was the Communist tactic of seeking an alliance with the Catalanist democratic parties. The other was the fact that in 1967 the PSUC set up the Comissió Obrera Nacional de Catalunya, in which it played the predominant role, in order to make up for its replacement the same year by the FOC as the leading party in the Comisión Obrera Central de Barcelona. Even so, despite its tactical motivations, the importance of the endeavour to bring the labour movement into the struggle for Catalan self-government should not be underestimated.

The debate within the CCOO over whether the organization should be based on zones or on sectors of production was indicative of a confrontation between one group which defined it as an 'anticapitalist union', whose mission it was to change the overall living conditions of the working class, and another which perceived of it as mainly concerned with short-term conflicts on the shop floor. In an attempt to adapt the organization to the prevailing climate, the Communists defined CCOO as a 'socioeconomic movement' and thus one with links to the urban movement of *associacions de veïns* (neighbourhood associations) which was extremely active during the 1970s. The adoption of more ambitious goals than in the rest of the European union movement was an attempt, none the less, to compensate for insufficient organization and to adapt in some strange way to the lack of union rights which, elsewhere in Western Europe, had been well-established for years.

Repression, wage freezes, the renewed determination of the 'vertical union's' bureaucracy to control collective agreements, and its own internal divisions, plunged the new labour movement into a severe crisis between 1967 and 1970. Then, following the disintegration of the FOC in 1969, as a result of controversy between unionists and left-wing avant-garde elements that was both parallel and somewhat similar to the split that occurred in the PSUC, the CCOO recognized the immediate necessity of concentrating its efforts on working conditions within firms and, from 1971, under the leadership of the PSUC, it entered a new period of expansion during which it recruited new members for Catalan communism.

The Catalan Church hierarchy clearly disassociated itself from the Franco régime in the field of labour relations in 1969 when, in the wake of arguments within the Church itself (which soon brought about the decline of the Catholic labour organization), all the bishops of Catalonia, including Marcelo González, issued a statement against the union bill proposed by the régime on the grounds that it failed to guarantee full representation for the workers.

During this new phase of growth, as the end of the Dictatorship approached, there was a tendency for the new labour movement to abandon the use of general strikes as a political weapon, though general strikes based on solidarity between workers did break out at local and district level. One example was the stoppage sparked off in the Barcelona suburbs of Baix Llobregat in 1974 by lay-offs at two firms, Elsa, in Cornellà, and Solvay, in Martorell. The success of CCOO in the 1975 union elections raised the possibility of that organization's taking over the 'vertical union' and converting it into a single labour organization. However, this proposal was somewhat unrealistic, for the attempt to unite the labour movement in this way was seen by some as the imposition from above of a single union which, however representative, would be in contradiction to the union pluralism implicit in the aim of political pluralism.

THE YEARS OF THE ASSEMBLY OF CATALONIA

The four years from 1967 to 1971 were years of crisis and fragmentation for the political opposition, which was suffering the consequences of a number of adverse circumstances: repression was increasingly severe; it was proving impossible to force the régime to undertake political and institutional liberalization; the various opposition movements had emerged from clandestinity; and left-wing radicals were opposing any gradual transition to democracy. In 1967 the PSUC had suffered a major division. The MSC split up in 1968. The FOC disintegrated in 1969. And the break-up of the FNC, which took place the same year, gave rise to the Partit Socialista d'Alliberament Nacional dels Països Catalans (Socialist Party of National Liberation of the Catalan Countries – PSAN) which sought to blend separatism with Marxism. Drawing inspiration from the national liberation movements of underdeveloped countries, the PSAN wanted the Catalan countries to become a separate state as part of a socialist revolution. Though the subsequent breakaway of revolutionary groups led to a fall in membership, the PSAN played an outstanding role in the Assemblea de Catalunya.

It was in the midst of this dispersion and fragmentation that the trend towards the development of a joint policy got underway in Catalonia. Following the creation of the SDEUB, a Taula Rodona (round table) of political parties had been set up to undertake joint action based on solidarity. This body was the forerunner of the Coordinadora de Forces Polítiques de Catalunya (Coordinating Body of Catalan Political Forces – CFPC), comprising the PSUC, MSC, UDC, and ERC, which was created in December 1969, the year of the state of emergency. The parties were finding it hard to bridge the gap that separated them from the masses and to repair the bad image created by disunity and confrontation. The Coordinadora did not succeed in bringing them out of their social isolation. It was the Assemblea de Catalunya (Assembly of Catalonia), set up in November 1971 in the parish church of Sant Agustí in Barcelona, which enabled an unprecedented number of people to join in the political mobilization. Most of them did not join any party or subsequently hold any public office: instead they withdrew once the basic demands of political, social, and national freedom for Catalonia had been met.

There was nothing strikingly original about the Assemblea de Catalunya, but it was a new phenomenon supported by skilful publicity. It was no easy task to agree upon the four basic demands that would act as a common denominator: freedom, amnesty, a statute of self-government, and the coordination of the Hispanic peoples against the Dictatorship. One favourable precedent had been the successful outcome of the meeting of two hundred and fifty intellectuals held in the Abbey of Montserrat on 12 December 1970 to issue a protest to international public opinion over the death sentences handed out to six ETA militants at the Burgos trial in an attempt to stop their execution.

The Assemblea de Catalunya was not simply the sum total of the parties making up the Coordinadora which convened it: it brought together organizations as different as CCOO, Grup Cristià de Defensa dels Drets Humans (Christian Group for the Defence of Human Rights), the Assemblea Permanent d'Intel · lectuals (Permanent Assembly of Intellectuals) born at the Montserrat meeting, Comunitats Cristianes de Base (Basic Christian Communities), Assemblea Permanent de Capellans (Permanent Assembly of Priests), delegations from certain professional associations and, later on, neighbourhood associations from the industrial working-class suburbs. Its dynamism was described by one of its leading personalities, Agustí de Semir, as essentially different from that of any organization based on compromise, and it succeeded in surmounting the barriers of underground action and taking up a stance of defiant illegality. Its action spread beyond the city of Barcelona, to which opposition had hitherto been largely confined. Delegations were set up in over forty Catalan localities, in most of which anti-Francoism had previously had little weight because of the much more difficult conditions which hampered its development in smaller towns.

The arrest of one hundred and fourteen members of its standing committee in the parish church of Maria Mitjancera in Barcelona in 1973, and sixty-seven more at a meeting held in a school belonging to the Escoles Pies religious order in Sabadell in September 1974, slowed down the activity of the Assemblea de Catalunya but did not halt it. This was due, not merely to the likelihood that the end of the régime was in sight after the assassination of the dictator's successor Admiral Carrero Blanco in December 1973, but to the participation of large numbers of ordinary citizens, drawn by the simple programme proposed by the Assembly. Many people identified with the objectives it pursued: political freedom, labour rights, total amnesty for political prisoners, the coordination of all the peoples of the peninsula in favour of democracy – with an implicit ambiguity as to the type of political régime – and a last objective which, in 1971, seemed the most Utopian of all, since it appeared unlikely that it would be part even of a post-Franco liberalization: the provisional re-establishment of the Catalan Statute of 1932 'as a step towards the full exercise of the right to self-determination'. The fact that the Assembly printed 20,000 copies of each of its leaflets gives some idea of the extent of its influence.

While some members of the Assembly saw it as a tool whose validity would cease to exist once political parties were legalized, others believed it should continue to play its part until the objectives laid down in 1971 were fully attained, including the disappearance of the previous régime and the establishment of democracy. In the end, the former opinion predominated over the latter. Even the PSUC, which was initially among the most intransigent, would later endorse the first option. Since the Assemblea de Catalunya did not aim to 'overthrow the Dictatorship' but to ensure that, once the Dictatorship finally came to an end, democracy was not suppressed, the outcome was predictable.

During the last years of Franco's life, the situation in Catalonia was markedly different from that in the centre of Spain: calls to mobilize roused a greater response from the Catalans. The Left was stronger and less divided in Catalonia. In the centre of Spain, liberal, social democrat, and Christian democrat groups were not so active and commanded less support than in Catalonia, where even the Communists and Socialists recognized their electoral potential and social base. It is particularly important to stress that the creation of a united opposition had advanced much further in Catalonia. Whereas the Assemblea de Catalunya was created in 1971, the totally inadequate Junta Democrática de España (Democratic Council of Spain) set up by the Communist Santiago Carrillo and the independent Rafael Calvo Serer, did not appear until July 1974, while the rival organization, the Plataforma de Convergencia Democrática (Platform of Democratic Convergence), made up of the PSOE and the Christian Democrats, was not formed until June 1975, and the two formations did not merge until March 1976.

The predominant party in the Assemblea de Catalunya was the PSUC, but it would be a mistake to consider the Assembly a mere tool of the Catalan Communists. Their influence was due to a variety of factors. The CCOO was able to provide large numbers of marchers for the demonstrations called by the Assembly. For instance, the SEAT motor company strikers formed the largest contingent in the most important of these demonstrations held on 1 May 1973 in Sant Cugat del Vallès. The PSUC was also the only party which could offer the Assembly a certain infrastructure, though the services rendered by some Catholic organizations and the discreet grants made by Jordi Pujol's group should not be overlooked. Other parties with a promising future ahead of them, such as the Socialists and Convergència Democràtica de Catalunya, were still at the organizational stage. Convergència Socialista de Catalunya

(Socialist Convergence of Catalonia – CSC) was born in July 1974 but did not become a party until 1976. Convergència Democràtica de Catalunya (Democratic Convergence of Catalonia – CDC) was founded in November 1974 but was not considered a party until the end of 1975. Finally, Marxism was still the anti-Francoist ideology *par excellence*, despite the disrepute of the Soviet model following the 1968 intervention in Czechoslovakia and the crisis of Leninist doctrine which was undermining the foundations of Communism. The PSUC succeeded at this time in assimilating rival left-wing groups or sweeping them along in its wake. One significant case was Bandera Roja (Red Flag), set up in 1968 to bring left-wing splinter groups together, some of whose members joined or returned to the PSUC in 1974, becoming leading figures and standard bearers of Eurocommunism. Though Eurocommunism was well-suited to the unitary needs expressed by the Assemblea de Catalunya, it became apparent, once the constitutional régime was established, that Eurocommunist revisionism was causing an identity crisis in Catalan Communism, which until then had been dazzled by the example of Italy. By adopting a democratic path to socialism, like the former social democratic movement, Eurocommunism was obliged to share the same political space as the Socialists, who in Catalonia were still defining themselves as Marxists. The bulk of the potential electorate would eventually be drawn towards the Socialists, who were the main beneficiaries of the climate created by the Assemblea de Catalunya. In those days, CDS was considered more nationalist than CDC and was in favour of the construction of Spanish Socialism on a confederal basis.

That the Assemblea de Catalunya imposed conditions and limits on the predominance of the PSUC is clear from one fact: the PSUC had to give up the idea of extending the Juntas Democráticas promoted by Carrillo and Calvo Serer to Catalonia. The Assembly was critical of the inadequate approach of the Junta Democrática to the Catalan nationalist question and remained the only joint opposition front in Catalonia. In so doing, the Assemblea de Catalunya encouraged the PSUC to retain its autonomy *vis-à-vis* the PCE.

Immediately after the death of Franco in November 1975, the Consell de Forces Polítiques de Catalunya (Council of Political Forces of Catalonia), in which the Communists and Socialists were in a minority, was set up. From then on the initiative shifted away from the Assemblea de Catalunya and towards the established political parties, though in 1976 the Assemblea de Catalunya was still organizing some of the largest demonstrations in its history, and in the same year labour disputes reached even higher levels than in 1975.

In Madrid the political crisis caused by the death of the Dictator was solved by the succession of his outworn administration by one which looked to the future, and which would later be endorsed by the electorate. Once all the parties had been legalized and the constituent Cortes had met, a united opposition was no longer vital: all that was needed was consensus with the government. In Catalonia, however, it was not merely the succession of the Franco régime that was at stake but the creation of a new Catalan administration with autonomous power. Consequently, the unity of the opposition had to be reinforced, even though such unity could not last indefinitely, since social and ideological differences in Catalonia could not remain dormant for long.

Note

1. The workers periodically elected their delegates at company level, though the top leaders of the vertical unions, whose membership included both employers and workers and which prohibited strike action, continued to be trustworthy Francoists who kept the structures of the single official union under their control.

16 Catalonia during the Transition to Democracy and Self-government

TOWARDS THE VICTORY FOR SELF-GOVERNMENT IN THE 1977 ELECTIONS

Catalonia and its demands attracted considerable attention on the Spanish political scene after the death of Franco, much as they had in the early 1930s, during the last years of the reign of Alfonso XIII and the first years of the Second Republic. All Spanish political forces, both those who supported a gradual transition to democracy and those in favour of an outright break with the past, had to define their position on the 'Catalan problem'. Catalonia, where society had taken a clear stance to the Franco régime and where the opposition had been united within a single organization with great powers of mobilization, could not simply be ignored.

Neither the promise of decentralization made by Arias Navarro, who was Prime Minister at the time of Franco's death, nor the plan for a Consejo General de Cataluña (General Council of Catalonia), similar to the 1914 Mancomunitat, drawn up by the then President of the Diputació of the province of Barcelona, Juan Antonio Samaranch,[1] succeeded in neutralizing the Catalan movement. The giant demonstrations that took place in Barcelona during the first three months of 1976 proved these proposals to be unviable. The government of Adolfo Suárez, who took over from Arias Navarro in July 1976, had to tolerate a turnout of 100,000 people in Sant Boi de Llobregat on 11 September. By this time, however, the initiative had passed from the Assemblea de Catalunya to the political parties and the goal of abolishing the previous régime had been replaced by negotiation with Suárez.

During 1976, several events gave Catalanists cause for satisfaction. *Avui (Today)*, the first daily paper in the Catalan language since the Civil War, was able to start publication. The first Catalan language radio station, Ràdio 4, began broadcasting. The Institut d'Estudis Catalans was officially recognized. In December 1976 Joaquim Viola was replaced as Mayor of Barcelona by Josep M. Socías Humbert, a product of the 'vertical union' but who was nevertheless willing to negotiate with the neighbourhood associations and appease rebellious municipal employees.

It was important to restore peace in municipal affairs because Suárez wanted to postpone the local elections until after the general election so as to keep the whole process under better control. He succeeded in doing what the Monarchy had failed to do in 1931: municipal elections were not held until two years after the first general election and, indeed, after the new Constitution had been approved and the second legislative elections had taken place.

The Suárez government also managed to persuade the last Cortes elected under the Dictatorship to approve the Ley de Reforma Política (Political Reform Bill), thus making the transition from the Franco régime to a totally different system possible without any institutional break. The democratic opposition was in favour of such a break, or *'ruptura'*. This would have amounted to submitting the Monarchy to a plebiscite and holding the non-reformist leaders of the former régime responsible for their acts. It therefore called on voters to abstain in the referendum held to endorse the Political Reform Bill. However, 69 per cent of the Catalan electorate voted in favour of the bill, and abstention, though higher than in the rest of Spain, was only 26 per cent. The opposition gave up its fight for a *'ruptura'*, and was content with a negotiated change-over, or *'ruptura pactada'*, without challenging the Monarchy or demanding a purge.

Suárez legalized the democratic unions, the PCE and the PSUC and, when already in government, formed the coalition which later became a political party. Known as Unión del Centro Democrático (Union of the Democratic Centre – UCD), it was made up of former reformist supporters of the Dictatorship and anti-Franco Christian Democrats. The opposition forces had prevented the survival of the corporativist dictatorial régime, but had failed to overthrow Francoism itself, and this proved to be the nature of the whole process.

In the general election held on 15 June 1977, the first democratic elections for forty years, the governing party was victorious, winning 35 per cent of the votes in Spain as a whole. The PSOE emerged, some considerable distance behind with 29 per cent, as the chief opposition party. The PCE won only 9.1 per cent of the votes, while Alianza Popular (Popular Alliance – AP), headed by Franco's former Minister of Tourism and Information, Fraga Iribarne, won 8.2 per cent. In Catalonia, however, where UCD lost and the elections were won by the Left, a different party system took shape. Furthermore, the 1977 elections in Catalonia turned into a plebiscite on the restoration of self-government in which 75 per cent of the electorate voted for autonomist parties, 50 per cent of them casting their votes in favour of the Socialists or Communists. In the congressional elections, the coalition formed by the Partit Socialista de Catalunya (Congrés) and the Catalan federation of the PSOE carried off 28 per cent of the votes, followed by the PSUC with 18 per cent (double the number won by the PCE elsewhere in Spain), while the Pacte Democràtic de Catalunya (Democratic Pact of Catalonia), an alliance headed by Jordi Pujol's CDC, obtained 17 per cent, practically drawing even with UCD. Alianza Popular barely obtained the 3 per cent it needed to secure one seat, while ERC, in an alliance with the Partido del Trabajo (Workers' Party), came sixth behind the Christian Democrat coalition. The senatorial elections, where the majority and not the proportional system was in force, were won by the coalition made up of Socialists, Communists and ERC, and a few independents.

The defeat of his party in Catalonia obliged Suárez to negotiate. Though the Assemblea de Parlamentaris (Assembly of Parliamentarians), made up of the Catalan senators and deputies, had the full backing of democratic election results, power was still entirely in the hands of the government, which had been legitimated by the same election in most of the rest of Spain. A tussle ensued between Josep Tarradellas, the President of the Generalitat in exile in France, and the Catalan parliamentarians for control of the negotiations with the Suárez government. As a result, the latter was able to neutralize the combined threat of nationalist demands and left-wing domination by negotiating directly with Tarradellas, instead of dealing with the leaders of the Socialist and Communist parties who had won the elections. In this way the creation of true self-government was delayed. Tarradellas travelled to Madrid on 28 June 1977 and then returned to France. The standing committee of the Assembly of Parliamentarians was left with no choice but to support the negotiations undertaken by Tarradellas who, like Suárez, had succeeded in skilfully playing on the rivalry between the main Catalan parties. None of these, however, was truly hegemonic since the electoral supremacy of the Socialists was offset by the larger membership and greater union influence of the Communists.

THE PROVISIONAL GENERALITAT

On 29 September 1977 a decree was issued establishing a provisional Catalan autonomous government and on 23 October Tarradellas returned to Barcelona as President of the Generalitat. For the time being he controlled only the Diputació of the province of Barcelona which, according to the programme drawn up by the Catalanist parties, was to disappear, along with the other Catalan provincial Diputacions. Tarradellas appointed an executive council including Socialists, Communists, members of the Pacte Democràtic, and UCD. In 1978 the Catalan language became a compulsory subject in Catalan schools and the first agreements were reached for the transfer of power from the State to the Generalitat.

During the period of Tarradellas' provisional rule, which lasted a little over two years, the still weak Generalitat was not governed by the Socialists and Communists, who were strong in Catalonia but comparatively weak in Spain. This discrepancy between social influence and political power undermined the strength of the Generalitat while the new Statute of Self-government was under discussion, despite the consensus between the PSC, the PSUC, and CDC. Defections and disillusionment would gradually reduce the vitality of Socialists and Communists.

In 1978, attention centred on the debate over the Constitution, upon which the Statute of Self-government depended. The commission responsible for drawing up the Constitution included Miquel Roca Junyent of CDC and Jordi Solé Tura, then of the PSUC. The 1978 Constitution, after affirming the 'indissoluble unity of the Spanish Nation, the common fatherland of all Spaniards', for the first time included a timid acceptance of the plurinational nature of Spain by recognizing the existence of various 'nationalities and regions' and presenting the outline of a future 'State of Autonomous Communities', more akin to a single decentralized model of government than to the federal solution preferred by the Catalanist parties. In 1984, for instance, only 5 per cent of the revenues of the State were transferred to the autonomous communities, whereas in federal states the percentage is usually around 50 per cent. The inviolability of the division of Spain into provinces and the wide range of matters reserved to the exclusive jurisdiction of the central government prefigured the narrow limits that would be imposed on the Catalan Statute. The State of Autonomous Communities caused Catalans to fear that, by granting self-government to regions where the demand for such status was not sufficiently deeply rooted, the central government was seeking to cut down the scope of Catalan self-governing powers, though the formula also had the advantage of not making Catalan and Basque self-government into isolated exceptions. It seems that the subsequent disintegration of UCD was affected by centrifugal tendencies and by the far-reaching repercussions of certain poor results in regional elections in the wake of the new division into self-governing communities.

After the approval of the Constitution a new Catalan Statute of Self-government was drawn up by a commission of the Assembly of Parliamentarians of Catalonia who met in Sau in June 1978. In December, the draft statute was presented to the Congress. The text took into account the terms of the Constitution, so this time the Catalan Statute could not be cut down in the light of provisions subsequently laid down in the Constitution, as had occurred in 1932. However, in the arduous negotiations in Madrid, the Catalan parliamentarians had to make numerous concessions. The provincial Diputacions and the civil governors were maintained and the post of Delegate of the Central Government in Catalonia was created; the Generalitat's 'exclusive' jurisdiction over education was replaced by the dangerously ambiguous expression of 'full' jurisdiction; the transfer of public order to the Generalitat had to be dropped, and the Catalan government was empowered only to set up its own police force; the State retained the administration of the national insurance scheme and the right to appoint the members of the Tribunal Superior de Justícia de Catalunya (High Court of Justice of Catalonia); and the criterion governing the percentage of State revenues that was to revert to the Generalitat was reduced. CDC was in favour of a system of economic agreements similar to that granted to the Basque Country, but the PSC was against.[2] The co-official status granted to the Catalan language fell short of the exclusive official status proposed. Thus legal sanction was given to a situation of bilingualism which was unfavourable to the status of the Catalan language, since knowedge of Spanish was obligatory in Catalonia while knowledge of Catalan was not.

Because of these amendments, which were accepted by all the Catalan parliamentarians with the exception of Heribert Barrera of ERC and the independent J. M. Xirinachs, it was not possible to consider the 1979 Statute as more favourable to Catalonia than that of 1932, which all the Catalanist parties had considered inadequate in 1977. The Catalan government had more extensive jurisdiction over education and the communications media than in 1932, and knowledge of Catalan in schools was guaranteed, but in the areas of justice, public order, and local administration the Generalitat was given distinctly inferior powers to those conferred in 1932. Furthermore, the maintenance of provincial Diputacions and civil governors duplicated the functions of the Generalitat, interfered between the latter and the boroughs, and hindered the division of Catalonia into the smaller natural territorial units known as *comarques*.

On 25 October 1979, the Statute of Self-government was ratified by the Catalan people in a referendum. The turnout, however, was a disappointing 59.6 per cent.

Some months earlier, in April 1979, the first municipal elections had taken place, immediately following the second general election held in March. The latter had produced the same balance of forces in Catalonia as in 1977, though the electoral base of UCD was reinforced. CDC had shifted from the social democrat position of its previous alliance with the Partit Socialista de Catalunya-Reagrupament, headed by Josep Pallach (who died in 1977) to a position closer to the centre as a result of its new and lasting alliance with the Catalan Christian Democrat party, Unió Democràtica de Catalunya. The latter, in order to avoid being absorbed by UCD, had to form an alliance with CDC, and the coalition took the name Convergència i Unió (Convergence and Union – CiU). Meanwhile the three existing socialist groups had united on 16 July 1978 to form the Partit dels Socialistes de Catalunya (Party of the Socialists of Catalonia – PSC) with Joan Raventós, the former leader of the Catalanist MSC, as its Secretary General. The new PSC formed links with the PSOE, though it initially appeared to have preserved a considerable degree of autonomy.

In the municipal elections of April 1979 the Socialists and Communists became the predominant forces in Barcelona and in thirty-four of the thirty-eight Catalan cities with over 20,000 inhabitants. Twenty-one mayors belonging to the PSC–PSOE were elected and thirteen belonging to the PSUC. For two years the difficult task of rebuilding the ramshackle municipal administrations was dependent on the Pacte de Progrés (Pact for Progress) signed by the PSC, PSUC, CDC, and ERC. According to the terms of this pact, in the absence of an overall majority the first candidate on the party list that had obtained the largest number of votes would become mayor, and consensus was to guarantee the governability of the borough councils. The outcome of these first municipal elections placed the Diputacions in the hands of parties which had stated their wish to abolish them. The wealthiest, that of the province of Barcelona, was controlled by the Socialists, as was that of Tarragona, while Girona was won by CiU, which would later gain control of all the Catalan Diputacions, except that of Barcelona.[3]

Following the first municipal elections, defection and apathy grew more acute. The neighbourhood and professional associations lost their leaders, who had been elected to the borough councils where they devoted their efforts to rebuilding local government with somewhat limited resources and not always with the necessary training. The left-wing parties, who had lost their aura of Utopianism after the concessions they made to the so-called *poders fàctics* (essentially the armed forces and the banks), helped to deprive civil society of some of its drive and tended to monopolize the representation and management of social groups and the community at large. This trend was anything but beneficial to Catalonia which needed precisely the opposite: to continue to develop all the social energies which had enabled it to survive the Franco régime and were now of crucial importance in building a national plan that would be attractive to the majority of the population.

DEMOBILIZATION AND UNEMPLOYMENT

Another factor that contributed to apathy and defection was the economic crisis and the rise in unemployment which undermined solidarity. The strategy of the left-wing forces had been conceived for a prosperous Catalonia with full employment, in which social mobility would facilitate the integration of Spanish immigrants and the participation of the working class. The crisis was more severe and long-lasting in Spain than in other Western European countries on account of the delay in applying economic policies based on austerity and the reduction of dependence on outside sources of energy. The UCD governments were not strong enough to impose the necessary measures because their energies were devoted to calming agitation and overcoming the legitimacy crisis which affected the State during the period of transition. Unemployment gave rise to disappointment and undermined factors conducive to integration into a Catalan national plan. It also produced a rapid decline in union membership, which, after the 1977–78 boom, began to drop until it reached one of the lowest rates in Western Europe. Nowadays, fewer than 10 per cent of wage-earners in Catalonia are union members. The emerging underground economy offset the social repercussions of the crisis at the price of destroying solidarity, creating disloyal competition, endangering jobs, and leaving many workers defenceless.

From the outset, Catalan employers rejected the creation of an autonomous Catalan labour organization for independent action, contributing instead to the establishment of state-wide organizations and opposing the creation of a specifically Catalan framework of labour relations. They feared the intervention of a possible Socialist and Communist-dominated autonomous government and the greater power of the labour movement in Catalonia. Major employers were also confident that centralization would give them better control. The unions in Catalonia were already affiliated to Spanish federations, both the predominant CCOO and the smaller UGT, and they took the same line as the employers.

The lack of enthusiasm of Catalan employers for self-government explains their mistrust of CiU, though they eventually concluded that the consolidation of the Catalan nationalist coalition was the only way to contain the rise of Socialists and Communists. The relations between the employers and the first parliamentary government of the Generalitat under CiU were not devoid of tension, however. The weakness and isolation of the strictly Catalan unions should be highlighted in contrast with the existence of major Basque national union organizations which operate alongside the Spanish unions but independent of them.

Notes

1. Samaranch, who had occupied the quasi-ministerial post of National Sports Delegate under Franco, was appointed in 1977 Spanish ambassador in Moscow. He later became Chairman of the International Olympic Committee, a post held until recently. For years he has also been the chairman of the leading Catalan banking organization, the Caixa de Pensions.
2. Under the agreement enjoyed by the Basque Country, tax revenues are initially at the disposal of the Basque government. The latter periodically negotiates the sum it is to pay the central government, instead of receiving a fraction of the taxes paid to the State.
3. The newly elected municipal councils elect the deputies of each provincial Diputació.

17 The Development of Catalan Self-government from 1980 to 1990

THE NEW CATALAN PARLIAMENT AND THE FIRST GOVERNMENT OF JORDI PUJOL

The first Catalan elections, held in March 1980, brought about a change in the internal correlation of political forces. Convergència i Unió[1] became the leading minority party, with 27.7 per cent of the votes, followed by the PSC–PSOE with 22.3 per cent, PSUC with 18.7 per cent, UCD with 10.5 per cent and ERC with 8.9 per cent. CiU had won over part of the former UCD and ERC electorate. It had also taken a number of votes from the PSC, and the Catalan Socialists suffered too from the abstention of certain voters who backed the PSOE in general elections. One negative factor for the new self-governing Catalonia was the fact that voter turn-out in regional elections was lower than in Spanish general elections.

Since 1977, CDC had gradually toned down its nationalist and social reformist policies. Following the unification of the socialists, CiU accused the Catalan Socialists of subservience to the Madrid-based PSOE, a charge they hoped would enable them to capture the part of the nationalist vote held by the PSC. In the 1980 Catalan elections, some voters opted for parties they perceived of as being more Catalan, i.e. those that were independent of Spanish parties. This trend was detrimental to the PSC and UCD and favourable to CDC and, to a lesser extent, to ERC. Furthermore, the Fomento del Trabajo Nacional viewed Jordi Pujol, the leader of CDC and of the CiU coalition, as a lesser evil than a Catalonia governed by Socialists dependent on Communist support.

The task of developing self-government and creating the government machinery of the new Catalan autonomous administration (or Generalitat) required consensus and a strong majority government. Jordi Pujol offered to form a coalition government with the PSC but, after internal discussions, the PSC turned down the offer. Had the Catalan Socialists agreed to enter the government of the Generalitat, their own distinct identity might have become blurred and they might have lost prestige to the PSUC which would then have formed the opposition. On the other hand, they would have made the new Catalan administration their own, and in conflicts with the central administration they would have been up against UCD governments. Their refusal to enter the Catalan government placed them in an equally difficult situation. The Generalitat had little power – at most it was a power to be built up – and thus little opposition could be offered it; and each time the PSC did oppose it, it was accused by CiU of indirectly supporting the central government and failing to cooperate in the development of self-government. The Socialist opposition, not unnaturally, was weak. For instance, the PSC did not support the motion of censure brought by the PSUC against the CiU government in 1982 and they refused to back Josep Benet as the Communist candidate for the presidency of the Generalitat against Jordi Pujol. Having established the PSC as the weak opposition to a weak power, Jordi Pujol's administration was able to reap all the benefits of launching a self-governing system which, by 1982, had succeeded in having 80 per cent of the powers attributed to it by the Statute of Self-government transferred from Madrid.

But its internal fragility prevented the PSC from governing alongside CiU in 1980. At its second congress, held soon after the Catalan elections, the PSC almost split up. Raimon Obiols and the unitary wing, which presented itself as more Catalanist and had the backing of the central PSOE leadership, defeated the Spanish nationalist wing, which presented itself as more labour-oriented.

The CiU government, with the support of the Socialists, had a law passed by the Catalan parliament to strip the four Catalan provincial Diputacions of their powers. The Suárez government in Madrid appealed to the Constitutional Court, which decided in favour of the central government. This delayed the new territorial division of Catalonia into the smaller natural regions or *comarques*.

Jordi Pujol's was a minority administration which needed the votes of ERC and the UCD in order to govern, and it was no easy task to reconcile three such widely divergent points of view. ERC gained nothing from the support it gave the Pujol administration since, in the following regional elections, some of its supporters decided to vote directly for CiU rather than for ERC. Since the Suárez government also needed the backing of the CiU deputies in the Spanish Congress (either in the form of votes or abstentions), the UCD and CiU agreed to support one another, a system that had some beneficial results for the Generalitat.

But the economic crisis was worsening. The UCD was disintegrating and Suárez had to resign; acts of terrorism had claimed two hundred victims in 1979 and 1980, one hundred and seventy-four of whom were attributed to ETA, the Basque terrorist organization; and a military plot was brewing. On 23 February 1981 members of the Spanish parliament and the new UCD government headed by Leopoldo Calvo Sotelo were held captive in the Congress building by Antonio Tejero and two hundred Civil Guards, while in Valencia General Jaime Milans del Bosch declared a state of war. The coup failed, but from then onwards there was talk of 'democracy under surveillance', the first consequence of which was an attack on the self-governing communities.

The Calvo Sotelo government reached an agreement with the PSOE over a new law known as the LOAPA (Ley Orgánica de Armonización del Proceso Autonómico – Organic Law for the Harmonization of the Process of Self-government). The LOAPA limited the areas under the exclusive jurisdiction of the self-governing communities and marked the beginning of the retrieval of powers by the central government, a trend which posed a severe threat to Catalan self-government. Before the LOAPA was promulgated, a manifesto was issued under the title *Por la igualdad de los derechos lingüísticos en Cataluña* (*For equal language rights in Catalonia*). Signed by some 2300 supposed intellectuals and civil servants resident in Catalonia, this document claimed that the Spanish language was in danger there and that the policy of giving Catalan official-language status discriminated against the Spanish-speaking population. The response was mass mobilization, supported by 1300 different organizations under the leadership of La Crida a la Solidaritat en Defensa de la Llengua, la Cultura i la Nació Catalanes (Appeal for Solidarity in Defence of the Catalan Language, Culture and Nation, popularly known as 'La Crida'). The campaign culminated in a rally on 24 June 1981 at the Camp Nou stadium of the Barcelona Football Club and a giant demonstration against the LOAPA on 14 March 1982. Thereafter La Crida ceased to be a unitary platform and became a tool of separatist groups.

The LOAPA put the Catalan Socialists in a very embarrassing position and caused acute tension within the party. Ernest Lluch, the PSC spokesman in the Congress, refused to present his group's amendments to the LOAPA and was dismissed, followed by Eduardo Martín Toval and Joan Prats. In an effort to avoid a split or a confrontation with the PSOE, the PSC remained on the sidelines. But its credibility as a Catalanist party had been undermined.

THE DECLINE OF THE COMMUNISTS AND THE CiU-PSC TWO-PARTY SYSTEM

At the same time, the PSUC was also undergoing a scission that was to deprive it of the position it had gained on the Catalan political scene. The growth of the PSUC in 1975 and 1976 had been due less to its Communist identity than to the fact that it had succeeded in situating the struggle for democratic and national liberties within its own historical context, to such an extent that some people were unable to envisage Catalan autonomy without Marxist predominance. Eurocommunism enabled the PSUC to rid itself of the shackles of Stalinism and the tarnished image of the Soviet model, but it failed to offer any new theoretical approach. Leninism and the dictatorship of the proletariat were a hindrance when it came to winning votes, yet the Leninist principal of democratic centralism remained untouched.

The more lucid Catalan Marxists have acknowledged the inadequacies and stagnation of Marxist ideas when applied to national movements. Some years ago the Communist Rafael Ribó remarked that most Marxist analyses of nationalism have been purely strategic in character and that there is no overall dialectical study of the matter. This accounts for the vacillating, contradictory positions taken up by Marxism at particular conjunctures, as well as its tendency to consider nationalism and the contradictions it engenders as something outside the revolutionary movement itself. In subordinating the national emancipation of one's own – or someone else's country – to the triumph of socialism or the working class, and at the same time denouncing the weak theoretical foundations of Catalan nationalism, Marxism apparently assumed that the concepts of socialism, the working class and the labour movement were unequivocal, whereas in terms of precise present-day phenomena they are just as problem-ridden and raise just as many questions as the concept of nation itself.

It has often been said that the action of the PSUC and PSC averted the danger of Lerrouxism (see Chapter 6) and prevented Catalan society from splitting into two separate communities, made up of native-born Catalans and immigrants and their descendents respectively. There can be no question that the Catalanism of Communists and Socialists in Catalonia did much to encourage immigrant workers to support self-governing Catalonia, thus preventing the establishment of cross-bred alternatives like the Partido Socialista de Andalucía (Socialist Party of Andalusia – PSA), which had two deputies in the first Catalan parliament. But this factor was only one among many others and its influence should not be overestimated, any more than it should be forgotten that Lerrouxism has also frequently been avoided at the cost of rather less emphasis on the outward and visible signs of Catalan national identity.

The fall-off in union membership weakened not only CCOO but the PSUC itself. In a situation of economic crisis, the PSUC found itself divided between those who felt the effects of the recession and those who did not. The intervention of Santiago Carrillo, the General Secretary of the PCE, in the affairs of the PSUC whenever there were signs of internal tension belied the apparent independence of the Catalan party from the PCE, whose leadership seemed determined to impose a single Eurocommunist line throughout Spain. In fact since Leninism had been revised and discarded the PSUC had come to occupy the same political space as the Socialists, but the latter had the advantage of not having to get rid of a useless tradition and of being in a position to free themselves much more easily of Marxism.

While Carrillo's attempts failed, they undoubtedly had an effect on the crisis within the PSUC. Eurocommunism was defeated at the PSUC's sixth Congress in January 1981 and a new party leadership was formed without Gregorio López Raimundo and Antoni Gutiérrez. However, the PCE vetoed the agreement and Antoni Gutiérrez got ready to return to his post as General Secretary of the PSUC, which he succeeded in doing in March 1982, following the split caused by the expulsion of the 'pro-Soviets', as the Eurocommunists called their adversaries. With the creation of the Partit dels Comunistes de Catalunya (Party of the Communists of Catalonia – PCC), the scission became a reality. But the return to the original orthodoxy brought no solution. The PCC was unable either to benefit from the fall of the PSUC or to compete against it. In the 1989 general election, the PCC won only 1 per cent of the votes as against 7.2 per cent for Iniciativa per Catalunya, the coalition headed by the PSUC (see below). The Communist identity crisis continued to worsen, aggravated by the fact that a vote for the PSC-PSOE was considered a 'useful vote' and by the disintegration of the PCE itself, and some of the leading Eurocommunists, including Solé Tura, went over to the PSC–PSOE.

The disastrous results of the PSUC in the 1982 elections led to the resignation of Antoni Gutiérrez and his replacement by Rafael Ribó who, in 1987, with the support of the left-wing nationalists, set up the coalition Iniciativa per Catalunya (Initiative for Catalonia – IC). In view of the overall crisis of European Communism, already revealed in the change in the name and symbols of the Italian Communist Party, the mere reunification of the Catalan Communists seems unlikely to provide a solution. If Iniciativa per Catalunya is to constitute a third option, alongside CiU and the PSC, it must become something more than a pact based on mutual convenience. But while Rafael Ribó seems to be making a genuine attempt to turn IC into something new, of which Catalan nationalism is an essential ingredient, Julio Anguita, the present Spanish Communist leader, still sees Izquierda Unida (United Left – IU) as a reconstituted PCE and demonstrates on occasions that the endorsement of the nationalist cause in Spain was a tactic adopted by the Communists during the transition in order to benefit from the pro-democratic energies of Spain's historic nationalities.

In the October 1982 general election, the break up of the PSUC caused the majority of former Communist voters to opt for the PSC. Indeed it seemed, in that election, that following the collapse of the UCD,[2] the only way to avert a new military coup was to bring the PSOE to power. The 1982 general election produced the highest voter turn-out in Catalonia of the entire period, comparable only to the first democratic elections of 1977. It was too early in 1982 for CiU to reap the benefits of the downfall of UCD, the immediate beneficiary being the right-wing Alianza Popular. But CiU considerably bettered its score over what it had achieved in the previous general election in 1979.

The results of the 1982 general election provided confirmation of one of the trends in electoral behaviour in Catalonia: part of the electorate tended to vote for different parties at different levels of government. Whereas in elections to the Catalan parliament, it favoured parties it perceived as more Catalan, that is, more independent of Spanish parties, in general elections it opted for parties that existed throughout Spain which had a better chance of influencing the central government machinery or of forming a government.

The previous multiparty system in Catalonia was giving way to a system based on two forces – PSC and CiU – tending to play the predominant role in state-wide and strictly Catalan elections respectively. It is possible to detect the existence of a group of voters who support state-wide parties in general elections and abstain in Catalan elections, a habit that is particularly harmful to the PSC–PSOE, while another group votes for CiU in Catalan elections and for state-wide parties, especially PSC–PSOE, in general elections. And finally there is a smaller group, concentrated mostly in the industrial belt around Barcelona, which votes for a variety of parties in the general elections and for the PSUC in municipal elections.

Between 1983 and 1986, CiU launched the Partido Reformista in an attempt to find a way out of this situation and provide itself with a Spanish partner with whom to create a political centre space for opposing the PSOE in the rest of Spain. The resounding failure of this operation, known as the Roca Operation because it was promoted by Miquel Roca i Junyent, a leader of Convergència Democràtica de Catalunya, revealed not only the difficulty of reconstructing the political centre in Spain, which was largely occupied by the PSOE, but also of doing so from Catalonia, since other Spaniards rejected Catalan leadership. Despite this, the electoral base of CiU has gradually increased in each successive general election.

Thus Catalonia has no single hegemonic party. The power of CiU is limited by the fact that it does not control the Barcelona City Council or the Barcelona provincial Diputació. The influence of the Socialists is similarly restricted by the failure of that party to win a majority in the Catalan parliament or to win the presidency of the Generalitat. Nor is the fact that the PSOE holds the reins of central-government power much consolation, since the latter tends to negotiate directly with the CiU government of the Generalitat, bypassing the PSC. Thus both the leading Catalan parties are in a position of forming the government in some institutions and the opposition in others. Despite the disadvantages of this situation, it has reinforced the pluralist outlook of the Catalans, which was in any case already much greater than elsewhere in Spain.

In the aftermath of the Socialist landslide victory in the 1982 general election, some Catalan Socialist leaders entered the Spanish central government. The Mayor of Barcelona, Narcís Serra, became Minister of Defense while Ernest Lluch was appointed Minister of Health. At the same time, some forty top officials of the PSC were given key posts in the central administration. However, there was certainly no Catalan take-over in Madrid, and the novelty of the presence of Catalans in the Spanish government has done nothing to reduce the restrictive attitude of the State regarding the self-governing communities. The first instance of this was the appeal launched by the central government against the Llei de Normalització Lingüística (Law of Linguistic Normalization), a moderate piece of legislation designed to guarantee the public use of the Catalan language which had received the unanimous approval of Catalan parliamentarians – including the Catalan Socialists – in July 1983.

In the 1983 municipal elections, Pasqual Maragall, Serra's successor at the head of the Barcelona City Council, was re-elected, and his authority grew still further when Barcelona was chosen in October 1986

TABLE 17.1   Election results in Catalonia in general (Gen.), Catalan (Cat.), and European parliamentary elections (Eur.): percentages of votes and voter turnout

	Gen. 15–6 1977	Gen. 1–3 1979	Cat. 20–3 1980	Gen. 28–10 1982	Cat. 29–4 1984	Gen. 22–6 1986	Eur. 10–6 1987	Cat. 20–5 1988	Gen. 29–10 1989	Cat. 15–3 1992
Turnout	79.3	68.5	62.1	80.7	64.2	69.9	68.5	59.4	67.7	55.0
PSC	28.4	29.2	22.3	36.5	30.2	40.6	37.2	29.6	35.3	27.3
PSUC	18.2	17.1	18.7	4.6	5.6	3.9	5.4	7.7	7.2	6.4
ERC	4.5	4.1	8.9	4.0	4.4	2.7	3.7	4.2	2.6	8.0
PDC	16.8	–	–	–	–	–	–	–	–	–
CiU	–	16.1	27.7	22.2	46.6	31.8	28.1	45.4	32.5	46.4
UC–DC	5.6	–	–	–	–	–	–	–	–	–
UCD	16.8	19.0	10.5	2.0	–		–	–	–	–
CDS	–	–	–	–	–	4.1	5.8	3.8	4.2	0.9
AP/PP	3.5	3.6	2.3	14.5	7.7	11.3	11.3	5.3	10.5	5.9

PSC: Partit dels Socialistes de Catalunya. In 1977 there was only an alliance between Partit Socialista de Catalunya (Congrés) and the Catalan Federation of the PSOE.

PSUC: Partit Socialista Unificat de Catalunya. In 1982 the Partit dels Comunistes de Catalunya (PCC) broke away. In 1986 the PSUC formed an alliance with left-wing nationalists which took the name of Unió d'Esquerra Catalana. In 1987 it became Iniciativa per Catalunya, an alliance between the PSUC, PCC and Entesa dels Nacionalistes d'Esquerra. In 1989 the PCC on its own obtained 1 per cent of the votes.

ERC: Esquerra Republicana de Catalunya. In 1977 this party formed an alliance with the Partido del Trabajo in the Congressional elections and with the PSC–PSOE and PSUC in the elections to the Senate.

PDC: Pacte Democràtic de Catalunya (Reagrupament), an alliance between Convergència Democràtica de Catalunya, Partit Socialista de Catalunya (Reagrupament), Esquerra Democràtica de Catalunya, and Front Nacional de Catalunya.

CiU: an alliance between Convergència Democràtica de Catalunya and the Christian Democrat Unió Democràtica de Catalunya.

UC–DC: Unió del Centre i la Democràcia Cristiana, an alliance between Centre Català and Unió Democràtica de Catalunya.

UCD: Unión de Centro Democrático.

CDS: Centro Democrático y Social, a party created by Adolfo Suárez in 1982 with part of UCD.

AP/PP: Alianza Popular, headed by Manuel Fraga Iribarne. After the replacement of its leader, the organization was restructured and took the name Partido Popular.

The elections to the European Parliament took place in 1987 on the same day as the municipal elections.

TABLE 17.2   Results of the municipal elections in Catalonia, in percentages of votes and turnout

	1979	*1983*	*1987*
Turnout	60.9	67.9	68.5
PSC–PSOE	26.6	39.4	37.1
PSUC	20.2	11.2	10.3
ERC	3.8	2.8	2.4
CiU	18.6	24.9	32.5
UCD–CDS	13.3	–	3.1
AP	1.3	9.2	5.7

TABLE 17.3   Number of municipal councillors elected in Catalonia by the two main political forces

	1979	*1983*	*1987*
PSC–PSOE	950	1739	1707
CiU	1765	3328	4365

to host the 1992 Olympic Games. However, the 1983 elections also saw a rise in the total number of municipal councillors belonging to CiU, owing to the nationalist coalition's greater hold over small and medium-sized boroughs. By 1987 CiU, which in 1979 controlled only the Diputació of Girona, had won those of all the Catalan provinces except Barcelona following its gains in the municipal elections, which are the basis for elections to the Diputacions.

In the 1984 elections for the Catalan parliament, CiU won a major victory, securing an overall majority in the parliament. Since 1978 the PSC, like Jordi Pujol and the PSUC, had abandoned the principle of national self-determination for Catalonia, but from 1983 onwards the PSC not only gave up Catalan nationalism, which it had previously claimed as its own, but began to give it negative connotations by attributing it to CiU, thus opening the way for the CiU to claim a monopoly over it. In the face of the onslaught against self-government much of the electorate felt that a majority in the Generalitat should be given to the political force that seemed best equipped to put up resistance. It should also be observed that the 1984 regional elections were held at a time when the economic policy of the PSOE government, which was unavoidably harsh as a result of the delayed Spanish reaction to the crisis of the 1970s, had not only failed to keep the promise made in 1982 to create new jobs, but had generated a rise in unemployment. Since there was no appreciable difference between CiU and the PSOE in terms of social and economic policy, the key issue in the 1984 elections was the threat to self-government, which was to the advantage of CiU.

The 1982 victory of the PSOE had increased the influence within the PSC of those who wished to focus the campaign on anti-Pujolism giving it ambiguous anti-nationalist connotations in the hope of finally winning the support of Socialist voters who tended to abstain in regional elections. Not only did this fail to occur, but CiU succeeded for the first time in 1984 in capturing the votes of a small but significant proportion of the Spanish immigrant population. Ever since a verdict produced by the Constitutional Court in 1983 against a considerable part of the LOAPA, the 'syndrome' generated by that controversial law continued affecting the PSC. What is more, in 1984 CiU succeeded in capturing former UCD voters from AP and took over part of the former nationalist electorate of the PSUC. While in other parts of Spain the PSOE had grown towards the centre, in Catalonia the centre was occupied by CiU, which could expand to the right without losing its centre-left voters.

While all this was happening, many Catalan banks were falling victim to the economic crisis, among them the most important, Banca Catalana. This marked the failure of one of the prime objectives of the 1960s and 1970s – that of making Catalan financial capital independent of the great Spanish banks. After a series of traumatic events, Banca Catalana was to finish up in the hands of Banco de Vizcaya. Immediately after the 1984 Catalan elections, an attempt was made to incriminate Jordi Pujol – one of the former heads of Banca Catalana – for supposed irregularities which had occurred in the bank prior to the crisis. Before the Barcelona regional court decided in November 1986 not to bring charges against Pujol over the Banca Catalana affair, a large sector of Catalan public opinion considered that their leader was being made the victim of a political campaign by the PSOE government designed to undermine the authority of the President of the Generalitat.

The Spanish theory that Catalonia had fallen into the hands of the reactionary right-wing was belied by the result of the referendum on continued Spanish membership of NATO. When the last UCD government had decided to take Spain into the Atlantic military alliance, the PSOE had opposed the step in the name of neutrality and disarmament, but once in power the PSOE saw a connection between continued Spanish presence in NATO and membership of the European

TABLE 17.4   Results of referenda in Catalonia in percentages of vote

		Yes	No	Blank etc.	Turnout
Political reform	(15 December 1976)	93.4	2.1	4.5	74.0
Constitution	(6 December 1978)	90.5	4.6	4.9	68.1
Statute of self-government	(25 October 1979)	88.1	7.8	4.1	59.6
NATO	(12 March 1986)	43.6	50.7	5.8	63.0

Community, which Spain had joined in 1986. The extent of the opposition to its pro-Atlantic policy led the government to hold a referendum in March 1986. The outcome was favourable to the government throughout Spain, except in Catalonia, the Basque Country, and the Canary Islands. While the PSC was obliged to recommend its supporters to vote for the government, CiU failed to take a clear stand, leaving its voters free to choose, while the PSUC and the left-wing nationalists headed the opposition against continued Spanish membership of NATO, a position that won many more votes in Catalonia than had been cast by Communist supporters.

The pro-European tradition had deeper roots in Catalonia than in most other parts of Spain. The result of the referendum showed that many Catalans made a clear distinction between Europeanism and a policy of confrontation between rival blocs, despite the fact that a negative vote had no prospects as a viable alternative.

FROM THE LONG CRISIS TO THE ECONOMIC RECOVERY OF 1985

Spain's entry into the European Community in 1986, the favourable international situation, and the public works projects needed to provide the infrastructure for the Barcelona Olympics brought about a revival of the Catalan economy, which in 1985 began to emerge from the long crisis that had affected its structure and undermined its position within the Spanish economy.

Between 1960 and 1973, the average cumulative growth rate of Catalonia's GDP had been 8.4 per cent, as against the Spanish average of 7.6 per cent. Following the first rise in the price of oil, investment began to fall off in 1973, and a ten-year recession set in. At the same time there was a move towards technological modernization, matched by a steady rise in unemployment.

Between 1973 and 1979, the Catalan GDP increased by an average of only 2.7 per cent per annum – similar to that of Spain – but between 1979 and 1985 growth fell to 0.7 per cent, below the Spanish average of 1.4 per cent. Unemployment in Catalonia soared from 8.9 per cent in 1979 to 22.8 per cent in 1985, above the Spanish average of 21.9 per cent for the same year, and well above the 8 per cent average for the EEC.

Then, in 1986, increased productivity and investment brought a rise in Catalonia's rate of economic growth, which reached 4 per cent in 1986 and 5 per cent in 1987, exceeding the corresponding rates for Spain in both cases. By 1989 the Catalan unemployment rate of 11 per cent was well below that of Spain as a whole (16 per cent). Instead of aiming at rationalization or substitution, as previously, investment was designed at stepping up production capacity, and Catalonia ranked first among the self-governing communities of Spain for the volume of foreign investment received, absorbing one-third of the total amount of foreign capital invested in Spanish firms.

In 1990, the deceleration of the economy and signs of a new crisis began to threaten its recovery as Catalonia approached the threshold of full integration into the European Community in 1992, a challenge which further increases its dependence on the world economy.

In 1991 industrial growth in Catalonia was less than 1 per cent. The North-American recession and the Gulf War had harmful effects. Unemployment rose to 12 per cent in Catalonia as compared to 16.4 per cent in the rest of Spain. Internal investment came to a halt and only foreign investment continued, and this mainly in the financial and property sectors. Recovery seemed to depend essentially on a lowering of interest rates.

THE PROGRESS OF CATALANIZATION

Considerable progress has been made over the past fifteen years towards linguistic 'normalization', that is, the return of the Catalan language to normal usage in all spheres, which is a key feature of overall cultural normalization. In 1987 only 9.7 per cent of the population of Catalonia still did not understand Catalan: 90.3 per cent understood it, 64 per cent could speak it, 60.5 per cent could read it and 31.5 per cent could write it. Data from municipal censuses held in the province

TABLE 17.5   Knowledge of the Catalan language in the province of Barcelona, in percentages of the population

	Do not understand Catalan	Understand it	Speak it	Write it
1975	25.7	74.3	53.1	14.5
1986	11.0	90.3	59.3	30.1

of Barcelona (the province with the greatest proportion of Spanish-speaking immigrants) reveal striking changes between 1975 and 1986 (see Table 17.5).

The percentage of the population able to understand and write Catalan has risen sharply. The existence of Catalan television and the increased presence of the language in public life have contributed to progress in aural comprehension. In 1985 only 60 per cent of Spanish-speaking inhabitants of Catalonia were regular viewers of TV3 – the Catalan-language television channel run by the Catalan government – but by 1990 the proportion had risen to 90 per cent. The audience of Catalan-language radio stations showed similar increases. The marked rise in the ability to write Catalan was due to the fact that Catalan is now taught in the schools and used as a medium of instruction, though it still has far to go before it is on an equal footing with Spanish as a language of instruction. Progress in the field of oral expression is considerably less because a change in communication habits requires the individual to take the more difficult step of changing linguistic codes. The type of instruction given in schools is still generally unconducive to reinforcing the command of Catalan of pupils whose mother-tongue is Spanish.

Another factor, of a political nature, should be mentioned in this respect. Whereas knowledge of Spanish is legally defined as a duty, knowledge of Catalan in Catalonia is only a right. Bilingualism would not be a negative factor if it were as widespread among the Spanish-speaking population as it is among Catalan speakers. As a result of the different status the two languages have held over a period of many years – and still have today – Catalan speakers tend to switch languages when addressing Spanish speakers, even though the latter may have been living in Catalonia for years and can understand Catalan. A survey carried out in 1989 at the Universitat Autònoma de Barcelona, where 85 per cent of the student population was born in Catalonia and 55 per cent of the parents of these same students are Catalan-speaking, provides an illustration of this: while 60.8 per cent of the lectures and classes in the University were given in Catalan, 82 per cent of the staff who teach in Catalan still answer in Spanish when addressed by students in that language in class. In a conversation between equals, language switching is even more frequent.

Official use of the Catalan language has spread, although in certain areas such as the legal system the introduction of Catalan has proved much more difficult. Colloquial use of Catalan by Spanish speakers, on the other hand, has advanced much less, and this is one of the explanations for the relatively small progress achieved by the Catalan language press. The existence of the four daily newspapers which are published in Catalan – two in Barcelona, one in Girona, and another in Manresa – is still somewhat precarious. The five Spanish-language dailies published in Barcelona, including the local edition of a Madrid paper, have a combined circulation of 346,000, as against 56,000 for the Barcelona Catalan-language papers which together account for only 15 per cent of the total. To this figure must be added the 17,000 copies of the Catalan-language dailes published in Girona and Manresa and the 14,000 copies of two other dailies published in Lleida and Tarragona respectively, which are partly in Catalan and partly in Spanish. In 1986, one hundred and fifty-five magazines of various types were being published in Catalan, while fifty-six more used different proportions of Catalan alongside Spanish.

The number of books published in Catalan has been rising steadily, both in terms of copies printed and of titles available. In 1963, two hundred new titles were published in Catalan; by 1968 the figure had reached five hundred; and in 1977 it was 918, or 3.7 per cent of the total number of new titles published in Spain and 9 per cent of those published in the Catalan-speaking regions. In 1980, 1496 new books were produced in Catalan, 5.3 per cent of the total for Spain. In 1986 the number was 3754, or 10.2 per cent of the Spanish total of 36,912 works, which also included three hundred and nine in Galician and four hundred and eighteen in Basque. The 4145 books published in Catalan in 1987 brought the number of new titles per year in Catalan to four and a half times what it had been ten years earlier.

Over a hundred public and private radio stations are currently broadcasting in Catalan. Catalunya Ràdio, created in 1983, now enjoys the highest audience in Catalonia of any UHF/FM station. The Catalan government-owned television channel TV3 also began broadcasting in 1983, while Televisión Española's Channel 2 regional service to Catalonia stepped up the number of hours in Catalan. Television programmes in Catalan have played a prime role in reinforcing the national identity of the country's inhabitants, though foreign productions dubbed in Catalan far outnumber home-produced programmes.

In a Europe whose creativity has been waning over the past few years under the onslaught of American songs, films, and television series, the transition of Catalan culture from the phase of recovery to that of expansion was bound to come up against problems, particularly since the public has become more demanding now that the days of mere cultural resistance are over. The production of Catalan films and records is very low, as is that of other sectors which are dominated by multinationals or concentrated outside Catalonia for reasons related to the capitalist economy and official grant money. Even so, the symbols of Catalan identity have been reinforced during the last decade, a fact which causes surprise among most foreign visitors. Not only are many signs now written in Catalan but the vitality of popular festivals is playing a prime role in integrating the population into Catalan culture. One example is the success and proliferation of local teams of *castellers*, who compete with one another to build daring human pyramids, and whose popularity has now spread over a much larger area than that around Valls and Tarragona where they originated. Another very recent phenomenon, whose potential importance has been compared with the Nova Cançó movement of the 1960s, is the resounding success of Catalan rock groups, whose members write the words to their own songs.

THE OBSTACLES TO CATALAN SELF-GOVERNMENT

Even so, serious difficulties still lie in the way of the development of Catalan self-government. Interference from the central government, which establishes principles and regulates basic matters in all areas, has considerably reduced the legislative and self-governing powers of the self-governing communities, giving rise to a host of appeals to the Constitutional Court. The ambiguity of the texts of the Constitution and the Catalan Statute of Self-goverment, and the different conceptions of self-government held by the central and regional governments respectively, have led the Spanish Constitutional Court to play what is probably a more important role than any other comparable court in the legal system of the State. Between 1981 and 1988, the State filed about a hundred appeals alleging unconstitutional action by the Catalan Generalitat and the latter filed one hundred and thirty-nine against the

State. The peak was reached in 1986, with nineteen appeals by the State and thirty-one by the Generalitat. The number subsequently declined, though more through weariness than as a result of any satisfactory agreement.

The ruling given by the Constitutional Court in overthrowing the LOAPA in 1983 pointed out that the State did not need to resort to a Law of Harmonization since it could attain the same objective by means of the *leyes de bases* (basic laws) over which it holds the sole prerogative. Since then the State has succeeded, with the support of the Constitutional Court, in gradually undermining the jurisdiction of the self-governing communities through the widespread use of the *leyes de bases* whose function is not to establish general guidelines for the self-governing communities, but to define matters reserved to the State on account of their importance, the precise degree of importance being determined by the central government itself. Objective legal studies have reached the conclusion that, in view of the shape being taken at the present time by the so-called *Estado del las autonomías* (State of self-governing communities), the actual self-governing capacity of the communities is more an unfulfilled objective than a reality.

This situation has often led the Socialist and Communist opposition in Catalonia to accuse the Catalan government of 'victimism', that is, of accusing the central government of obstructionism in order to conceal its own inefficiency. It is true that the new autonomous administration has sometimes lacked the necessary imagination and energy to deal with the social, cultural and economic problems of the country and has mirrored certain defects of the central administration, such as excessive bureaucratization, routine, and *clientelismo* (governing in the interests of political supporters). But the action that can be taken by the Catalan government in day-to-day affairs is limited, and citizens tend to see it as a body with little effect on their everyday problems.

Disenchantment with the development of self-government has led to the appearance of a radical type of nationalism unconnected with the small extra-parliamentary groups which had previously seemed to monopolize it. Catalonia has no separatist party, like Herri Batasuna in the Basque Country, that is able to win votes in elections. Nor has terrorism in support of the separatist cause succeeded in taking root in Catalonia, where it has met with almost unanimous rejection. But the depenalization of the aspiration to independence, the search for a new concept of independence amid the sweeping changes of the contemporary European scene, and the attempt to map out a plausible non-violent path towards the liberty of Catalonia as a nation, are features of a new radical form of Catalan nationalism which, for the time being, is not identified with any one party.

The unimpressive electoral results of ERC – the most nationalistic of the parties with parliamentary representation – are frequently invoked by the parties that share political power in Catalonia as an indication that if the voters did not agree with the policy pursued respectively by CiU and the PSC, ERC would win more votes. However, since the first Convention for National Independence, held in Barcelona in March 1987, a group of influential independent intellectuals have lifted the taboo that previously surrounded the repressed wish for independence.

In an economically unified Europe, Spain is no longer the protected market of Catalan industry, and in a Spain that is part and parcel of the European Community the danger of military coups seems a thing of the past. A survey carried out in Catalonia in 1988 indicated that 44.8 per cent of the respondents would answer 'yes' to an imaginary referendum on gradual progress towards independence. Among native Catalans the proportion was 60 per cent, while among Spanish immigrants it was a surprisingly high 33 per cent. Another survey published in the *Diari de Barcelona* on 23 April 1988 yielded similar results.

On 12 December 1989, at a time when the Spanish government's support of the concept of self-determination in the unification of Germany and the progress of the Baltic republics of the former USSR towards self-determination seemed to be viewed with approval in Spain, and especially in Catalonia, the Catalan parliament passed a resolution declaring that 'observance of the Constitution does not imply the Catalan people's renunciation of self-determination'. The PSC voted against the resolution and members of the Partido Popular (Popular Party – PP, the right-wing successor of Alianza Popular) were absent from the Chamber. The Spanish government reacted with threats. But the resolution subsequently proved to be a gesture with no further consequences, and the strategy of CiU has not changed. Radical nationalism still affects only a minority and for the time being has no bearing on the electoral process.

The shortcomings that have marked the development of self-government have led to a debate on the reform of the Catalan Statute of Self-government. However, the Catalan parties which exert the greatest responsibilities and influence are reluctant to engage in this process since it would involve some degree of reform of the 1978 Constitution. Jordi Pujol considers that the pact underlying the 'State of self-governing communities' has not been fulfilled and that the struggle to secure its implementation must go on. It is clear, none the less, that if the pact has not been enacted it is because of its ambiguities. The Catalan Socialists, for their part, launched a proposal for the federalization of Spain without constitutional reform, a formula they claim would put an end to the perpetual strife between the State and the Generalitat which they see as beneficial to CiU and harmful to themselves, since they are caught between two fires. But aside from the fact that the PSOE is against federalism, some nationalists also believe that the historic nationalities might be in greater danger in a more uniform, federal Spain, than in a State like the present one comprising different levels of self-government. ERC is in favour of the reform of the Statute of Self-government while the Communists are not against it.

In the short term, however, both ERC and the PSUC aspire to making Catalonia into a single province in order to abolish the present four provincial Diputacions, thus pulling the carpet from under civil governors and the provincial delegations of the Spanish ministries. The functions of the Diputacions may well soon be limited in any case by the Consells Comarcals (regional district councils) set up under the Llei d'Ordenació Territorial (Law of Territorial Organization) which was passed by the Catalan Parliament in April 1987. This same law abolished the Corporació Metropolitana de Barcelona which had brought together twenty-seven boroughs comprising half the population of Catalonia. The Consells Comarcals are also a means towards decentralization.

In 1990, the correlation of internal and external forces hardly seemed more favourable than it was in 1978–79 to the reform of the Statute of Self-government: on the contrary, it would be no easy matter to achieve a consensus among Catalan parties such as existed at that time. There have been signs of a closening of positions between the PSC and CiU since the 1989 general election at which, for the first time in any election, CiU obtained more votes in the city of Barcelona than any other party, though its advance was due more to the decline of the Socialists than to its own gains. The prestige of the Spanish central government, however, both at home and abroad, was at that time higher than in 1978. The old illusion that the Spanish Left was better disposed towards Catalan self-government than the Spanish Right had vanished. The strength of the PSOE government was undoubtedly waning after so many years in power, but the break with the UGT and the general strike declared by the UGT and CCOO on 14 December 1988 failed to change the balance of forces in the 1989 general election, aside from the votes the PSOE lost to Izquierda Unida. In the last general election of June 1993, the PSOE lost its overall majority in the Spanish parliament. It therefore found itself obliged to come to an accommodation with the Catalan and Basque nationalist MPs in order to be able to continue in government. The self-governing communities – the Basque Country excepted – have not acted with the expected degree of political autonomy. The participation of Catalan ministers in the central government and Catalan intervention in a Spanish party like the PSOE have had no impact on self-government, and the failure of the attempt to create a Spanish party with Catalanist support – the Partido Reformista – has dispelled all hope of backing from the rest of Spain.

At the end of the Franco régime, the prestige of assimilatory Spanish nationalism was low. But a powerful form of Spanish neo-nationalism has emerged, purified by the baptismal waters of democracy, liberated from feelings of guilt, and clad in progressive garb. This new Spanish nationalism, expressed through the Madrid press and the central administration, pursues the same objectives as its predecessor.

However, before attempting to overcome the ambiguities of the Constitution and the Statute of Self-government, Catalonia's priorities must be to build up her strength on the home front, to show clearly and visibly the authority of the Generalitat by means of the Catalan police force, to promote Catalonia's international relations and her presence abroad, and to work for the establishment of a single province. She must Catalanize education, respond efficiently to the problems of her citizens, pursue a cultural policy based on authenticity rather than ostentation, and avoid bureaucratization and opportunism.

The elections for the Catalan parliament in March 1992 produced a significant increase in the nationalist vote since ERC, proposing independence by peaceful democratic means, succeeded in almost doubling the number of its members of parliament from only six to eleven, and thus became the third most powerful party in the Chamber, above Iniciativa per Catalunya and the PP. The rise of ERC was not at the cost of the ruling CiU coalition which was able to regain its absolute majority with 46.4 per cent of the votes cast and the addition of one seat. Having managed to pick up votes in the industrial suburbs of Barcelona, CiU came close to the figures obtained by the PSC and produced better results than Iniciativa per Catalunya in that area.

The increase of votes for CiU and ERC represented a weakening in the vote for parties with connections with the Spanish State, except for the PP. The PP kept its vote and actually gained one seat, rising from six to seven members of parliament, but even so it was relegated to bottom place in the parliament. The PSC lost two seats despite its excellent electoral campaign and being able to capitalize on the Olympic Games. Iniciativa per Catalunya, directed by the PSUC, also lost two seats, falling from nine to seven. IC in 1992 was unable to attract the votes of Socialist defectors, which was what the campaign set out to do.

The drop in the number of votes cast, calculated at 55 per cent, did not affect either radical or willing-to-compromise nationalism, but it did affect the PSC and IC, both of which lost votes in the suburbs and surrounding districts of Barcelona where abstention was highest.

In March 1992, Jordi Pujol was elected to a fourth consecutive term of office after twelve years as President of Catalonia.

Although it is a very positive element, political stability in Catalonia cannot by itself solve all the difficulties. It is not normal in a country like Catalonia for 45 per cent of its citizens to be so indifferent to self-government that they do not even bother to vote, either because they think the government is incapable of sorting out the problems that worry them or because they are disillusioned with it. Pragmatism as a main line of policy can produce apathy. Such a high rate of abstention would be of less concern in a country with more sovereignty of its own than Catalonia, but Catalonia needs much determination and conscious participation on the part of citizens of all types if she is to solve her problems without giving up her identity in the harsh political rat-race.

Apart from observations of this kind, prompted by the present situation (Spring 1994), it is still too early really to gain a balanced view of what the last sixteen years have actually meant for Catalonia and its nationalist movement.

AGAINST THE BACKGROUND OF EUROPE

Certain features of the present European scene may prove beneficial to Catalonia as a nation. Among these are the slow weakening of the role of States and their assimilatory nationalisms and the entry into the European Community of Eastern European countries with experience of the perils of Jacobinism (provided always that their transformation is brought to a successful conclusion). For the time being, however, we still find ourselves in a Europe of States rather than a Europe of

Peoples based on nations and regions. The surrender of State sovereignty to the European Community has not brought with it the participation of political regions in the overall destiny of Europe consistent with the future of its peoples. The Europe of political regions, in which Catalonia would have a role to play, remains to be built.

Certain facts appear to deny the great hopes that Catalanism had put in the European movement. In the 1987 elections to the European Parliament, Spain was made into a single political unit and the Spanish government turned down the possibility of considering the self-governing communities as separate electoral elements.

Direct contact with Europe and European unity itself was a factor for renovation and emancipation for the Catalan national movement over many years, a factor towards enabling Catalonia to escape from gradual absorption by Spain. The effects of the loss of cultural creativity in Europe are now being felt in a Catalonia that has succeeded in slowing down the denationalization process but must go on to the more difficult phase of creation in order to continue to exist in its own right.

In a European Union that is now caught up in the task of redifining its own nature, its position in the world, and its future projects, at a time when the Single Act of 1992 seems more a part of yesterday than of tomorrow, stateless nations like Catalonia are becoming increasingly marginalized. The Europe of the Twelve affords such nations no political channels for defending their identity and it may be that, instead of seeking associations with regions, they should be building alliances with small independent nation states which are justifiably apprehensive of the absolute dominion of the larger states.

But Europe's own cultural identity is in crisis. A syncretic European culture, derived fundamentally from American mass culture and conveyed through the mass media, is emerging, and this culture, among other things, is having a destructive effect on national cultures, a process whose consequences are especially harmful to those cultures which lack State support. Europeans now see the authentic forms of culture of the various European countries as exotic, while jazz and rock are viewed as universal.

The nation-state is undergoing a crisis of structure, but no substitute for it has yet been found as a means of 'nationizing' individuals and converting them into citizens. By mythifying the nation, states have been able to ensure that the inhabitants identify themselves as citizens of the State, thereby creating a basic social cohesion and a certain rationalization of social and political action. This, however, applies only to those who are fortunate enough to belong to the nation singled out by the State, and not to members of nations that have come to be considered hindrances to be suppressed by it. Formal democracy has been founded on the nation-state and, despite the latter's obvious decadence, no alternative framework has yet emerged to replace it. Up till now, cosmopolitan ideologies have always served the influence of a particular nation whose objectives were presented as universal.

Progress towards European unity cannot ignore the problem of collective identity, which is basic to the personalization of individuals. The solution – though it may today appear Utopian – lies in the dissolution of the conventional nation-states, nearly all of which are in fact plurinational, and in the reconstruction of the historical territories of nations, based on their languages. Failing this, the future of the civic values engendered by Europe hangs in the balance, and all that will remain will be a common market, governed by transnational companies and a European bureaucracy, and devoid of democratic parliamentary control. Europe no longer rules the world. If Europe is to be reconstituted, priority must be given to the cultural values of territorial communities with a language of their own over the expansionist, authoritarian values of State nationalisms which cannot serve as a foundation for a politically united Europe.

The European Union was conceived of as an ideal bound up with democracy and a sense of solidarity and egalitarian reconciliation among the states of Western Europe, eschewing all notions of rivalry and hegemony in the wake of the two European wars that had become World Wars.

Following the disappearance of internal trade barriers in 1993 the next objective is monetary union, and this in turn means the acceleration of economic integration within the parameters of the most developed of the twelve countries of the Union, with a consequent threat to the less developed of them. For this reason, forced integration could have the effect of dismemberment of the Union. There is so far no agreement about whether this process will be favourable or unfavourable to the Catalan economy.

For its true legitimation, economic union requires political unity and for this it will be necessary to solve the problem of the democratic shortcomings that the construction of Europe has brought with it. The European Parliament is at last to receive some powers of control, but the political regions that now possess full and/or delegated powers can have no more than an ornamental role to play in it, in spite of the fact that it is they who are a stronger driving force in the unification of

Europe than the bureaucracies of the central states themselves. The unity of Europe is, in fact, devoid of a democratic basis and it denies the regions and the nations with political autonomy, like the German *länder* for example, the right to participate in dialogue within the political and administrative areas in which they possess their powers. The German *länder* have already warned that they are not prepared merely to use their powers as rubber-stamps for Brussels, without entering into some sort of dialogue on the issues. European political unity cannot be based on a uniformist Jacobin model, the only one in existence until the Second World War except for the German federal model. If this last may be seen as no more than partially valid in that it applies to one single nation, then it follows that it will be necessary to adopt the model of the Swiss confederation, which is able to accommodate within itself communities that are patently different from each other.

The end of the Communist régimes in Eastern Europe has given rise to centrifugal currents in Western Europe, despite the fact that the EFTA countries wish to participate in the customs union, and this cannot but have political implications. Some maintain that the present structure of the institutions of the European Community, already difficult enough to run with twelve nations, will not be viable with twenty-three. Meanwhile the countries of Eastern Europe are also knocking on the door.

The European Community had to accept the reunification of Germany, justified though it was, as a *fait accompli* and as a sort of referendum about self-determination that moved frontiers and altered a *status quo* that until then had been considered untouchable. On the other hand, the European Community refused to recognize the same right of self-determination for Slovenia and Croatia. This reluctance has cost many thousands of lives and much destruction, for indirectly it encouraged military action by the Serbs. In the end, under German pressure, the European Community was forced to recognize Slovenia and Croatia, and a doctrine was cobbled together which was also valid for the nations of the former Soviet Union, today known as the CIS. And so the right of self-determination, thought of after the Second World War as something that applied only to the world outside Europe, is once again applicable in Europe itself. Certain governments like the Spanish and the British have already declared that they will use their veto to prevent the recognition of new states within the existing European Community. But the divisions in Belgium and the renewed vigour of Scottish nationalism are now clearly a part of the Western European scene. And the civilized divorce of Czech from Slovak could be an example of the kind of common sense that we have not seen in Europe since Norway acquired its independence peacefully in 1905.

The European states have lost sovereignty, and common or shared sovereignty seems to be the only effective way of maintaining what is left of it in the face of the only surviving superpower and against the unilateral economic onslaught of Japan. The meaning of sovereignty is different today from what it was a few decades ago. But that is no argument for the European Community's denying nations like Catalonia, the Basque Country or Scotland the amount of sovereignty necessary to make the self-government they already have efficient self-government within an association of states that hardly seem to be losing political strength, given that in Western Europe the public sector accounts for between 40 per cent and 50 per cent of their GNP.

A Europe of regions is not a Europe of tribes. It is a Europe of units that each gives cultural identity to the citizens of a world that is otherwise a mass, standard world. At all events the tribal way-of-being that threatens the European ideal is that of the old nation-states that took up arms to impose their will and deny collective rights to peoples who had individual identities and were clearly different, for these are the real wealth of Europe and only become problems if they are turned into vestigial pieces of folklore. Many thought this is what the nations tied to the Russian Empire and to the extinct USSR were!

The end of the threat of nuclear disaster and the old Iron Curtain has presented Europe with a whole series of new challenges to which technocratic pragmatism has no answer. Decentralization was forced on highly centralist states by reason of the inefficiency of public administration when faced with wider responsibilities. The Brussels administration cannot but follow the same road.

Catalonia is now an encouragement and a stimulant for other European peoples. Instead of looking outside for a model to follow the Catalans have to build and set in motion their own model.

Only as a normal nation can Catalonia contribute to the difficult construction of Europe, and Europe today needs all the contributions it can get. It is not the old ex-imperialist State apparatuses, but nations and peoples, both with and without states of their own, that have most interest in building the united Europe which yet remains to be defined.

Notes

1. CiU, an alliance comprising Convergència Democràtica de Catalunya (Democratic Convergence of Catalonia – CDC) and Unió Democràtica de Catalunya (Democratic Union of Catalonia – UDC).

2. Unión de Centro Democrático (Democratic Centre Union – UCD), which played a decisive part in the transition to democracy, failed to become a party with a clearly defined orientation and to overcome internal divisions caused by the diverse origins of its members, as well as suffering from opportunism and the lack of a clear leadership. It split up as a result of internal divergences among possible allies in a parliament in which it did not command an overall majority. In January 1981, its leader Adolfo Suárez resigned. He had part of the financial sector and many top army officers against him. Leopoldo Calvo Sotelo was chosen as his successor and the unsuccessful coup of February 1981 took place in the midst of the UCD crisis. Calvo Sotelo was unable to contain the split. Following poor results in the regional elections in Galicia and Andalusia, the Social Democrat wing approached the PSOE, while the Conservative wing made overtures to Alianza Popular, and Suárez himself left UCD to found a new party, Centro Democrático y Social (Democratic and Social Centre–CDS).

Further Reading in English

(A full chapter-by-chapter bibliographical essay of works in Catalan, Spanish and French is to be found in the Catalan and Spanish editions of this book.)

Alba, V., *Catalonia: a Profile* (London, 1975).

Allison Peers, E., *Catalonia Infelix* (Liverpool, 1937).

Amelang, J. S., *Honored Citizens of Barcelona: Patrician Culture and Class Relations, 1490–1714* (Princeton, NJ, 1986).

Arnau, J., and H. Boada, 'Languages and School in Catalonia', in *Journal of Multilingual and Multicultural Development* (Clevedon, Avon, 1986).

Azevedo, M. M., 'The Reestablishment of Catalan as a Language of Culture', *Hispanic Linguistics*, II (1984).

Azevedo, M. M. (ed.), *Contemporary Catalonia in Spain and Europe* (Berkeley, CA, 1991).

Balcells, A., 'An Example of the National History of a Stateless Nation: Catalonia', in *Conceptions of National History: Proceedings of the Nobel Symposium, 78* (Berlin, New York, 1994).

Balfour, S., *The Remaking of the Spanish Labour Movement: Social Change, Urban Growth and Working-class Militancy, Barcelona 1939–1976* (London, 1987).

Bisson, T. N., *The Medieval Crown of Aragon: A Short History* (Oxford, 1986).

Boyd, A., *The Essence of Catalonia: Barcelona and its Region* (London, 1988).

Brenan, G., *The Spanish Labyrinth* (Cambridge, 1969).

Carr, R., *Spain 1808–1939* (Oxford, 1966).

Carr, R., *Modern Spain 1875–1980* (Oxford, 1980).

Case of the Catalans Consider'd, The (London, 1714) (facsimile ed. and trans into Catalan by M. Strubell, Barcelona, 1992).

Catalan Statute of Autonomy, The, 3rd edn (Generalitat de Catalunya publ., Barcelona, 1987).

Connelly Ullman, J., *The Tragic Week: A Study of Anticlericalism in Spain, 1875–1912* (Harvard, 1972).

Corbella, J. M., *Social Communication in Catalonia* (Generalitat de Catalunya publ., Barcelona, 1988).

Deplorable History of the Catalans, The (London 1714) (facsimile ed. and, trans into Catalan by M. Strubell, Barcelona, 1992).

Elliott, J. H., *The Revolt of the Catalans: A Study of the Decline of Spain (1598–1640)* (Cambridge, 1963).

Giner, S., *The Social Structure of Catalonia* (Anglo-Catalan Society, Sheffield, 1984).

Hall, J., *Knowledge of the Catalan Language (1975–1986)* (Barcelona, 1990).

Hansen, E. C., Schneider, J. and Schneider, P., 'From Autonomous Development to Dependent Modernization: the Catalan Case Revisited: a Reply to

Pi-Sunyer', in *Comparative Studies in Society and History* (Cambridge, 1975).

Hansen, E. C., *Rural Catalonia under the Franco Régime: the Face of Regional Culture since the Spanish Civil War* (Cambridge, 1977).

Hughes, R., *Barcelona* (London, 1992).

Jones, N. L., 'The Catalan Question since the Civil War', in P. Preston (ed.), *Spain in Crisis* (London, 1976).

Llubera, J., 'Catalan National Identity: the Dialectics of Past and Present', in Tonkin, McDonald and Chapman (eds), *History and Ethnicity* (London, 1989).

Llubera, J., 'The Idea of *Volksgeist* in the Formation of Catalan Nationalist Ideology', in *Ethnic and Racial Studies*, VI, no. 3 (London, 1983).

McDonough, G. W., *Good Families of Barcelona: a Social History of Power in the Industrial Era* (Princeton, NJ, 1986).

Meaker, G. H., *The Revolutionary Left in Spain, 1914–1923* (Stanford, CA, 1974).

Orwell, G., *Homage to Catalonia* (London, 1938).

Parés i Maicas, M., *et al.*, *Approach to Catalonia* (Barcelona, 1985).

Payne, J., *Catalonia, Portrait of a Nation* (London, 1991).

Pérez Alonso, J., 'Catalan: an Example of the Current Language Struggle in Spain: Sociopolitical and Pedagogical Implications', in *International Journal of the Sociology of Language* (New York, 1979).

Pi-Sunyer, O., 'Catalan Nationalism: some Theoretical and Historical Considerations', in Tiryakian and Rogowski (eds), *New Nationalisms of the Developed West* (Winchester, MA, 1985).

Pi-Sunyer, O., 'Elites and Non-Corporative Groups in the European Mediterranean: a Reconsideration of the Catalan Case', in *Comparative Studies in Society and History* (Cambridge, 1974).

Pi-Sunyer, O., 'Occupational Images and Ethnicity: Some Observations on the Attitudes of Middle-class Catalans', in *Human Organization* (Washington, 1975).

Pi-Sunyer, O., *Nationalism and Societal Integration: a Focus on Catalonia* (Amherst, MA, 1983).

Pi-Sunyer, O., *The Stalled Transformation: Six Years of the Autonomy Process in Catalonia* (Amherst, MA, 1986).

Puigjaner, J. M., *Catalonia: a Millennial Country* (Generalitat de Catalunya publ., Barcelona, 1989).

Read, J., *The Catalans* (London, 1979).

de Riquer, M., *et al.*, *Catalonia* (Luna Wennberg, Barcelona, 1983).

Sabater, E., 'An Approach to the Situation of the Catalan Language: Social and Educational Use', in *International Journal of the Sociology of Language* (New York, 1984).

Schneidman, L., *The Rise of the Aragonese–Catalan Empire* (New York, 1970).

Setton, K., *The Catalans in Greece* (London, 1975).

Siguan, M., 'Language and Education in Catalonia', in *Prospects*, vol. 14 (1984).

Sobrequés, J., Vicens, F., and Pitarch, I., *The Parliament of Catalonia* (Barcelona, 1981).

Stephens, M., 'The Catalans', in *Linguistic Minorities in Western Europe*

(Llandysul, Dyfed, Wales, 1976).

Strubell i Trueta, M., 'Language and Identity in Catalonia', in *International Journal of the Sociology of Language*, vol. 47 (1984).

Terry, A., *Catalan Literature* (London, 1972).

Thomson, J., *A Distinctive Industrialization: Cotton in Barcelona, 1728–1832* (Cambridge, 1992).

Trueta, J., *The Spirit of Catalonia* (Oxford, 1946).

Vallverdú, F., 'A Sociolinguistic History of Catalonia', in *International Journal of the Sociology of Language*, vol. 47 (1984).

Vergés, O., and Cruañas, J., *The Generalitat in the History of Catalonia* (Generalitat de Catalunya publ., Barcelona, 1991).

Webber, J. and Strubell i Trueta, M., *The Catalan Language: Progress towards Normalisation* (Anglo-Catalan Society, Sheffield, 1991).

Wollard, K. A., *Double Talk: Bilingualism and the Politics of Ethnicity in Catalonia* (Stanford, CA, 1988).

Index